Praise for *Because They Hate*

"Brigitte Gabriel's story is at once intensely personal and possessing global significance . . . the story of her family and her childhood encapsulates the threat that faces the entire free world today. Brigitte Gabriel's words should be read, and studied carefully, by all the law enforcement and government officials of the West—as well as by everyone who values freedom."

—Robert Spencer, author of
The Politically Incorrect Guide to Islam (and the Crusades)

"Her writing is eloquent and her passion tremendous."

—*Publishers Weekly*

"Brigitte Gabriel eloquently reminds America what is truly at stake in this struggle against terrorism: our families, our way of life, and our hopes. Ms. Gabriel's personal account of her own experience is riveting, compelling, and spellbinding. This is a must-read for the entire American public. . . . *Because They Hate* contains monumental revelations that will shock and disturb you. But it is also a story of an indomitable spirit—Brigitte's—that will move you."

—Steve Emerson, author of *American Jihad:
The Terrorists Living Among Us*, and executive
director of the Investigative Project on Terrorism

"[Brigitte Gabriel's] writing is a critical wake-up call to Americans as we face the threat of takeover by jihadists. We are glad to be able to help her share her story with God-fearing, patriotic Americans who care about the truth and want to learn about the threat every nation throughout the world is facing from radical Islam."

—Paul F. Crouch, Jr., vice president of administration,
Trinity Broadcasting Network

"A compelling and captivating personal story with a powerful lesson about threats to freedom in our time."
—R. James Woolsey, director of Central Intelligence, 1993–1995

"*Because They Hate* should be read by all to understand radical Islam. . . . This book gives dire warning of what is to come if the democratic and Western world does not take responsible action to protect its people and societies. The United States is the primary target as Islamic Radicalism attempts to spread its worldwide dominance."
—Paul E. Vallely, Maj. General U.S. Army (Ret.), FOX News Channel military analyst, and coauthor of *Endgame: The Blueprint for Victory in the War on Terror*

"Part memoir and part analysis of the social, political, and religious factors that created the current situation in the Middle East, Gabriel issues a clear warning."
—*The Tampa Tribune*

"Gabriel makes her case, but also offers a sound and powerful program of what we have to do as a nation and as individuals to stave off defeat by radical Islam."
—*The Bulletin* (Philadelphia)

"Gabriel believes the West is complacent about the threat posed by radical Islam. She learned while growing up Christian in Lebanon that Islamofascists are serious—and if we want to survive we better take them seriously. She speaks with the passion of a survivor who has seen death and destruction firsthand—and doesn't want America to suffer the same future as Lebanon."
—*World* magazine

"*Because They Hate* is powerful, passionate, and full of divine purpose."
—Dr. John C. Hagee, senior pastor of the Cornerstone Church and author of *Jerusalem Countdown: A Warning to the World*

THEY MUST BE STOPPED

Scarlet Hicks

December 28 2012

Also by Brigitte Gabriel

Because They Hate:
A Survivor of Islamic Terror Warns America

THEY
MUST
BE
STOPPED

**Why We Must
Defeat Radical Islam
and How We Can Do It**

BRIGITTE GABRIEL

 ST. MARTIN'S GRIFFIN 📖 **NEW YORK**

www.stmartins.com

The Library of Congress has catalogued the hardcover edition as follows:

Gabriel, Brigitte.
   They must be stopped : why we must defeat radical Islam and how we can do it / Brigitte Gabriel.—1st ed.
      p. cm.
   ISBN 978-0-312-38363-3
   1. Terrorism   2. Terrorism—Religious aspects—Islam.   I. Title.
   HV6431.G23   2008
   363.325'16—dc22   2008018642

ISBN 978-0-312-57128-3 (trade paperback)

D   10 9 8 7 6 5 4 3

In memory of

Krystyna Bublick

my dearest friend

She was a passionate activist, a light in a world of darkness, a patriotic American who embodied the best of what America had to offer. She was a courageous fighter who stood on her principles. She spoke against evil and understood what is at stake. She was a source of profound encouragement, and a champion to those who could not defend themselves. With profound sadness for her loss and joy for the privilege of calling her my best friend, I dedicate this book in her loving memory.

Contents

12. Winning the War on Islamofascism:

INTRODUCTION

A great deal has changed since *They Must Be Stopped* was first published. Right on the heels of the book's release came a global economic meltdown, the most serious financial crisis since the Great Depression. Stock markets fell, banking institutions collapsed, and governments coughed up massively expensive bailouts to keep whole sectors of the economy afloat. The meltdown thoroughly dominated the news media and sent citizens into a panic about losing their jobs, homes, and life savings. For a country that had gone seven years since the fall of the Twin Towers without another terrorist attack, this meant that as candidates for the upcoming 2008 presidential election approached the finish line, the campaign issue of national security was relegated to the back burner.

The economic collapse proved to be a critical factor in the elections that fall. It crippled Republican credibility and lent a greater allure to the Democratic candidate's mantra of "hope and change." Voters who were weary of war, complacent after seven years of domestic security, and desperate for change elected their first African-American president, Barack Hussein Obama. He promised a fresh, less confrontational approach to dealing with Islamic extremism—an "open hand" policy that promised to win Muslim hearts and minds around the world by offering them respect and redress for their perceived grievances against the West, while at the same time humbling the "arrogant" American superpower by apologizing to allies and enemies alike for our "cowboy diplomacy" and imperialist transgressions. Accordingly, Barack Hussein Obama wore his middle name as a badge of honor during the swearing-in ceremony. Barack Hussein Obama gave his very first television interview as president to the Arabic-language news network Al-Arabiya. He reassured the viewers, "My job to the Muslim world is to communicate that the Americans are not your enemy."[1] Unfortunately, politely explaining to an enemy that we're not the enemy is hardly an effective wartime strategy, particularly against radical Muslims, who believe they are driven by a holy commandment to fight the infidels in holy war and who view this outreach as weakness. The fact is, Muslim extremists long ago decided that America, the Great Satan, *is* the enemy, and attacked us on our own soil. We are at war whether we wish it or not.

Mr. Obama's efforts to communicate nonaggression and respect included such gestures as bowing to the Saudi king upon meeting him in London. This was a stunningly submissive act that could only be perceived in the Arab world as a symbolic victory: There was the American president, the leader of the world's sole superpower, virtually genuflecting to the leader of Saudi Arabia, the home of the most active exporters of the fundamentalist ideology that seeks our very destruction.[2] Not even the weakest Muslim president or leader in the Middle East has ever bowed to the king of Saudi Arabia. Only a subservient bows to a king, not his equal, a head of state. Obama also downplayed America's Judeo-Christian roots, saying in his speech to the Muslim world from Turkey that "we no longer think of ourselves as a Christian nation," while bizarrely (and incorrectly) pronouncing us on French Television during an interview with a French Canal Plus reporter "one of the world's largest Muslim countries" instead—endowing our small Muslim-American population, 2.3 million Muslims living in a nation of 300 million people, with a demographic significance far out of proportion with reality.

In a highly anticipated address to the Muslim world from Cairo, Mr. Obama even presented himself as a defender of Islam, declaring, "I consider it part of my responsibility as president of the United States to fight against negative stereotypes of Islam wherever they appear."[3] This is a strange duty for an American president to embrace, not only because the "negative stereotypes" stem from ongoing Islamic terrorism itself (over 14,000 attacks by Muslims across the world since September 11), not people's misperceptions, but also because he said nothing about countering the vile stereotypes of Christians and Jews that are rampant in the Muslim world, not to mention in the West itself. He went on to make a number of other laudatory misstatements about the contributions of Islam to the modern world, including portraying the religion as having a "proud tradition of tolerance," when in fact one of Islam's hallmarks throughout history is a demonstrable *intolerance*. From the 600s all the way up to the early twentieth century with the killing of 2 million Armenians in Turkey, Islam is responsible for the murders of 270 million people across the world—more than any other religion on earth. The speech conveyed to the world—and especially to our enemies—that the new president had adopted a weak, conciliatory stance against Islamist aggression, a position that can only result in the Islamist sharks smelling blood and drawing a tighter circle around their victim.

The Obama administration's approach to the war against radical Islam has been to avoid treating it like a war at all, and to revert to a pre-9/11 strategy of handling international Islamic terrorism as a law enforcement matter. For example, Obama wants to extend Miranda rights to nearly all captured terrorists, even those snared on the fields of battle in Iraq and Afghanistan. He is also threatening Bush administration officials and CIA interrogators with prosecution over harsh interrogation methods used against terrorist detainees—methods that resulted in the capture of leading jihadists, the disruption of terrorist plots, and the preservation of American lives. The idea of persecuting CIA agents, as former terrorism prosecutor Andrew McCarthy points out, is "a legal nightmare that would certainly hamper our intelligence-gathering efforts, put fear of prosecution into the hearts of our law enforcement agents, and embolden our enemies to resist torture and demand justice in our courts."[4] The president has also publicly committed to closing the prison facility for terrorist suspects at Guantánamo Bay by January 2010 despite not having a clear plan for how to dispense with the 250 or so enemy combatants being held there or how to ensure that these trained jihadists will not rejoin the battle if released—as scores of them already have.[5]

Treating enemy combatants like mere criminals also necessitated softening the language of aggression. Shortly after Obama took office, the Department of Homeland Security began purging its terminology of wartime references like "enemy combatant"[6] and "war on terror," and banning terms like "jihadists" that might suggest we are at war with Islam[7]; instead, the DHS and Obama administration began substituting comically amorphous terms like "transnational challenge" (for global jihad) and "man-caused disaster"[8] (for acts of terrorism). The changes didn't end with the language. The DHS also redirected its focus from the very real menace of al Qaeda and related Islamic terror groups to an exaggerated threat of "right-wing domestic extremists" and "disgruntled military veterans." How can we ever hope to confront radical Islam and win our battles if our president and his leadership lack the moral clarity, the knowledge of Islamic history, and the focus to even call our enemy by name, let alone confront it until victory?

Further undermining the West's security, President Obama has allowed Iran's nuclear power program to continue unabated, despite the fact that Iranian president Mahmoud Ahmadinejad has repeatedly and openly declared his apocalyptic, genocidal intentions toward Israel and America. This summer saw an astonishing popular uprising against the Iranian leadership by citizens hungry for true democracy and freedom—a rebellion brutally repressed by Ahmadinejad and the mullahs. But rather than back the revolutionaries in the streets and send a clear message to the people of Iran that America and its people stand with them in their fight for freedom, President Obama showed his support for the regime by allowing the bloody repression to carry on for days before issuing a tepid condemnation. The Obama administration followed that with yet another offer of direct talks regarding concerns about Iran developing nuclear weapons, an offer which was met by a now-familiar refusal to negotiate. The Iranian leadership is already dangerously close to being in possession of a nuclear bomb,[9] and Obama's affirmation of their right to "legitimate"[10] nuclear ambitions buys them more time to accomplish that.

In fact, the Obama administration has abandoned all pretense of preventing Iran from developing nuclear weapons. This is the opinion of sources as diverse as *The Christian Science Monitor*, the authoritative Iranian newspaper *Kayhan*, and many experts gathered at an August 10–13, 2009, international conference on Iran organized by the Konrad Adenauer Foundation. The Obama administration has accepted that Iran is going to develop nuclear weapons, and believes that with clever and/or muscular diplomacy, Iran can be "deterred" from using them.

Obama's entire strategy for "deterring" a nuclear-armed Iran consists of a combination of entreaties, enticements, empty threats, and self-deceptions. In the category of "empty threats," Secretary of State Hillary Clinton floated the idea that the United States would extend a "defense umbrella" over the Middle East "once [the mullahs] have a nuclear weapon." Secretary Clinton doesn't say ". . . *if* they *get* a nuclear weapon . . ."; instead she says ". . . *once* they *have* a nuclear weapon."[11] However, once they have a nuclear weapon, and *use* it in their planned "Scud-in-a-Bucket" EMP attack on the United States, Secretary Clinton's putative "defense umbrella" will remain neatly folded in the State Department umbrella stand.[12]

The mullahs know this. To them, Obama, his policy, and his representatives are the subjects of ridicule and contempt. Khamenei's house organ *Kayhan* states that the Obama administration is "begging Iran for dialogue—in very disrespectful language, like uncultured cowboys."[13]

Remember they are not talking about the "uncultured cowboy" George W. Bush. They are calling Barack Hussein Obama, he of the extended hand, a "begging . . . uncultured cowboy."

Our president's belief that he can defuse Islamist hostility and their supremacist agenda by being more deferential and conciliatory; by refusing to acknowledge the theological roots that drives Islamic terror itself; by exalting Muslim contributions to American culture while downplaying the glory of our own Judeo-Christian, democratic, capitalistic heritage; and by offering to engage the enemy in still more unproductive "dialogue"—all of which the Islamists consider signs of weakness—is a naïve, dangerous fantasy. His attempt to connect with the Islamists through his father's Muslim heritage and through his own youthful upbringing in Muslim Indonesia has done nothing to abate the snowballing momentum of Islamic extremism. Indeed, the terrorists have made it clear that it doesn't matter who or which political party occupies the White House—America remains the ultimate target. The fugitive al Qaeda leader, Osama bin Laden, issued another taped message to the West in September 2009 that emphasizes this very point—in it he criticizes Obama for following in former president George W. Bush's footsteps.

And so Islamic terrorism against the infidel continues, with two spectacular attacks against Western and Jewish targets in the last year in Jakarta and Mumbai. But we don't even have to look abroad—violent jihad is erupting again within our own borders. As I write this update, a massive FBI probe, focused on a Denver-based terror cell, launched raids in Queens and has uncovered a plot to detonate up to nine backpack bombs on the New York City subway system, reminiscent of the 2005 London attacks that killed 52 people and the 2004 Madrid train bombings that killed 191,[14] such a plot could easily have resulted in more deaths and devastation than the London and Madrid attacks combined. Two other major attacks were foiled as well: one in Dallas, Texas, the same day another one was uncovered in Springfield, Illinois—both planned by Muslims who subscribe to the jihadist ideology of the supremacy of Islam and its war against infidels. One was a Jordanian who had overstayed his visa in Dallas, the other an American born and raised in the good old U.S. of A.

On a smaller scale, this summer an American-born Muslim convert named Carlos Bledsoe shot and killed one American soldier and wounded another outside a Little Rock, Arkansas, military recruitment center, saying the act was "done for the sake of Allah" in retaliation for the U.S. war on terror.[15] The heavily armed jihadist apparently had other potential targets in mind as well, including a local synagogue and Christian churches. Bledsoe is only one of a wave of converts with murderous, traitorous potential.

Counterterrorism expert Steven Emerson of the Investigative Project on Terrorism writes:

> We're seeing a new phase . . . here in the radicalization of American citizens as well as American-born Muslims. In the past six months alone there have been more than forty arrests of either American-born Muslims or of Americans who converted to Islam and tried to carry out plots either overseas or in the United States. This is indicative of what has happened in Europe over the last ten years where the environment there and some of the calls by the Islamic groups have radicalized the Muslim population there.[16]

Converts aren't the only threat. Muslim immigrants to the West have begun returning to their homelands to engage in jihad. At least twenty Somalis from Minnesota alone have recently returned to Somalia to fight in the civil war there and participate in terror training camps,[17] with at least six being killed, including a white American convert[18] (one hundred or more have streamed from England into Somalia since 2004[19]). When these trained veterans of jihad return to the West (as Bledsoe returned from a mysterious trip to Yemen), are they likely to turn their newfound deadly skills on us?

But acts of terrorism are only the most dramatic and visible front in our war with radical Islam. We also continue to face an insidious "cultural jihad" from Islamist groups such as the ubiquitous Muslim Brotherhood, who hide behind so-called civil rights organizations like CAIR, the Council on American-Islamic Relations, which press for special legal, social, and cultural concessions for Muslim-Americans. The Brotherhood's goal is the gradual imposition of Sharia law and erosion of our freedoms in the West, and ultimately the downfall of America.

These "stealth jihadists" take advantage of Western openness and a deeply ingrained political correctness to chip away at some of our precious liberties like free speech, for example, rendering criticism of Islam off limits. The result is often cultural capitulation in the form of self-censorship. Recently, while doing research for his new introduction of *A Week in December*, British novelist Sebastian Faulk read the Koran and was disturbed by what he found there, calling it "depressing" and "the rantings of a schizophrenic" in an online *Telegraph* interview, claiming "it has no ethical dimension like the New Testament, no new plan for life." In short order, the link to the interview was pulled and a mere day or two later, Faulk wrote a follow-up for the *Telegraph* in which he recanted every criticism, and instead cravenly apologized for hurting any Muslim sentiments, accepting that the Koran "is by definition beyond criticism."[20] It could not have been more painfully and disappointingly obvious that Faulk received either threats over his initial statements or advice that, were he not to publish a retraction, he might end up like fellow British novelist Salman Rushdie, who lived for many years under the threat of a death fatwa pronounced by Iranian Ayatollah Khomeini twenty years before over Rushdie's book *The Satanic Verses*.

Such self-censorship is becoming a Pavlovian instinct in the publishers themselves. Just before *They Must Be Stopped* appeared in bookstores, the imminent publication of *The Jewel of Medina*, a racy historical novel about Mohammed's nine-year-old bride, Aisha, was postponed by publisher Random House over fears that it might incite Muslim violence against anyone involved, from its author, Sherry Jones, to the publisher to booksellers stocking the novel. And in fact, weeks later when the book found a new publisher in a small London press, the publisher's home was firebombed by three young Muslim men.[21] In a forthcoming book about the Danish cartoon controversy that sparked worldwide Muslim rage and violence in 2006 over satirical depictions of Mohammed and Muslims, Yale University Press consulted two dozen authorities, whose reportedly unanimous recommendation was that the cartoons themselves should not be reprinted in the book.[22] The director of Yale University Press explained, oddly, that the cartoons are freely available on the Internet and can be "accurately described in words," so reprinting them could be interpreted as "gratuitous." The truth is probably better explained by one of the consulted experts, who said, "You can count on violence if any illustration of the prophet is published. It will cause riots, I predict, from Indonesia to Nigeria."[23] We in the West have reached the point where not violence, not even the *threat* of violence, but the mere *suspicion* that Muslim violence is likely to occur is enough to pressure us to curtail our own free speech. Our founding fathers, who gave up their lives to give us the freedoms we have, are turning in their graves.

The grip of political correctness and cultural self-flagellation is so strong in Europe that in February 2009, Geert Wilders, Dutch parliamentarian and outspoken critic of Islam, was barred from entering Britain, a fellow European Union country. Now he is actually scheduled to be put on trial in his home country in January 2010 on charges of racism and hate mongering.[24] Outrageous though this charge may seem, there is already a European precedent for conviction; in August 2009 a Finnish court convicted a Helsinki councilman of "defamation of religion" for criticizing Mohammed and Islam on the councilman's blog.[25]

Thanks to our own cultural retreat, seditious Islamist groups have been emboldened to begin operating more openly in America. Hizb ut-Tahrir, the pro-jihadist movement whose aim is to establish a worldwide Islamic state, or caliphate, and whose prominent alumni include terrorists like 9/11 mastermind Khalid Sheikh Mohammed, recently held a conference in Chicago, suggesting that the group is unafraid to rev up its recruiting efforts in the United States.[26] Also in the last year, the worldwide spread of Islamic law has accelerated. Sharia's more draconian punishments, such as stoning adulterers to death, are gaining traction wherever Sharia law is becoming more strictly enforced, such as Somalia and Nigeria. In Indonesia's Aceh province, a law recently passed making adultery punishable by stoning, and also imposes severe sentences for rape, homosexuality, alcohol consumption, and gambling.[27] Islamic law is taking hold in the West as well. It is estimated that more than eighty-five Sharia courts are operating in Britain.[28] Muslim immigrants to the West are becoming more insistent about judging according to Allah's law and rejecting the validity of man-made laws. When former Georgia Tech student Syed Haris Ahmed was found guilty this year of conspiring to provide material support to terrorists in America and overseas, his father said, "He's not guilty of any crimes *in the eyes of Allah*. He's guilty of *U.S. laws*."[29] [Emphasis original to the quote.]

Many are dismissive of fears that Sharia law could ever be implemented in the United States. But few people are aware that it is already gaining traction here through "Sharia-compliant finance" or "Islamic banking," which requires banking practices to conform to Sharia law. The economic crisis of last autumn emboldened Islamists who saw it as a sign that the capitalist West was collapsing under its own immoral weight—and Sharia finance was poised to take its place. Hugely influential fundamentalist cleric Yousef al-Qaradawi exulted that "the collapse of the capitalist system, which is based on usury and securities rather than commodities in markets, shows us that it is undergoing a crisis and that our integrated Islamic philosophy, if properly understood and applied, can replace Western capitalism."[30] Extremist organization Hizb ut-Tahrir's recent Chicago conference was entitled "The Rise of Islam and the Fall of Capitalism," and offered such panel discussions as "Capitalism Is Doomed to Fail" and "The Suffering Under Capitalism."[31]

Indeed, the West has already begun to accommodate Sharia finance. The UK, for example:

> now has five fully "Sharia-compliant" banks . . . while another seventeen leading institutions including Barclays, RBS, and Lloyds Banking Group have set up special branches or subsidiary firms for Muslim clients.
>
> The $18 billion in assets of Britain's Islamic banks are said to dwarf those of Muslim states such as Pakistan, Bangladesh, Turkey, and Egypt. And there are also fifty-five colleges and professional institutions offering education in Islamic finance in Britain—more than anywhere else in the world.[32]

There are Islamic banking institutions operating in over seventy-five countries with assets estimated at around $700 billion, a figure which is growing rapidly.[33] Some of the West's leading financial institutions, including Citibank, Goldman Sachs, Dow Jones, Merrill Lynch, Morgan Stanley, and others have created "Sharia Advisory Boards" staffed with Islamic clerics and scholars to keep their financial practices in line with Islamic law. Bankers claim that this is simply good business, but as *Londonistan* author Melanie Phillips explains, "acceptance of Sharia finance furthers the Islamist objective of gradually legitimizing Islamic Sharia law more generally in the West."[34]

Sharia law is not the only alarming aspect of Islam to gain a greater foothold in the West during the last year. Honor killings are on the rise around the world, and they are no longer limited to Arab territories like Jordan[35] and Gaza (where there have been ten so far in 2009),[36] but also now appear in countries such as Spain,[37] Italy,[38] Canada, Germany,[39] the UK,[40] and even America. In one gruesome instance, a leading Muslim-American businessman, the owner of a New York State TV network (which he founded to counter negative media stereotypes of Muslims) who was touted by all major media as the exemplatory "moderate" Muslim, beheaded his wife after she announced that she wanted a divorce.[41] As I write this, a controversial tug-of-war is playing out in Florida over teenage girl Rifqa Bary, a convert to Christianity who ran away from her strict Muslim parents in Ohio rather than possibly face murder at the hands of her own father for apostasy, the Sharia penalty for which is death. But the court, skeptical about such foreign concepts as honor killings and apostasy, is considering whether to return her to her parents. Her case, which has brought the issue of honor killings to national awareness in this country, is still pending. Frank Gaffney of the Center for Security Policy notes that "Rifqa Bary is a proverbial 'canary in the mineshaft,' a warning to all of us that toxic Sharia is leeching into America."[42]

A year after the hardcover edition of this book hit bookstores, we seem to be losing ground in the clash of civilizations. As impossible as it may seem, the eight-year-old memory of the terrorist attacks of September 11, 2001, is beginning to fade for many, even for those in our government. But to relax our vigilance and pretend we are not at war is suicidal, willful blindness; the reality is that, if anything, the danger is greater than when *They Must Be Stopped* first appeared. The recently exposed plots in New York, Dallas, and Springfield are glaring reminders that we still face the threat of devastating terrorist attacks, including the possibility of a weapon of mass destruction being unleashed on our shores, an attack which would dwarf 9/11 in horrific scale. Is there hope? Of course, and there are signs that many are waking up to the danger, including politicians who are eager to take back the reins of government and reverse the naïve stance of the Obama administration toward radical Islam. My own grassroots organization, ACT! for America, is empowering tens of thousands of American citizens to resist Islamofascism and rise in defense of our security, our liberty, and our values. ACT! for America is the largest national security grassroots movement in the United States with over three hundred chapters nationwide and a full-time lobbyist on Capitol Hill. But we cannot afford the luxury of complacency, and there is no time to lose. Every day Islamists push for successes large and small; therefore this is our time to rise in defense of freedom, not only for our sake, but for the sake of our future generations. We owe it to our founding fathers as well as to our grandchildren. The longer we wait to push back, the more difficult it will be to reverse the momentum and emerge victorious against a lethal enemy bent on destroying everything we stand for.

Now more than ever, they must be stopped.

1

ISLAM 101:
THE EAST THROUGH WESTERN EYES

While I was growing up in Lebanon, I was able to see what the United States and the Western world was all about. Radio and television connected me to the West. I knew what the latest trends and fashions were, who was famous, what was in and was out. Radio gave us the news and TV was loaded with American programming. However, there has always been a lack of information coming from East to West. In fact, there has been a great deal of misinformation and misunderstanding about the Middle East over the centuries. Shrouded in a language foreign to many, its heavily censored media controlled and influenced by Islamic leaders and dictators, the mystery continues to this day.

Westerners do not understand Middle Eastern culture, its religion, Islam, and how Islam as a political and religious ideology drives and impacts every aspect of the culture and its people. Westerners come from a Judeo-Christian background, where the teaching of faith centers on love, tolerance, and forgiveness. They do not understand that the sword of Islam—so glamorized on film—represents hatred, intolerance, murder, and the subjugation of anyone not Muslim.

The West's perception of the mysterious Middle East began to come into focus during the past forty years with the rise of the PLO and Ayatollah Khomeini. The world watched one terror attack after another: the 1971 Munich Olympic massacre, the hostage crisis in Iran, the bombing of the marines in Lebanon, the *Achille Lauro* hijacking and murders, the Pan Am flight that exploded over Scotland, TWA flight 847, and the killing and taking of hostages in Lebanon. At every airport security checkpoint and with every X-ray machine, the crackdown on security at airports drove the dangers home. Terrorism began to be a recognizable problem—but not really in the forefront of our minds. Countries and governments failed to connect the dots and realize that even though these terrorist attacks happened in different countries and an different continents, the perpetrators, regardless of their names or what group they belonged to, had something in common: they were Muslims, and their intended victims were always Westerners, Christians, and Jews.

September 11 brought this reality home. At 8:46 A.M. on September 11, 2001, the clear blue skies above the New York skyline were changed forever by an explosion of fire and smoke. In less than two hours four airplanes struck U.S. targets. The compelling and horrific images remain etched not only upon the psyche of America, but of all humanity. Via instant live news coverage, people around the world experienced the mass murder of innocents unfold before their eyes. People across the globe shared the new reality of fear and sorrow inflicted on a massive scale by terror in the name of Islam and Allah.

We needed to learn more about those who in the name of Islam and in homage to Allah would kill and murder not only Americans but anyone who would stand against the tenets of their ancient religion. These warriors of Islam had come to the shores of America not only to destroy the towers in a major U.S. city, but to make a statement. Indeed, they had been making their statement of hatred, intolerance, and bigotry for some time through terrorist activities around the globe. On September 11, 2001, radical Islamists demonstrated they were ready, willing and able to take on any city, culture, or country—even the most powerful nation in the world—until they alone would rise to be the masters of all humanity.

The West began to ask questions: Who really knew what Islam stood for? What was the truth about Islam? Is it a religion of peace or not?

If most of the world has been confused by Islam's relationship to terrorist attacks worldwide, then Yahiya Emerick, the author of *Understanding Islam*, offers this simple explanation. It's all been a misunderstanding, he claims, perpetrated by the distorted views presented of Muslims in such films as *Not Without My Daughter, True Lies, Black Hawk Down, Under Siege,* and *Delta Force.* He declares that these films and their stereotypical media messages have "served to paint Muslims as wife-beaters, bomb-throwers, and swarthy immigrants whose loyalty cannot be trusted."[1]

So let's test these claims against the "true" religion. Let's see if the actual statements found in the Koran support this view. Is Islam a peaceful religion? Or do the proponents of this "peaceful" religion have a hidden agenda? Does Islam pose a threat to Jews, Christians, and others who possess a religious worldview other than Islam? And do we really need to be all that concerned about the declaration of jihad throughout the world?

To begin answering these questions we must first take a look at the Arab Middle East, the birthplace of Islam, to learn how its people, their heritage, their customs, and their origins contribute to the twenty-first-century phenomenon called Islamofascism or Islamonazism. Unless we understand where Islam originated, who adopted it, and what they stand for, we will not be able to understand what is driving terrorists today—terrorists who commit murder in the name of Islam and claim it is their God-given right to do so.

Before the advent of Islam, the people of Arabia were polytheists and worshiped many gods, among them divinities such as Al-Lat, the sun goddess; Manah, the goddess of destiny; Al-'Uzza, the most mighty; and Venus, the morning star.[2] They performed rituals and made sacrifices and offerings to deities embodied in trees and or sacred rocks.

The year 600 A.D.—just prior to the life of Mohammed and the birth of Islam—found Christians and Jews with rich and flourishing settlements in Arabia where they had built strongholds in the city and vicinity. The city of Yathrib, later to become known as Medina, lay in an oasis 250 miles north of Mecca, and was especially prosperous. Mecca was important because of its location halfway along the west coast of the Arabian peninsula. The city was a commercial hub for traveling nomads. Merchants prospered and grew in numbers as trade and business opportunities increased with the influx of travelers and merchants.

In addition to commerce, Mecca had another attraction that drew visitors: a sacred rock, a black stone enshrined in the Kaaba representing multiple Arabian gods, and where Arabs worshiped for many centuries prior to Mohammed and the advent of Islam. (The Kaaba is an example of how Islam appropriated aspects of previous religions as its own, just as it appropriated the Jewish Temple Mount in Jerusalem as Mohammad's point of ascent into heaven.)

Mohammed was born into the Quyrash tribe in Mecca around 570 A.D.[3] Around the age of forty, he began receiving revelations which would become the foundation for a new religion later to be called Islam and its followers Mohammedans. In the Koran, this event is described as a sudden explosion one night on Mount Hira where Mohammed spent a month each year. He was visited in his sleep by the angel Gabriel who commanded him to begin reciting. There was about a three-year gap between these first revelations and those that would follow in fragmented fashion, making up what is now known as the Koran.[4]

Mohammed preached that the Koran is the correctly written word of God, and any other work allegedly written by God is tainted. The Koran is not only the only untainted version of God's word, but is also a "full and final revelation."[5] It is because of this understanding and belief in Islamic doctrine and its teaching that radical Muslims today believe that Islam is the superior religion on earth and should be treated accordingly. Therefore, no man-made laws, contracts, negotiations, or conduct that contradicts the Koran should be respected. They believe that all nations must submit to Islam and that Sharia law (Islamic law) should be the governing code of conduct throughout the world.

• • •

Five basic Islamic doctrines are embedded in the Koran, and there are five foundational pillars by which those who espouse Islam practice and carry out the beliefs of their religion.

The first doctrine is that there is only one God and He is self-sufficient and without partners. God is all-knowing, all-powerful, and the creator of all that was and is and what will be. The second doctrine is that there have been many prophets sent by God. These prophets include Noah, Abraham, Jesus, Moses, and Mohammed. The third doctrine is that while God is self-sufficient, He also created angels, of which there are both good and evil. The fourth doctrine is that the Koran, not the Bible, is God's entire and final message to the people. The fifth doctrine is that a final judgment day is approaching for all, when the evil will descend into hell, while the good will ascend into heaven.[6]

THE FIVE PILLARS OF ISLAM:
FOUNDATIONS OF FAITH AND EMPIRE

Profession of Faith: Iman.

Iman is the basic belief in the Oneness of God and the Prophet Mohammed. It is the creed, pivotal confession, and profession of Islam (Shahadah) which declares, "Allah is the greatest. There is no god but Allah and Mohammed is His Prophet." Each Muslim must profess these words. For Muslims it confirms that God, as they know Him, is a unique being, unlike any other.

Prayer: Salat.

Second, Muslims adhere to regularly scheduled prayers, or Salat, that take place five times during the day. These are physical prayers and are considered a critical act of worship. During the prayers, which Muslims can do alone or with a congregation of other believers, they face Mecca. Through a series of ritual prayers that are said at dawn, noon, mid-afternoon, sunset, and nightfall, they reconfirm themselves and submit to Allah in every area of their lives.

It is important to stress how important the daily prayers are to the Islamic faith. Once the Islamic faith has been embraced, it is *expected* that the follower perform this prayer ritual five times daily. The prayer is used as a form of worship for Allah and a link for the follower to commune with Him, away from any other distractions. It is required that the prayers be said in Arabic, not in the person's native tongue, as Arabic is the perfect language of the Koran as given by Allah and is unchangeable.

Giving of Alms: Zakat.

Third, practicing Muslims agree to a financial obligation or Zakat, which is a form of almsgiving or charity. Muslims believe that all they have belongs to Allah. Any wealth they may possess is given by God and entrusted to them. But Islam gets a little more specific about what is expected in the way of giving. Zakat requires that Muslims annually donate one fortieth of their income to the needy.[7] Only the poor are exempt from this form of prescribed charity.

Fasting: Sawm.

Fourth, every year, at the celebration of Ramadan, Muslims fast or perform Sawm. From dawn until sundown, believers do not eat, drink, smoke, or have sexual intercourse. All those who are well enough must fast and abstain in this way for the entire duration of the holy month of Ramadan in the Islamic calendar.

Pilgrimage: Haj.

The fifth pillar of Islam requires everyone who is able to make a pilgrimage, or Hajj, to Mecca. This trip must be undertaken once during the lifetime of every Muslim. It takes place during the twelfth month of the year and demonstrates a final act of submission to Allah.[8] Muslims congregate at the shrine of the Kaaba in Mecca. They kiss and touch the black stone as they circle the Kaaba dressed in white to symbolize purity.

• • •

The five pillars of Islam describe the duties of every Muslim. As the main religious text of Islam the Koran is a record of the exact words revealed by God through the angel Gabriel to the Prophet. The Koran is the divine and sacred foundation of Islamic law. It is written in 114 chapters, also called "suras." It contains guidance, commandments, rules, ethical regulations, historical recreations, and wise sayings that pertain to every aspect of daily life. Not one word has been changed over the centuries.[9]

The Hadith is the accompanying book of the Koran, from which Muslims derive spiritual nourishment and daily guidance for life. The Hadith is a written record of the oral traditions, passed down from Muslim to Muslim, about the Prophet Mohammed's life, actions, and deeds. The Hadith is a record of what the prophet was supposed to have said and done and is second in authority only to the Koran.

An additional body of text vital to Islam is Sharia, the Islamic holy law. *Sharia* is an Arabic word meaning "way." Islamic jurists gave this name to a set of laws to govern and guide Islamic believers. The Sharia spells out an obligatory set of rules, designated by God the supreme legislator, to be followed and obeyed. Sharia law discusses in detail rules governing marriage, divorce, child rearing, interpersonal relationships, food, clothing, hygiene, prayer, and even commercial and criminal law. These rules are meant to help Islamic believers to live and maintain a harmonious society.

Many Islamic practices, such as fasting, tithing, daily prayers, and profession of faith, have much in common with Christianity and Judaism. However, what makes Islam different from other religions is its call to kill and subjugate all other members of other faiths. The terrorists of today as well as imams in mosques throughout the world are calling for the death of millions of people around the world in the name of Islam. They are calling for jihad against the infidels, citing suras and verses from the Koran and Hadith to support their call to action. In order to understand why terrorists quote the Koran as the foundation behind their actions, we must come to understand Islam as a political and religious ideology.

ISLAMIC IDENTITY

Islam is central to the lives of Muslims. Understanding this very important fact is key to understanding the Islamic world and how it relates to the rest of the world. For Muslims, their loyalty and identity revolve around their religion. Even though Muslims and non-Muslims may live in the same community and have the same nationality, in the Islamic world it is religion and not national identity that defines their society and determines who belongs to it and who does not. For example, a Muslim Palestinian will feel a closer bond with and loyalty to a Muslim Albanian than to a Christian Palestinian even though the two Muslims speak different languages and come from different countries. Both Muslims share a divinely guided past and common sense of destiny. Both belong to the supreme religion of earth—Islam—and both are superior beings blessed by Allah and given authority over all other people because of their faith as professing Muslims.

The Ummah: Political Authority and Communal Life

Muslims believe that Allah is the sole true sovereign. He revealed to Mohammed all matters of life, politics, and religious law, and gave him authority to rule over all. The ummah is the political and religious community of Islam. It unites Muslims in all nations and makes them equal to one another, with Allah as their god and Mohammed as their political authority.

The Prophet Mohammed founded and ruled an Islamic empire not only as prophet but also as head of state. His political and legal authority was accepted only because of his religious status. Because of the precedent set by the Prophet Mohammed, the religion of Islam is not merely one segment of life, it regulates life completely, from the social and the political to the diplomatic, economic, and military. This combination of religion and politics as one is the foundation of Islam, an inseparable political/religious ideology of Islamic governments, and the basis of Muslim loyalties.

In Islam's view, the world and mankind are divided into two irreconcilable groups: Dar Al Islam, the house of Islam, which is made up of believers, and where Islamic law reigns; and Dar Al Harb, the house of war, made up of non-Muslims, where infidels (known as *kuffars*, or nonbelievers) live. This of course refers to those of us who do not believe and profess Islam.[10]

In Islamic teaching, all people will one day accept Islam or submit to its rule. Based on Islamic teaching Islam cannot recognize political borders or permanent peace treaties. According to Ibin Taamiyah, a fourteenth-century Muslim jurist, any act of war against Dar Al Harb is morally and legally justified, and exempt from any ethical judgment. It is this ideology and belief that is the driving force behind those radical Muslims who work to impose Islam in its seventh-century practices upon the civilized world.

"Fight them until all opposition ends and all submit to Allah."[11] (Koran 8:39)

Radical Islamists are commanded to wage jihad until victory.

Jihad

Jihad is another very important component of Islam, and we must learn about it by examining history, not by listening to the Council on American Islamic Relations or other Islamic talking heads on television. Jihad is a communal religious duty for all Muslims young and old throughout the world. The Koran informs its followers that there is always a holy war being fought, and instructs its followers to participate. During the early centuries of Islamic expansion, fighting with the sword against the enemy infidel was the main commandment of jihad. Many Islamic pundits in the West today explain that jihad is mostly a spiritual struggle and not a military one. However, when you examine the history of Islam and the commandments of the Koran that endorse jihad as a military tool, it becomes clear that the term jihad refers mostly to war against nonbelievers. For example, the Koran sura 9:29 commands Muslims to "fight against those who do not believe in God or the judgment day, who permit what God and his messenger have forbidden, and who refuse allegiance to the true faith."

The objective of military jihad is not only to convert people to Islam, but also to gain political control and exercise Islamic authority over a population so that society lives and abides by the principles of Islam. The Koran emphasizes that those who die in military jihad automatically become martyrs and are awarded a special place in paradise.[12]

Today Islamists across the world commit terrorist attacks against people in the belief that this holy war must be fought to the death, that infidels must be killed for their lack of faith in the Koran. These beliefs are so strong that Islamists consider jihad to be a sixth pillar of the faith. When I lived in the Middle East the only meaning for the word "jihad" that we as Christians understood was the military jihad against us. Today, there are those moderate Muslims who believe that the jihad is a war with words, not the sword.[13] The problem is, however, that any debate between moderates and radicals about what jihad means is almost always won by the radicals, who can quote suras from the Koran supporting their position that it means war and the elimination or subjugation of nonbelievers.

MISUNDERSTANDING ISLAM *7th Century*

Since the birth of Islam, the Christian West has had difficulty understanding Islam as a religious ideology and a phenomenon that differs from Christianity. In the early seventh century, when Muslims began conquering nations, they were referred to by different names. When they conquered the Iberian peninsula in the eighth century they were called Moors. In the rest of Europe Muslims were referred to as Turks. In Asia Minor, Christians called Muslims Tartars and other ethnic names.

When Europe finally understood that Islam was not an ethnic group, it then mistakenly perceived it as a religion comparable to Christianity with Mohammed as its central figure, as Jesus is to Christianity. Muslims were referred to as Mohammedans and to Islam as Mohammedism. This lack of understanding of Islam as a political movement persists today. After September 11, 2001, people still describe a mosque as a Muslim church, refer to the Koran as the Islamic bible, and equate sheikhs and mullahs with priests and rabbis. Nothing could be farther from the truth. Mosques are frequently used to preach hatred and killing in the name of Allah, and are places where militants can hide, store ammunition, and discuss strategy of war. The Koran, unlike the Bible, calls for a political movement for which all Muslims must fight, kill, and subjugate those of other faiths until Islam rules the world. And sheikhs and mullahs are political figures who urge their followers to fight and become martyrs in the name of God.

Today Islam is seen through a Western prism, which reflects a Western worldview as well as a lack of knowledge in Islam as a religious and political identity. The West identifies leaders as belonging to the left or the right. They perceive Yasser Arafat as moderate, the king of Saudi Arabia as a conservative, and Khomeini or Osama bin Laden as radicals. The West fails to understand that all these leaders will stand together as one on the Islamic side of the fence against the infidels when the call of *Allah Akbar* (Allah is the greatest) is made.

Westerners also assume that the Islamic understanding of peace, justice, and freedom are the same across the cultural divide. They do not realize that these words have completely different meanings in the mind of Muslims.

The word peace in Arabic does not mean harmony between groups or nations, as is the Western understanding of the word. It only means *salam*, which is the absence of conflict at this time between two fighting parties or countries. The word *sulha*, or reconciliation, is the translation of Western *peace*. In contrast, for true peace in Western terms to be achieved, the fighting parties must end their conflict, agree to stop fighting, announce that they have reconciled past problems, and move forward in a true harmonious relationship.

The word "freedom" in the West means the ability of individuals to make decisions affecting their lives in every way, especially the election or removal of people in government and power who impact their everyday lives. It means the right to choose and make decisions. You are free to choose your religion, your leaders, your politics, your way of life as an individual. Freedom in the West is the basis for a democratic society.

In the Islamic world, the word "freedom" means the freedom from foreign powers that have ruled the Islamic world in modern times. They associate freedom with independence from foreign power and control over their land, which they associate with tyranny. Muslim leaders talk about justice when they talk about peace, not freedom. Justice in Islam is the opposite of tyranny. Justice in the eyes of

Muslims is the return of the Islamic caliphate to rule over the world, uniting the Islamic Ummah throughout the world, free of Western influence and culture and returned to supremacy.

An analysis of the political and religious underpinnings of the Muslim Middle East and the ability to piece together a complete understanding of the culture is vital when discussing our options to end terrorism. The sad reality is that the export of killing and terror in the name of Islam has exceeded and overshadowed anything positive about the Middle East. Unless we stand up in a united effort to expose and discuss the problem and come up with solutions to counteract the radicalism spreading around the world, civilization will pay a heavy price for its apathy and ignorance.

2

ISLAMIC TERRORISM:
THEN AND NOW

Twelve years after he received his prophethood, Mohammed decided to relocate to the city of Yathrib in the hope of recruiting more followers—especially the successful Jews and some Christians—to his religion. In 622 A.D. Mohammed emigrated with about fifty of his men to Yathrib from Mecca, a 200-mile journey. This journey is referred to as the Hijra, which historians see as marking the beginning of an era in which Islam was spread not only as a religion but also as a political and military movement. The Hijra marked a turning point: the political reign of Islam had begun. It was at this point that Mohammed and his men began to fight and win battles to spread Islam and begin 1,400 years of Islamic terrorism and domination. The effects of the Hijra on the population of Yathrib, and to future societies and nations, are significant today.

Following the Hijra to Yathrib (which was later renamed Medina), which was then the center of Arab Jewish life, Mohammed aggressively tried to persuade the Jews to accept him as a true prophet and Islam as the true religion. In his attempt to win them over he adopted many of their customs and rituals, such as fasting, prohibiting the eating of pork, and circumcision.

When the Jews refused to accept him or his religion, Mohammed received this revelation from Allah:

> "And the Jews will not be pleased with you, nor the Christians until you follow their religion. Say: Surely Allah's guidance, that is the (true) guidance. And if you follow their desires after the knowledge that has come to you, you shall have no guardian from Allah, nor any helper."[1] (Koran 2:120)

With Allah letting Mohammed know that He had parted ways with the Jews, Christians, and anyone else who would follow their beliefs, Mohammed had the license to declare war on Jews and Christians as being apart from Allah. He began a campaign of terror, attacking them, taking their goods, and driving them into exile. Later, in his attacks on other tribes, cities, and countries, Mohammed and his men slaughtered Christian and Jewish males and took their women and children as slaves.

> "Some ye slew, and ye made captive some. And He caused you to inherit their land and their houses and their wealth, and land ye have not trodden . . ." (Koran 33:26–27)

After exiling the Jews Mohammed and his followers became stronger in Medina. He began attacking the Meccan trade caravans that passed through the major routes near Medina. This lead to three major battles between 623 and 630 A.D. These three battles set the course and parameters for Islamic terror that we are experiencing today. Leading Muslim figures both nationalistic and religious, from the late Yasser Arafat to Osama bin Laden, still invoke these battles as well as the treaty of Al-Hudaybiyah to exhort crowds and plan terrorist strategy. Understanding these events helps us understand where our enemies get their inspiration as well as the rationale behind their beliefs.

THE BATTLE OF BADR

In March of 624, Mohammed and 315 of his men attacked a 900-man Meccan caravan that was passing near Medina. Mohammed's small force fought and defeated the Meccans in a brave fight inspired by their belief in God and paradise. Mohammed's small army returned to Medina loaded with treasure and prisoners. Four-fifths of the booty went to the Islamic jihadists and one-fifth went to Mohammed for the good of the general community.

In addition to being a military victory, the battle of Badr had a profound religious significance to the Muslims, who felt that the success of the battle of Badr was God's deliverance after years of hardship. Finally God had awarded them victory over their powerful enemy. The Koran describes the battle of Badr: "You did not kill them but God killed them." (Koran 8:17)

THE BATTLE OF UHUD

In March of 625, in an effort by the Meccans to defeat the Muslims and remove their threat to the regional commercial operation whose lifeline was the trade caravans, 3,000 Meccans attacked the Muslims in Uhud, a hill near Medina. Seventy-five Muslims were killed while the Meccans lost only twenty-seven men. The fighting ended only when the Meccans believed they had killed Mohammed.[2]

Even though the Meccans failed in attaining their goal of

removing Mohammed, the Muslims felt that the loss was theirs, spiritually. Because of the greater loss of men, they felt that they had lost Allah's favor—military and religious issues were inseparable in their minds. If God's handing them victory in Badr was a sign of vindication, their loss in Uhud signified the loss of God's favor.

Mohammed came to the conclusion that the Muslims had forgotten their duty to God because they had become more interested in the booty of war. Therefore Allah punished them for abandoning him, and allowed the defeat in Uhud. This soul-searching, self-criticism and return to pure Islamic traditional values in the face of defeat and failure has become an enduring theme throughout Islam to this day. Those inclined to take up a cause for Allah's sake and for the new caliphate know they are winners when they win, and think they are winners when they lose—even if they die they become martyrs, receiving Allah's rewards in heaven. They know Allah is on their side when they succeed and try harder to please him when they fail. Many Muslims throughout the world today, especially those in the Middle East, believe that Allah has blessed Saudi Arabia with wealth as a reward for their strict practice of Islam (as it was practiced in the days of Mohammed). Many Islamic leaders use the example of Saudi Arabia's wealth and success as an Islamic kingdom to inspire other jihadists to become more observant and religious so they may be blessed by Allah.

THE TREATY OF AL-HUDAYBIYAH

In 628 Mohammed traveled toward Mecca with 1,400 of his followers and made camp nearby at Al-Hudaybiyah. Fighting was avoided when Mohammed and the Meccans agreed on a treaty to suspend hostilities toward one another for ten years. Based on that treaty,

Mecca viewed Mohammed as nonaggressive and disposed to friendliness. Mohammed, however, had a long-term strategy to incorporate Mecca into Islam. He knew that he couldn't win the battle with the Meccans if he fought them now, so he used the time granted by the treaty to build his army, and strengthen, recruit, and rejuvenate it, and then declared war on Mecca two years later when least expected.

THE SIEGE OF KHAYBAR

A few weeks after the treaty of Al-Hudaybiyah was signed Mohammed led the Muslims in an attack against the Jewish oasis of Khaybar. He tortured, murdered, plundered, and enslaved many people.[3] After a fierce battle in which ninety-three people were killed, the Jews negotiated a surrender agreement, which would allow the Jews to continue working the land but stipulated that they give up half of their harvest to the Muslims as a "tribute tax," known as jizyah. As Mohammed had the upper hand, his negotiations reserved for him the right to change his mind, break the agreement, and expel the Jews, if he so chose.

As Mohammed and Islam became more and more powerful, he conquered all the Christian and Jewish tribes of Arabia. The Christians and Jews surrendered to the Muslims and began paying the Jizyah, which was both their protection and acknowledgement that they were inferior to Muslims, and became known as Dhimmi. Jews and Christians who did not convert to Islam were allowed to live because they were "people of the book" but became second-class citizens and had to pay the jizyah.

"Fight those who believe not in Allah nor the Last Day, nor hold that forbidden which has been forbidden by Allah and

His Apostle, nor acknowledge the religion of Truth [even if
they are] of the people of the Book, until they pay the Jizyah
with willing submission, and feel themselves subdued." (Koran 9:29)

The pact of Khaybar set the bar for relations between victorious Muslim and defeated Christians and Jews, while Islamic con-
querors expanded beyond Arabia. The world was now divided
into two: Dar Al Islam (the house of Islam) and Dar Al Harb (the
house of war). The house of war meant any territory that is not
conquered, dominated, and subjugated by Islam and its practices.
This is the basis of the Islamists' drive to fight all infidels until
they either convert to Islam or be killed. The jihadists today consider all countries not under Islamic rule as Dar Al Harb, and are
obligated to fight until Islam is declared victorious in the land of
infidels.

THE CONQUEST OF MECCA

By 630 Mohammed had achieved power over a wide area. The
Meccans had their guard down, as the treaty of Al-Hudaybiyah led
them to believe Mohammed had no intention of fighting them. In
Mohammed's mind, the treaty was just a tool. Two years after signing the treaty, Mohammed and his warriors attacked Mecca, conquering it and converting the population to Islam. He destroyed all
the idols of the Kaaba and rededicated the shrine to Islam, declaring Mecca as the holy city of Islam. To assure Mohammed and Islam's dominance, non-Muslims were forbidden entry to Mecca
upon penalty of death.

By 631 Mohammed the prophet, warrior, and ruler, with revelations from the angel Gabriel in one hand and a sword in the

other, led his Muslim believers to conquer and subjugate all the nomadic desert tribes of Arabia.

> "When the forbidden months have passed, slay the idolaters wherever ye find them, and take them (captive), and besiege them, and prepare for them each ambush . . ." (Koran 9:5)

ISLAM EXPLODES OUT OF ARABIA

After Mohammed's death (in 632 A.D.), Islam continued to grow, led by four caliphs. In 634 the second caliph Omar began referring to as himself "commander of the faithful." With the sword and the Koran in hand, caliph Omar began a vicious expansion of Islam, conquering vast masses of land stretching from the Middle East into Africa.

With each military victory the Muslims' belief that Allah was on their side was reinforced. Conquered Christians and Jews, terrorized by the ruthlessness of the Islamic invaders on a mission from God, were able to buy their right to remain alive and practice their religions only if they agreed to pay tribute.

The first jihadists on their holy mission of Islamic dominance conquered the Persian armies, capturing Babylonia, Mesopotamia, Armenia, and Persia. To the west they conquered the Christian provinces of the eastern Mediterranean, from Syria and Palestine to Egypt, Tunisia, Algeria, and Morocco. In 711 they conquered the Iberian peninsula and established a foothold in Europe, which led to conquering Spain and Portugal a few years later. By 751 Islam had conquered India and Central China.[4] In just a little more than a century after Mohammed's death, Islam, a political-religious-totalitarian ideology, covered and ruled more of the earth than the Roman empire at its peak.

With their sights set on world conquest again, let's get an idea of what could be in store for future generations if the Islamists, headed by the likes of Osama bin Laden and President Ahmadinejad of Iran, carry out their dreams for the next caliphate.

THE STATUS OF CHRISTIANS AND JEWS UNDER ISLAM

Christians and Jews were made to pay the jizyah at humiliating public ceremonies. In offering up the jizyah, the Dhimmi had to "hang his head while the official took hold of his beard and hit him on the protuberant bone beneath his ear."[5] In some areas, Christians and Jews were made to wear a receipt for the Jizyah around their neck as a mark of their dishonor.

Christians and Jews were forbidden to construct new churches, temples, or synagogues. They were also forbidden from ringing their church bells or blowing the shofar to begin services, just as they are forbidden today in Saudi Arabia and Iran.[6] Dhimmi were forced to wear distinctive clothing; it was Baghdad's caliph Al-Mutawakkil, in the ninth century, who designated a yellow badge for Jews under Islam, which Hitler copied and duplicated in Nazi Germany centuries later.[7]

Islam conquered its way across continents and oceans through ruthless terrorism, causing devastating tragedy on millions of people. Muslims saw themselves as the rightful heirs of civilization, culture, and history. They changed the names of many cities into Islamic names. Constantinople became Istanbul. Jerusalem became Al-Quds. They took credit for the inventions and accomplishments of the people they conquered. Mosques were built on top of churches; the most famous mosque in the world, the Al-Aqsa mosque, was built on top of the Jewish Temple Mount.

THE RISE OF THE WEST

By 1061 resentment and confrontation were brewing between the Islamic empire and Christendom. Christians and Muslims fought as Christians attempted to liberate themselves and their lands.[8]

Christians were incensed that Islam ruled Jerusalem, the cradle of Christianity. Many Christians had converted to Islam under the constant pressure, humiliation, and suffering imposed by the Muslims. The first Crusade was launched after Pope Urban II urged Christians throughout Europe to take back the land of Christ and return it to Christianity.[9]

In 1099 Christian crusaders liberated Jerusalem. Less than a century later Muslims lead by Saladin reclaimed it and drove out the Christian infidels. Jerusalem remained under Islamic control until Israel liberated it in 1967. It was the first time in two thousand years that the entire city of Jerusalem was united as one under Jewish sovereignty, where Jews were able to pray on the Temple Mount occupied by an Islamic mosque.

From 1099 through the next three hundred years, Christian Crusades were launched from Europe in an attempt to liberate Christian land conquered by Islam, only to be defeated each time. It would take not an army nor faith, but the coming of the Industrial Revolution, to give the West the economic power to defeat Islam.

Around 1600, major changes were brewing in Christian Europe. The Renaissance, which had unique respect for commerce and entrepreneurialism had led to the scientific revolution and the discovery of the Americas. Christian Europe turned this development into a military and economic advantage.

By the eighteenth century, Europe's Industrial Revolution gave them the economic power to expand globally. It gave the armies pushing the Muslims back into the Middle East the endurance and military superiority earlier crusaders did not have. As Europe expanded and liberated Christian lands, it freed Christians and Jews from paying the protection tax. This was a huge economic blow to Muslim growth and prosperity, which had been buoyed up by the attainment of wealth built on Christian and Jewish slavery.

Europe's industrial dominance fueled its quest to retake countries invaded by the Muslims. In 1798 Napoleon Bonaparte's technically advanced army marchted into Egypt. The heart of Muslim territory, Dar Al Islam, was pierced.[10]

By 1877 the Islamic Empire had surrendered Romania, Bosnia, Herzegovina, Montenegro, Bulgaria, and Cyprus. France invaded Algeria, Morocco, and Tunisia. Britain invaded Egypt, Italy invaded Libya, while the Russians and British divided Persia. By 1905 the West had liberated its territory previously conquered and savaged by Islam, and declared an economic and military victory, thus marking the end of 1,400 years of Islamic rule and jihad. During this period, Muslims had killed 270 million people across the globe: 120 million Africans, 60 million Christians, 80 million Hindus, and 10 million Buddhists.[11]

• • •

As Islam lost control over massive territories and millions of people, suffering a huge defeat at the hands of infidels, Muslims experienced pain and humiliation previously unknown to them. How could Christianity have overcome Islam? The infidels are inferior to Islam, they are cursed by Allah, they have submitted to Islam for fourteen centuries. Their religions are inferior to Islam, the true path and Allah's religion on earth. The Ummah were and still are in shock.

Muslim religious leaders, thinkers, and scholars concluded that

Muslims lost their power because Allah had taken it away from them. They believed that Islam had lost its way from the true path of Allah revealed to them by the Prophet Mohammed. Therefore Allah punished them to teach them a lesson. Only through a return to the true, authentic Islam practiced in the days of the Prophet will Islam return to its glory and reclaim its superiority. Only then will Allah again reward Muslims throughout the world. However, Islamists today have their eyes set on world conquest—again! Muslims today are using their oil wealth and prosperity, the very same thing that allowed the Europeans to defeat Islam, to finance terrorism and spread Islam throughout the world.

Understanding the history of Islam and how it influences radical Islam today is vital to our survival. For example, the history of the treaty of Al-Hudaybiyah shows us that using temporary treaties and lying to infidels to advance Islam is not only acceptable, it is sanctioned and blessed by the Prophet.

After the signing of the Oslo Accords, as the West and the Israelis rejoiced and celebrated the long-awaited peace between the two nations, Yasser Arafat also was rejoicing, but for a different reason. Arafat was able to return to the Palestinian territory, establish the Palestinian Authority, and have it financed by infidels—even having Israel train and supply his police force with weaponry, knowing fully that he had no intention of ever having peace with Israel. His peace accord was nothing more than an Islamic strategy of war practiced and preached by the Prophet Mohammed after the truce of Al-Hudaybiyah.

Arafat began referring to Al-Hudaybiyah shortly after signing the Oslo Accords in 1993 (His first mention was in a speech given in English in South Africa.) In an interview on Egyptian television on April 18, 1998, Arafat was asked about the Oslo Accords. He again cited Al-Hudaybiyah as the basis of his peace with Israel.

Then, when Arafat was questioned in an interview by *Al-Quds* newspaper in May 1998 as to whether he felt that he had made a mistake in agreeing to Oslo, Arafat replied: "No, no. Allah's messenger Mohammed accepted the Al-Hudaybiyah peace treaty, and Saladin accepted the peace agreement with Richard the Lion-Hearted." In a statement to the Palestinian Legislative Council on May 15, 2002, he said: "Let us remember the Al-Hudaybiyah conciliation accord out of our concern for the national and pan-international solidarity with your people and your cause."[12] Arafat referred to Al-Hudaybiah over and over again in many statements.

I have referred to Yasser Arafat's statements because they are the most glaring examples of Islamic principles at work in modern political negotiations. Meanwhile the West wallows in a state of denial and ignorance, bullied by political correctness and refusing to listen to our enemies who have an understanding of peace and tolerance different from ours. While many today would argue that Arafat was not an Islamist but a nationalist, no one can argue with the fact that he used Islamic principles based in the Koran and on the actions of the Prophet Mohammed as the basis for his negotiations and strategy of war.

MODERN ISLAM:
THE RISE OF ISLAMIC SUPREMACY

Islam is rising up after 300 years of slumber and decline to avenge its ancient glory, using its historic success formula whereby Islam rules by the sword and the teaching of Mohammad; whereby religion and state are one and the same; whereby the Ummah is governed by Islamic rule and all other religions are suppressed.

Since the Iranian revolution in 1979, Islamic fascism and

worldwide Islamic terrorist acts have escalated to a level beyond anyone's imagination. The scourge and fear of Communism has been replaced by the scourge and fear of Islam. Every day, the media bring the world evidence of the murder of innocent civilians in the name of Islam by Muslims. Since September 11, 2001, there have been more than ten thousand Islamic terrorist attacks worldwide carried out by men and women who believe that dying for their religious beliefs is more important than life itself. When and where did this phenomenon start? And what was the signal sent to Islamists worldwide to rise up in a holy war against the West?

The defeat of Shah Mohammad Reza Pahlavi's Iranian regime in 1979 by Ayatollah Ruhollah Khomeini reignited the radical Islamists' dream of uniting Muslims around the world and establishing a caliphate that would dominate world governments with Islamic political and theological ideology. Formerly secular, moderate Muslims became fervent in their Islamic nationalism and were indoctrinated by radical Islamists into the world of Islamic fascism.

The Iranian Revolution

Khomeini's rise to power as supreme ruler of the Islamic Republic of Iran in February of 1979 was the culmination of events that began prior to the Iranian revolution and the overthrow of the shah. During his reign, the shah of Iran had become less and less receptive to the needs of his people, especially the country's rising middle class.[13] As Iran's oil revenues increased, the shah felt less dependent on loans and grants from the United States and less inclined to appease the United States government by continuing to govern his people with certain democratic policies.[14]

After the death of his mentor, Ayatollah Boroujerdi, in 1962, Khomeini embarked on his journey to reject the ideas and cultures of Westernized countries and to establish a global Islamic state through Islamic jihad. As the "Father of Modern Jihad" Khomeini reintroduced the cultural mind-set of committing atrocities for the sake of a political ideology based on fundamental religious beliefs.[15]

Khomeini began his protests against the shah in 1962, after becoming more and more frustrated by the governing policies of democracy in a majority-Shiite nation. Khomeini detested the shah's relationship with the West and his swift and often brutal punishment of religious dissidents. In 1963 the shah exiled Khomeini to Turkey. Khomeini soon moved to An Najaf in Iraq, where he developed, taught, and authored his views of national governance through Sharia law, and sent them to Iran to be distributed in the mosques.

In 1978, Khomeini fled to France where he initiated the overthrow of the shah and his regime from a Paris suburb. Yasser Arafat and the Palestinian Liberation Organization (PLO) were instrumental in deposing Shah Pahlavi and establishing Khomeini as ruler. (Khomeini's friendship with the PLO was later essential because the conflict between Israel and the Palestinians deflected the menacing and alarming activities implemented by Khomeini and his faithful clerics in Iran. Khomeini was able to commit atrocities on a daily basis without too much news coverage until the Iran hostage crisis.)

The Carter administration publicly sought Khomeini's friendship and vocally supported him through the 1979 Iranian revolution, which quickly deposed the shah and established Khomeini as Iran's dictator.[16] To the world, in particular our enemies, the United States had been too quick to discard an old, reliable ally who had been helpful during the cold war. The Soviet Union was one of our enemies that took notice, and in December 1979, the USSR invaded Afghanistan just six months after Carter signed a new arms treaty with Russian president Brezhnev.[17][18]

Ironically, and to the world's chagrin today, former President (1976–1981) Jimmy Carter saw the shah as a great abuser of human rights when he cracked down on dissidents that were a threat to dismantling his government. In his naiveté, Carter intentionally overlooked that Iran was a secular nation ruled by a man who implemented laws similar to that of a democratic society. Instead, Carter instituted a campaign to depose the shah because of his abuse of human rights. In a further ironic twist, Carter denounced the shah's imprisonment of some three thousand political prisoners, many of whom, when Khomeini came to power in 1979, were executed along with an additional ten thousand to twenty thousand pro-Western ones.[19][20] In fact, the Ayatollah butchered more people during his first year as supreme ruler of Iran than the Shah had during his entire twenty-five year reign.[21]

President Carter offered his opinion about a country whose culture he did not understand, at a moment that was critical to the birth of a worldwide radical movement. America not only betrayed one of its allies but also gave Khomeini (who invented the phrase "America, the great Satan") the power with which to spread his venom elsewhere.

In a similar political/cultural situation, America today is calling for democracy in the Middle East, which is a wonderfully noble idea. However, if elections are encouraged in places that are not prepared for and ready for democracy, terrorist organizations end up ruling the land: for example, Hamas in Gaza, Hezbollah in Lebanon, and effectively the mullahs in Iran. America again is faced with decisions either to stand by and support most of the current leaders of the Middle East or to encourage democratic elections across the board. If democratic elections were held in Egypt or in Jordan we would end up with radical Islamic governments in both of these two secular countries. The only thing that is keeping the radicals in check

is the tight control on those radicals maintained by King Abdullah of
Jordan and President Mubarak of Egypt. As much as we dislike the
Saudis and the other royals of the Middle East, they are now the
lesser of the two evils when compared to Islamic radicals.

From 1979 to 1989, Ayatollah Khomeini set Iran back one hundred years. Soon after becoming supreme ruler, Khomeini established a strict interpretation of Sharia law and incorporated it into
his personal doctrine of a religious political government. Iran was
now a theocracy, governed by a group of fundamentalist clerics
and led by a dictator bent on establishing a fundamentalist Shia
Iran as a world superpower.

The new rules of law denied men and women their basic rights.[22]
Shia ruthlessness sacrificed thousands of Iranian students and children who were sent to their deaths clearing mine fields during the
Iranian-Iraq war in the name of preserving Shia Islamic nationalism. Students were also used as human shields and were sent to blow
up Iraqi tanks with bombs strapped to their bodies.[23] Khomeini's
concept of suicide bombers set a precedent for this inhumane
method of "warfare." The PLO, Hezbollah, Hamas, and Iraq's sectar-
ian terrorist militias began incorporating suicide bombings into
their strategies, and other Islamic terrorist groups soon followed.[24]
The Iranians' world as they had known it before Khomeini had just
spiraled deeper into hell.

Khomeini's government set the stage for a significant gathering
of like-minded Muslims around the world who bore resentments
to the West. Khomeini brilliantly rallied the Muslim warriors to
stand up against the corrupt West and organize into groups of
resistance, committing terrorist attacks worldwide in the name of
Islam.

On November 4, 1979, Islamic radicals stormed the United
States embassy in Iran and held fifty-two Americans hostage for

444 days. Ironically, Khomeini's choreography of the Iranian hostage crisis cost Carter the reelection to the presidency in 1981.[25] Carter willingly helped establish a theocratic society in an oil-rich region that is now exporting terror and developing nuclear power to fight the West. Even though he had good intentions, the end result is the same: Carter's naivete and his democratic impulses were used as a tool to end democracy.

The United States' clandestine support of the Taliban against the soviets in Afghanistan strengthened and armed radical Islamists around the world. As a result, from the roots of the Afghani/Soviet war came the birth of Al Qaeda, and from a region now steeped in Islamic nationalism and religious zealots came the Iranian-born Hezbollah and other terrorist groups.

For the first seventy years of the twentieth century Islamic terrorism had mainly been confined to the Middle East, India, Africa, and the Balkans' Caucasus region during World War II. On September 5, 1972, much to the astonishment and horror of the world, Arafat's assassins, members of the auxiliary division of the PLO terrorist group Black September, prepared for their world debut in Munich's Olympic Village. At 4:30 A.M., they silently made their way into the rooms of the Israeli wrestling team and eventually murdered eleven Israelis and a German policeman. The terrorists' demands? They wanted Israel to release 234 Arab terrorists from Israeli jails who had committed acts of violence against Israelis and, of course, they demanded safe passage out of Germany.[26]

Since this act of terrorism, there have been countless horrifying and unspeakable terror campaigns by fundamentalist Muslims. For the reader unfamiliar with the extent of Islamic mayhem, the following summarizes Islamic/Arabic aggression leading up to 9/11. As the number of terrorist acts worldwide since 2001 has been too numerous to list here, I have included only a few to provide a general picture. (This list also appeared in my book *Because They Hate*; it is updated here).

WORLDWIDE TERRORIST ACTS BY
ISLAMIC MILITANTS 2001–2007

2001

Terrorism against Israel.

September 11: The attacks kill almost 3,000 in a series of three hijacked airliner crashes into two U.S. landmarks: the World Trade Center in New York and the Pentagon in Arlington, Virginia. A fourth plane crashes in Somerset County, Pennsylvania.

Paris embassy attack plot foiled.

Richard Reid, attempting to destroy American Airlines Flight 63, is subdued by passengers and flight attendants before he could detonate his shoe bomb.

2002

March: The PLO, aided by Hamas and Hezbollah, murder 130 Jews in one month in Israel, mostly civilians.[27]

The following list has been compiled from (IPD) Information Please Database, 2007 Pearson Education, Inc., unless otherwise footnoted.

April: Explosion at historic synagogue in Tunisia leaves 21 dead, including 11 German tourists.

May: Car explodes outside hotel in Karachi, Pakistan, killing 14, including 11 French citizens.

June: Bomb explodes outside American consulate in Karachi, Pakistan, killing 12.

October: Boat crashes into oil tanker off Yemen coast, killing 1.

October: Nightclub bombings in Bali, Indonesia, killing 202, mostly Australian citizens.

November: Suicide attack on a hotel in Mombasa, Kenya, killing 16.

2003

January: In Manchester, England, Detective Constable Stephen Oake is stabbed to death, and 4 other officers are injured, in a police raid. The murderer, Kamel Bourgass—a suspected Al Qaeda operative who spent time training in Afghanistan—was later convicted of a plot to spread the deadly poison ricin on the streets of Britain. Manchester has become one of Britain's main havens for Islamic terrorists, according to security experts.[28]

May: Suicide bombers kill 34, including 8 Americans, at housing compounds for Westerners in Riyadh, Saudi Arabia.

May: Four bombs kill 33 people, targeting Jewish, Spanish, and Belgian sites in Casablanca, Morocco.

August: Suicide car bomb kills 12, injures 150 at Marriott Hotel in Jakarta, Indonesia.

November: Explosions rock a Riyadh, Saudi Arabia, housing compound, killing 17.

November: Suicide car bombers simultaneously attack 2 synagogues in Istanbul, Turkey, killing 25 and injuring hundreds.

November: Truck bombs detonated at London bank and British consulate in Istanbul, Turkey, killing 26.

2004

March: Ten bombs on 4 trains explode almost simultaneously during the morning rush hour in Madrid, Spain, killing 191 and injuring more than 1,500.

May: Terrorists attack Saudi oil company offices in Khobar, Saudi Arabia, killing 22.

June: Terrorists kidnap and execute American Paul Johnson Jr. in Riyadh, Saudi Arabia.

August: Al Qaeda's plan to blow up 11 British airliners over American soil foiled.[29]

September: In Beslan, Russia, group of 33 Islamist rebels storm a school and take about 1,200 children and adults captive. The siege ends after three days with the deaths of at least 339 hostages, about half of them children, and 500 injured.[30]

September: Car bomb outside the Australian embassy in Jakarta, Indonesia, kills 9.

December: Terrorists enter the U.S. consulate in Jeddah, Saudi Arabia, killing 9 (including 4 attackers).

2005

July: Four Al Qaeda suicide bombers strike central London's public transportation during morning rush hour, killing 52 and injuring 700.[31]

October: Twenty-two killed by three suicide bombs in Bali, Indonesia.

November: Fifty-seven killed at three American hotels in Amman, Jordan.

2006

January: Two suicide bombers carrying police badges blow themselves up near a celebration at the police academy in Baghdad, killing nearly 20 police officers. Al Qaeda in Iraq takes responsibility.

June: In Ontario, Canada, 17 are arrested, foiling a series of planned terrorist attacks in southern Ontario. None of the targets are identified, but authorities say the Toronto subway system has not been among them. Police and intelligence officials make the arrests after the group accepted delivery of three tons of ammonium nitrate, a common fertilizer that can be explosive if combined with fuel oil. This is part of a shocking wave of young Canadian Muslims who have become radicalized.[32]

June: In Denmark, police intensify their focus on honor killings and other related crimes after nine convictions in the murder of eighteen-year-old Ghazala Khan, who married against her family's wishes. With nearly 50 reports of honor-related crimes, police are finding that the problem may be worse than previously believed.[33]

August: Police arrest 24 British-born Muslims, most of whom have ties to Pakistan, who had allegedly plotted to blow up as many as 10 planes using liquid explosives. Officials say details of the plan are similar to other schemes devised by Al Qaeda.

2007

April: Suicide bombers attack a government building in Algeria's capital, Algiers, killing 35 and wounding hundreds more. Al Qaeda in the Islamic Maghreb claims responsibility.

April: Eight people, including two Iraqi legislators, die when a suicide bomber strikes inside the parliament building in Baghdad. An organization that includes Al Qaeda in Mesopotamia claims responsibility. In another attack, the Sarafiya Bridge that spans the Tigris River is destroyed.

June: British police find car bombs in two vehicles in London. Reportedly, the attackers tried to detonate the bombs using cell phones but failed. Government officials say Al Qaeda is linked to the attempted attack. The following day, an SUV carrying bombs bursts into flames after it slams into an entrance to Glasgow Airport. Officials say the attacks are connected.

Khomeini's Islamic revolution paved the way for the proliferation of Islamic terrorist acts throughout the world. His mandate to establish an Islamic caliphate, and transform Iran into a world superpower, has been handed down from one Iranian leader to the next and is ongoing. In November of 2007, the International Atomic Energy Agency (IAEA) reported that although Iran had increased its quantity of centrifuges (machines used to enrich uranium), Iran was still well below the capability to enrich enough uranium to produce nuclear weapons. In December of 2007, the United States stated that it would still pursue sanctions on Iran, although at the United Nations Russia and China will probably veto any additional economic sanctions.[34] In a December 2007 article in the *Washington Post*, John Bolton, former ambassador to the UN, discussed five weaknesses that affect the Iran nuclear report. Bolton believed that the individuals who studied Iran's nuclear program were biased toward Iran and were naïve about Iran's intentions concerning nuclear proliferation. Furthermore, Iran has tightened their security, and this has made it very difficult to solicit intelligence information.[35]

Iran's vision for developing nuclear weapons through the production of highly enriched uranium could come to fruition as early as 2010.[36] [37] They will use any tool within their grasp to accomplish their mission of producing a nuclear bomb. In the words of Ayatollah Khomeini:

> We know of no absolute values besides total submission of the will of the Almighty. People say: "Don't lie!" But the principle is different when we serve the will of Allah. He taught man to lie so that we can save ourselves at moments of difficulty and confuse our enemies. Should we remain truthful at the cost of defeat and danger to the Faith? We say not. People say: "Don't kill!" But the Almighty Himself taught us how to

kill. Without such a skill man would have been wiped out long ago by the beasts. So shall we not kill when it is necessary for the triumph of the Faith? . . . *Deceit, trickery, conspiracy, cheating, stealing, and killing are nothing but means.* [emphasis added] On their own they are neither good nor bad. For no deed is either good or bad, isolated from the intentions that motivated it.[38]

What is driving the Iranian mullahs is a messianic vision of bringing back the Mahdi, the twelfth imam, who is the Islamic messiah. The Mahdi disappeared centuries ago and can return only after an apocalypse. Iranians believe they can bring back the Mahdi by creating the world disaster required to usher in his return, then Islam reigns supreme in the universe and all people live peacefully in an Islamic heaven. Some say this is insanity and that the Iranians do not really believe this.

But listen to the words of President Ahmadinejad when he called for the Mahdi in his speech at the United Nations in 2005: "O mighty Lord, I pray to you to hasten the emergence of your last repository, the promised one, that perfect human being, the one that will fill this world with justice and peace."[39]

During the cold war we found safety from the nuclear-armed Soviet Union in the policy of mutually assured destruction. It worked because neither we nor the Russians wanted to die. What makes Iran different than other powers is that for Iran mutually assured destruction means death to America and assured paradise for the martyred Iranian population. They push the button with a smile on their face, and seventy-two virgins are just around the corner.

3

PURISTS DRINK THEIR ISLAM STRAIGHT

"Your Lord inspired the angels with the message: 'I am with you. Give firmness to the Believers. I will terrorize the unbelievers. Therefore smite them on their necks and every joint and incapacitate them. Strike off their heads and cut off each of their fingers and toes.'" (Koran 8:12)

Radical Islam is a danger not only to Western society, but also to moderate Muslims and the rest of the world. Radical Islamists are dedicated Muslims following the instructions of the Koran and walking in the steps of their Prophet Mohammed, whom they consider "the perfect man"—Al-Insan Al Kamil. All because they truly believe in the Koran, their holy book, and believe it contains Allah's words and commandments.

They do not have to make up any of their sources of motivation. It is there in black and white. In this war on Islamofacism we are not fighting a few people who hijacked a peaceful religion. We are fighting devout Muslims who drink their Islam straight. No water, no ice, no nothing. The Koran states very clearly that Islam is the superior religion on earth; all others are inferior and must submit to Allah and accept Mohammed as his messenger and the last of the prophets.

As images of hostages begging for mercy before they were beheaded became a regular occurrence on world television, Westerners wondered how such barbarity could exist in the twenty-first century. The Judeo-Christian consciousness could not fathom that any religion would advocate such barbarity. We refuse to believe that terrorism has anything to do with religion but is instead a twisted ideology hijacked by fringe elements. Many think it is poverty and oppression that drive suicide bombers and terrorists to kill and be killed as a last resort, out of sheer desperation. Others think that the Palestinian-Israeli conflict is the source of the Islamists' anger with the West, especially toward America, Israel's strong ally. They also believe that America's presence in Islamic countries is the driving factor behind martyrdom operations and terrorism as well.

After attacks in New York, London, and Madrid, government leaders raced to the nearest mosque to assure Muslims that they know that the most recent murderous events have nothing to do with their religion, it is someone else's fault, and that we are sure these terrorists do not understand Islam. Our leaders fell over themselves to address Muslim groups and to reassure them as to how convinced we are that Islam is a religion of peace. Even President Bush demonstrates this ignorance: "I believe that Islam is a great religion that preaches peace. And I believe people who murder the innocent to achieve political objectives aren't religious people. . . ."[1]

President Bush, all our elected officials, and our nation will be well served by educating themselves as to what the Prophet Mohammed taught in the Koran and instructed millions to follow:

"When you clash with the unbelieving Infidels in battle, smite their necks until you overpower them, killing and wounding many of them. At length, when you have thoroughly subdued them, bind them firmly, making (them) captives. Thereafter either generosity or ransom (them based upon what benefits Islam) until the war lays down its burdens. Thus are you commanded by Allah to continue carrying out Jihad against the unbelieving infidels until they submit to Islam." (Koran 47:4)

Former British prime minister Tony Blair has said, "True Islam is immensely tolerant and open,"[2] and "Of course the fanatics [are] attached to a completely wrong and reactionary view of Islam . . ."[3] What's tolerant about the passage quoted above? What's reactionary about dutifully following what Allah commands?

Blair and Bush would be advised to take a course on Islam. It will serve them and freedom well.

"Fight and kill the disbelievers wherever you find them, take them captive, harass them, lie in wait and ambush them using every stratagem of war."(Koran 9:5)

"So fight them until there is no more Fitnah (disbelief [non-Muslims]) and all submit to the religion of Allah alone (in the whole world)."[4] (Koran 8:39)

Why do our leaders need to hold meetings to assure Muslims that non-Muslims know Islam is a religion of peace? Why aren't *Muslims* telling us Islam is a religion of peace while apologizing for what their brethren are doing? The sad reality is that most Muslims are silent about the jihadists' terrorism. After all, this is what the Koran and the religion of Islam is all about. For most Muslims to denounce what the jihadists do in the name of their religion would be denouncing the Prophet and the words of Allah, who instructed Muslims to do exactly that—declare war on non-believers and fight them until they become subdued. Even though most Muslims are moderates and will not carry out terrorist operations themselves, some of them approve of the jihadists' behavior and the rise of Islam throughout the world. They mistakenly believe that the radicals are not going to affect them. They need only look back a few years and remember what the Taliban did in Afganistan.

Even though the majority of Muslims are peaceful, law-abiding citizens who do not wish to fight or declare jihad on their neighbors and colleagues, such moderates are irrelevant in the war we are fighting. Most Germans were moderate as well. Their moderation did not stop the Nazis from killing 14 million people in concentration camps and costing the world 60 million lives. Most Russians were peaceful as well. However, Russian Communists cost the world 20 million lives. The same goes for most Japanese prior to World War II. Yet Japan was responsible for the killing of 12 million Chinese. The moderate majority was irrelevant.

Most moderate Muslims do not know the words of the Koran and are not religious enough to read the Hadith and the Sira, which have even worse commandments regarding declaring war on the infidels and killing them. Whenever moderates and radicals get into a debate about Islam, radicals always win because they back their statements with "facts" from the holy book while nonreligious Muslims cannot.

Even though we are fighting a radical minority, that minority is the one we need to focus on and address. It is like fighting terminal cancer. Even though you may have one cancerous tumor in your brain, the fact that you have many other healthy cells becomes irrelevant. Unless you zero in on that one tumor and do whatever is required to eliminate it, the cancer is going to eliminate you and all your other healthy cells.

I have met wonderful professional moderate Muslims in my

travels across the United States, outstanding and respected members in their communities. When I asked them to join ACT!'s Muslim Islamic Council, to speak against the radicals, every person I asked said no. They said they can work with me behind the scenes but did not want anyone to know that they are involved, out of fear and the risk of public outcry and being cast out of the Islamic community. Their moderate views became irrelevant in the fight against radical Islam. If moderate professionals refuse to stand up and speak publicly against radical Islam in their communities, then our expectations and treatment of those communities should be adjusted accordingly.

The frightening thing is that radical Islamists who are willing to commit martyrdom operations may be clothed in professional attire and possess professional degrees, which makes them even more dangerous. In June 2007, eight doctors were discovered plotting to blow up civilians in England using car bombs. Even liberals were shocked that physicians could have become part of the Islamic death-and-martyrdom cult. Apologists who offered excuses as to why terrorists become suicide bombers couldn't find one reason that would make a doctor want to kill himself and others. Actually, there are quite a few reasons given in the Koran and Islamic teachings, but none of the bury-your-head- in-the-sand types want to hear them.

In the West, doctors are a figure of professional and financial success. Why would they want to kill themselves if they have a dream home with a swimming pool and a Mercedes in the garage? What Westerners fail to realize is what the power of faith in a god, in an afterlife, and in promises written in a holy book given by this god to a prophet, can do to the human psyche. Islam creates believers who are so impassioned about their faith and their ideology, they are willing to die for the glory of Islam, to make their religion supreme, and to receive the rewards promised in its name.

> Koran 85:11 "For those who believe and do good deeds will be gardens; the fulfillment of all desires."

> Koran 56:8 "Those of the right hand—how happy will be those of the right hand! . . . who will be honored in the Garden of Bliss . . .

> Koran 56:13 "A multitude of those from among the first, and a few from the latter, (will be) on couch-like thrones woven with gold and precious stones. Reclining, facing each other. Round about them will (serve) boys of perpetual (freshness), of never-ending bloom, with goblets, jugs, and cups (filled) with sparkling wine. No aching of the head will they receive, nor suffer any madness, nor exhaustion. And with fruits, any that they may select; and the flesh of fowls, any they may desire. And (there will be) Hur (fair females) with big eyes, lovely and pure, beautiful ones, like unto hidden pearls, well-guarded in their shells. A reward for the deeds."[5]

Establishing Islam as the dominant religion on earth and making the whole world submit to it becomes the ultimate goal. These devout Muslims are not restricted by Western social constructs. Murder is perfectly acceptable as a way to accomplish their goal. After all, this is exactly how Prophet Mohammed spread Islam throughout many nations and continents. The precedent was set by "the perfect man," Al-Insan Al Kamil, Prophet Mohammed himself.

book, *Schmoozing with Terrorists: From Hollywood to the Jihadists Reveal Their Global Plans to a Jew!*, Aaron Klein interviewed terrorist leaders and suicide bombers to learn why they are blowing themselves up to kill infidels. While Westerners think that suicide bombers blow themselves up because of the occupation in Israel, the occupation of Iraq, and U.S. presence on Arab soil, nothing could be farther from the truth. One of the recruited bombers Klein interviewed scoffed at claims that he decided to become a bomber in response to Israeli actions and called that "Israeli propaganda." He went on to say:

> The will to sacrifice myself for Allah is the first and most major reason. It is true that the Zionists are occupying our lands and that it is our religious duty to fight them, including through suicide attacks. The goal is not the killing of the Jews, but that this is the way to reach Allah. . . . Martyrs have special status in the next world and have bigger chances to watch Allah's face and enjoy the magnificent pleasures he offers us."[6]

These terrorists take great pride in their religion and in their work to spread that religion: they are willing to talk to anyone, to brag to anyone. They do not have secrets, they do not have a hidden agenda. On the contrary, they advertise their views on Web sites, and write articles to encourage others and to explain why all Muslims are called to serve such a mighty cause. They are willing to sit with reporters and share their pride of purpose and thoughts in order to ensure that the West understands what they want. Their passion and commitment is unmatched in any other religion today. The terrorists of today are very savvy in using the media and technology to their advantage. They have developed a well thought out public relations campaign that has produced videos and mission statements that have been seen and read by millions. The Islamic terrorists' publicity machine is targeted, high-tech, and frighteningly successful.

"FOURTH-GENERATION WARFARE"

Al Qaeda has its own biweekly Internet magazine: *Al-Ansar*. An issue published in early February 2002 contains an article written by Abu Ubeid Al-Qurashi, one of Osama bin Laden's closest aides. Al-Qurashi describes Al Qaeda's war against the infidel as "fourth-generation warfare," a new name for the same hallowed concept: terrorism. He states:

> The fourth-generation wars would, tactically, be small-scale, emerging in various regions across the planet against an enemy that, like a ghost, appears and disappears. The focus would be political, social, economic and military. [It will be] international, national, tribal, and even organizations would participate (even though tactics and technology from previous generations would be used).[7]
>
> The Islamic nation has chalked up the most victories in a short time, in a way it has not known since the rise of the Ottoman Empire. These victories were achieved during the past twenty years, against the best armed, best trained, and most experienced armies in the world (the U.S.S.R. in Afghanistan, the U.S. in Somalia, Russia in Chechnya, and the Zionist entity in southern Lebanon) and in various arenas (mountains, deserts, hills, cities). In Afghanistan, the mujahedeen triumphed over the world's second most qualitative power at that time. . . . Similarly, a single Somali tribe humiliated America and compelled it to remove its forces from Somalia. A short time later, the Chechen mujahedeen humiliated and defeated the Russian bear. After that, the Lebanese resistance [Hezbollah] expelled the Zionist army from southern Lebanon.[8]

In case his message eluded you, "fourth-generation" warfare, meaning terrorism, will be directed at the West's political, social, economic and military assets.[9]

Note that Al-Qurashi speaks of the "Islamic nation." By this, Al-Qurashi removes all doubt that we are in a religious war. Al-Qurashi understands his religious duty to unite all Muslims into a supranational entity that aims to destroy the infidel, the infidel's world, what it stands for, and everything in it. In the same edition of *Al-Ansar*, he lists the victories that have accrued to the "Islamic nation" as a result of its adoption of fourth-generational warfare. He boasts of more victories in the last twenty-five years than at any time since the rise of the Ottoman empire.

These victories, however, do not satisfy the "Islamic nation." The fresh taste of blood whets its appetite for more. Victory serves only to highlight the weaknesses of the enemy, and to reveal opportunities for further conquest. Victory is the motivation to further plunder and lay waste to the land of the infidel.

Al-Qurashi displayed his disdain for the modern Western world in recapping the "Islamic nation's" victories on September 11 in the February 26, 2002, issue of *Al-Ansar*:

1) No form of surveillance can provide early warning or permit rapid decision making. Even the Echelon satellite surveillance system, which cost billions of dollars . . . did not . . . stop the 19 mujahedeen wielding knives.

2) The American's marketing of the war is totally inefficient. America could not even find an acceptable name for the campaign. Neither "Crusader War," "Absolute Justice," or "Infinite Justice" allowed the American propaganda apparatus to overcome the feelings of hatred for America. They could not even remove internal American qualms.

3) The Islamic nation is struggling against globalization, [and has a] negative attitude towards Western rhetoric and explanations. The Westerners' rage increased once it became clear . . . that [Muslims] could use the same computers . . . without espousing the same values. . . . [Islamic] culture cannot be shattered by technology.

4) The West ignores the power of faith. Western civilization, . . . based on the information revolution, cannot distance the Muslims from the Koran. The book of Allah brings to the hearts of Muslims a faith deeper than all the . . . [lies] of the tyrannical Western propaganda machine.

5) Symbols never lose their value. Sheikh Osama [bin Laden] has become a symbol for the repressed from the four corners of the Earth—even for non-Muslims.

6) [Size] did not keep [the Western propaganda machine] from being defeated by Sheikh Osama. . . . The aggressive Westerners became accustomed to observing the tragedies of others—but on September 11 the opposite happened.[10]

Al-Qurashi makes five points that cannot be overstated: 1) The Islamic holy warriors, the mujahedeen, lack the military technology to compete on our level; 2) Therefore, they will seize the West's weapons and turn Western technological strengths against us. 3) We cannot use this same strategy against them. 4) They understand what makes us tick and can manipulate our emotions. 5) We cannot deter or influence them. They are believers, confirmed in their faith and motivated to press on to victory against an enemy that lacks the fire, courage, and motivation to oppose them to the bitter end.[11]

NO NEED FOR COMPROMISE

The lack of international recognition and support from Western countries for the mujahedeen's jihad and their cause need not discourage them, Al-Qurashi writes, because it is actually their strength. It obviates the need to compromise or "to continually lower the threshold of their demands" in order to gain recognition from their enemies.[12] So great is the mujahedeen's faith in terror and the power of psychological manipulation that they do not doubt their ability to demolish all obstacles. Thus they can dispense with the need to accommodate, in any way, the imperatives of their enemies.

I spend hours monitoring Islamic chat rooms on the Internet in order to monitor terrorist groups' activities and to keep my hand on the pulse of the radical mind and its reactions to current events or developing news around the world. I infiltrate sites associated with Al Qaeda, Hamas, Hezbollah, and a variety of other smaller, less-known groups. The remarkable thing is, no matter which site I am on, they all sound the same: the same rhetoric and same reactions to current events. The only difference is in the dialects of the people involved in the conversation. These radicals are driven by the same form of authentic, "straight" Islam as is written in the Koran, and are singleminded in their desire to fight the infidels until Islam emerges victoriously in the West.

The main driving force behind all Islamic terrorism is the Koran. What drives these passionate soldiers of Allah is Islam itself and the promises made to them by the Prophet Mohammed. They are convinced that it is only a matter of time before the caliphate is brought back and Islam is established as supreme throughout the world. They are repulsed by Western societies that permit free sex, drugs, prostitution, nudity, and especially a woman's right to be a man's equal. They are repulsed by Western women's freedom, their dress code, and their independence. The position of women in the West is abhorrent in Islam's view and gives fuel to those purists who want to bring Allah's justice to earth and punish those who gave women such freedom and undermined God's will.

Islamists use women's rights in the West as a rallying point to show that unless stopped, this corruption, headed by the United States, is coming to their Islamic communities and countries. They use this point to recruit and motivate Muslim men, young and old, to stand up and fight to protect from Western invasion and preserve the honor code and family values of Islamic societies. They blame the deterioration of Western societies on women's rights, which allowed women to initiate divorce and destroy the family. They reinforce the Islamic teaching that women need to be controlled and beaten for the protection and preservation of culture and society.

To them, Western women who bare their legs, arms, hair, and make up their faces are bait for sin. And we are not talking about the likes of Britney Spears dancing half naked with a live snake draped on her body. We are talking about any woman who wears shorts and a tank top to go to the grocery store to pick up some milk.

On one occasion when I was speaking at a large gathering of community leaders and activists who came to hear my lecture on terrorism, I discussed the 9/11 hijackers, their ideology, and the ritual they performed the night before the attacks. A very nice, friendly woman in her forties stood up and asked me, "But since they lived among us, didn't they see how nice we are? Didn't they see that we are not all corrupt?" I looked at her and paused for few seconds. She was wearing business attire: a skirt above her knees showing her legs, a short-sleeved shirt baring her arms, with a V-neckline that allowed her chest to be visible in a conservative way. Her hair was worn up, revealing her neck, and she wore a beautiful necklace. Knowing that she was a business owner, I looked at her and said: "You are what they despise about our culture. You are the example of a beautiful woman, who in their eyes is baring it all for men to see. I can see your legs, your arms, your neck, face, and hair, and your cleavage." She was a bit shocked by my frankness but I continued. "You are the picture-perfect image of an independent woman who can provide for herself and her family without having to depend on a man. You have proven you have a brain and an ability to use it, rendering men irrelevant in your life by your independence." This female freedom and independence is one of the greatest sins in Islam and is one of devout Muslim purists' greatest justifications for terrorism against Western societies.

> Koran 33:59 "Prophet! Tell your wives and daughters and all Muslim women to draw cloaks and veils all over their bodies (screening themselves completely except for one or two eyes to see the way). That will be better."[13]

Conversations in Islamic chat rooms often focus on the purity of a Muslim life and how the Prophet Mohammed instructed his people to live according to the will of Allah. They believe that it is the Muslim's religious duty to fight in the way of Allah against nonbelievers regardless of who they are or how nice they may be. Personality has nothing to do with religion and God's orders. They believe that they are the chosen ones who must fight to reclaim Islam's greatness and to establish the caliphate that infidel nations destroyed.

> "Not equal are those believers who sit at home and receive no injurious hurt, and those who strive hard, fighting jihad in Allah's cause with their wealth and lives. Allah has granted a rank higher to those who strive hard, fighting jihad with their wealth and bodies to those who sit (at home). Unto each has Allah promised good, but He prefers jihadists who strive hard and fight above those who sit home. He has distinguished his fighters with a huge reward."[14] (Koran 4:95)

In the years following 9/11, the West still has not recognized that we are fighting a devout enemy motivated by religion who is willing to destroy the whole world in order to achieve our complete submission under Islam.

In 2006 the Pentagon assigned intelligence analysts to write a report about the source of Islamic extremism flaring around the world. They wanted to find out what is driving educated young men, and in some cases women, to commit such horrible acts of suicide and murder. The outcome of the briefing was politically incorrect and explosive. It is the Koran, the holy Islamic book, that is driving them. It is the religion itself, straight from the mouth of the Prophet Mohammed, the perfect man, according to Muslims.[15]

The Pentagon briefing paper was titled "Motivations of Muslim Suicide Bombers." The analysts had studied the Koran and Islamic scripture to try to understand Islam and see how extremists had hijacked a peaceful religion. What they found out was that suicide bombers were carrying out the teachings of the Koran. They found out that the more a Muslim understood the Koran and its teaching, the more immoderate he became as he headed toward the purer form of what Mohammed taught.

The report concludes: "Suicide in defense of Islam is permitted, and the Islamic suicide bomber is, in the main, a rational actor."[16] It's time we stop mincing words. What we are calling radical Muslims are nothing more than devout purists. Here are just a few quotes from the Koran that prove my point.

> "Fight those who do not believe until they all surrender, paying the protective tax in submission." (Koran 9:29)

> "Fight them until all opposition ends and all submit to Allah." (Koran 8:39)

> "Fight them and Allah will punish them by your hands, lay them low, and cover them with shame. He will help you over them." (Koran 9:14)

> "O Prophet, urge the faithful to fight. If there are twenty among you with determination they will vanquish two hundred; if there are a hundred then they will slaughter a thousand unbelievers, for the infidels are a people devoid of understanding." (Koran 8:65)

> "Fight the unbelievers around you, and let them find harshness in you." (Koran 9:123)

> "Say (Mohammed) to the wandering desert Arabs who lagged behind: 'You shall be invited to fight against a people given to war with mighty prowess. You shall fight them until they surrender and submit. If you obey, Allah will grant you a reward, but if you turn back, as you did before, He will punish you with a grievous torture.' "

The Pentagon briefing states:

> His [the suicide bomber] actions provide a win-win scenario for himself, his family, his faith and his God. . . . The bomber

secures salvation and the pleasures of Paradise. He earns a degree of financial security and a place for his family in Paradise. He defends his faith and takes his place in a long line of martyrs to be memorialized as a valorous fighter. . . . And finally, because of the manner of his death, he is assured that he will find favor with Allah. . . . Against these considerations, the selfless sacrifice by the individual Muslim to destroy Islam's enemies becomes a suitable, feasible and acceptable course of action."[17]

The briefing was the culmination of endless hours of work by the Counterintelligence Field Activity, a Pentagon intelligence unit. The briefing cites many Koranic scriptures relating to jihad and martyrdom. It also recounts how suicide bombers prepare for an attack by reciting passages from six surahs, or chapters, of the Koran: Baqura (surah 2), Al Imran (3), Anfal (8), Tawba (9), Rahman (55), and Asr (103).[18]

The following are more examples of holy scriptures that drive and validate their belief, ideology, and sincere determination to do the right thing according to their religion:

"I shall terrorize the infidels. So wound their bodies and incapacitate them because they oppose Allah and His Apostle." (Koran 8:12)

"The infidels should not think that they can get away from us. Prepare against them whatever arms and weaponry you can muster so that you may terrorize them. They are your enemy and Allah's enemy." (Koran 8:59)

"Fight and kill disbelievers wherever you find them, take them captive, beleaguer them, and lie in wait and ambush them using every stratagem of war." (Koran 9:5)

The astonishing thing is that the Pentagon briefing was completely ignored by the media, as though its subject was toxic and harmful to the touch. Even after this study by what is supposed to be the American military heartbeat, the White House insisted that Islam is a religion of peace and that it is not the religion that is radical but rather those corrupt individuals who hijacked it.

Not only are the radicals drinking their Islam straight but the holy book they read is like a bartender who keeps refilling their glasses, reinforcing and motivating them toward greater atrocities, to be committed while in their religious stupor. We are committing cultural suicide by turning a blind eye to the danger Islam spells out continually.

Here is a shot straight from the hundred-proof bottle. The Palestinian Authority–controlled daily *Al-Hayat Al-Jadida* ran this message on September 11, 2001:

> The suicide bombers of today are the noble successors of their noble predecessors . . . the Lebanese suicide bombers, who taught the U.S. Marines a rough lesson [murdering 241 Marines and 63 civilians in the 1983 bombing of the Marines headquarters and U.S. embassy in Beirut]. . . . They are the salt of the earth, the engines of history . . . the most honorable persons among us.[19]

Putting aside the astounding coincidence of extolling suicide bombers on the very day that suicide bombers attacked the United States, the Palestinian Authority's reference to them as "the salt of the earth" should tell us all we need to know about how killers are glorified and praised in Islamic culture.

Moreover, this message comes directly from the radicals' own mouthpiece! The suicide bomber is the highest embodiment of Palestinian culture and Islamic culture in general, where murder is not only justified in the name of the religion and by the religion, but encouraged as a special obligation of jihad. The triumphant and celebratory atmosphere within the Arab Muslim world on 9/11 was a logical extension of this core Islamic belief.[20] They were dancing, blowing car horns, and throwing candy in the streets.

This love and veneration of suicide bombers extends throughout the Islamic nations. Sheikh Muhammad Jamaal spoke to 28,000 worshipers on December 14, 2001, at the Al Aksa mosque on Jerusalem's Temple Mount. With no apparent inhibition, he prayed:

> May the fire of Allah burn down the USA; may He drown America's ships and down her aircraft; may Allah afflict the USA with earthquakes; may Arab oil—imported by America— exterminate U.S. leaders![21]

Violence is exhorted by the highest religious authorities throughout the Muslim world from their houses of worship. And for Muslims, the mosque is much more than just a place to pray. As noted on an Islamic website:

> The mosque means much more than a mere house of divine worship . . . ; it is the real centre for the society of Islam in a certain locality. . . . The mosque is also the cultural centre of Islam. . . . The mosque, being the essential meeting place of Muslims five times a day, [is] also a general centre where all important matters relating to the welfare of the Muslim com- munity [are] transacted and where Muslims [gather] on im- portant occasions. . . . The mosque [is] thus not only the spiritual centre of Muslims but also their educational, politi- cal and social centre, their national centre in a general sense.[22]

For Muslims, the mosque is their *cultural* center. The preaching of violence from mosques speaks volumes about the culture that

permits it, encourages it, and endorses it. The Palestinian Authority regularly broadcasts Sheikh Jamaal's sermons on television and
radio. On December 28, 2001, he advised:

> Oh believers . . . do not count on the evil USA, which hates
> Muslims and Islam . . . Infidel countries, led by the USA, have
> launched a dirty war against Islam.[23]

The aggressor cries victim! And don't give me the line, "They
are just trying to get back what the Jews took from them." The land
of Israel has been in existence for thousands of years. Muslims are
upset that Jews are living on a sliver of what was originally theirs
and that the United States is supporting and protecting them. Israel is the only region of democracy, modernity, and civilization in
a vast land of ignorance, backwardness, and barbarism.

Clerics routinely educate Muslims to believe that the United
States is an enemy of Islam. Believers are exhorted to pray for devastation to befall America. Is it surprising that the Islamic world's
anger, hatred, and paranoia find their outlet in suicide and bombings? America and the West did not declare war on Islam. It is the
purest form of Islam that has declared war on the infidel—and Islam taken straight has no leniency.

As a warrior, Prophet Mohammed set the example that continues to inspire jihad. He ordered twenty-seven military campaigns
and led nine personally. Howard Bloom, the author of *The Lucifer
Principle,* states:

> According to some Koranic interpreters, any leader who
> fails to "make wide slaughter" in the land of the infidel is
> committing a sin. A statesman is only allowed the tempo-
> rary expedient of peace if his forces are not yet strong
> enough to win."[24]

Radical Islam abhors sin. In particular, it abhors the sin of Muslims' failure to slaughter and subjugate large numbers of infidels.

The call to hatred and jihad in mosques throughout Western nations should send shivers down the spines of every freedom-loving, God-fearing, tolerant Westerner who just wants to live and let live. As Americans who believe the founding father's views on free speech, we are now faced with a conundrum. While we afford Muslims the freedom to express their thoughts and their religion in our land, they are using our freedoms to incite hatred and are working to end our democracy. They are free to say what they want to do. It's up to you and me to make sure they don't do what they say.

Western civilization has bestowed on us the blessings of freedom and individual conscience. It has granted us opportunities for accomplishment and productivity to an extent unseen in any other culture. We are obliged to appreciate these gifts and see the difference in what our enemies are proposing for us. Theirs is a culture that shamelessly glorifies violence against the infidel. In their culture, there is no higher calling than that of the suicide bomber.

Before 9/11, Islamic terrorist entities—that is, state-sponsored terrorist organizations or terrorist states—had successfully executed suicide operations not only in Judea, Samaria, Gaza, and Israel, but also in Afghanistan, Algeria, Argentina, Chechnya, Croatia, Kashmir, Kenya, Kuwait, Lebanon, Pakistan, Panama, Russia, Tajikistan, Tanzania, Saudi Arabia, Yemen—and against the United States.[25] Islamic terrorists targeted ordinary citizens of every nationality, foreign embassies, two U.S. embassies (in Kenya and Tanzania), American warships and military personnel, and world leaders.[26] They even attempted to assassinate the pope during his visit to the Philippines in 1995.[27]

After 9/11, the killing continues unabated in all of these countries, with bombings against civilian and tourist targets in Kenya,

Indonesia, Turkey, Russia, India, Israel, Bali, England, and other locations too numerous to mention.

September 11 was not the first Islamic terrorist attack inside the
United States. However, it was the signal event that, finally, removed all doubt that the United States was now a permanent fix-
ture on our enemies' radar.

Radical Islam is determined to destroy us and it has a plan. Its
followers harbor no shame for their murderous desires, brazenly
publicizing their intentions. Theirs is a militaristic culture that rejects and aims to destroy the outsider. They consider themselves victims of an enemy that seeks to humiliate and destroy them. At the
same time they eye the infidel West as a choice morsel, impotent and
defenseless, just waiting to be consumed. Can we match their zeal-
ous hatred with our own passionate commitment to defend our way
of life, the values we believe in, and the fruits of our civilization?

Bin Laden's closest aide, Lieutenant Al-Qurashi, recognizes our
apparent disadvantage. He sees a contrast between the commitment
of the "believer" and that of the "infidel." He notes that the principle
of deterrence that prevented war between the United States and the
former Soviet Union cannot be used by the West against radical Islam. The principle of deterrence is worthless, he says, "when dealing
with people who don't care about living but thirst for martyrdom."[28]
Such people, he continues, are completely independent in their decisions and seek conflict from the outset. "How can such people, who
strive for death more than anything else, be deterred?" he asks.[29]

WE HAVE NAMED OUR ENEMY

It is not yet politically correct to talk about a religious war. But this
is exactly what we are facing: a religious war declared by devout

Muslims. At least at this point it is acceptable to call it radical Islam. Daily we see President George W. Bush and his administration take pains to insist that the war on terrorism is not a religious conflict.[30] President Bush continues to refer to radical Islam's terrorists as "evildoers, rather than devout Muslims."[31] Better a vague declaration against terrorism in general! After all, we know that speaking candidly when it comes to Islam can be hazardous to one's health. But this choice, however practical, hands radical Islam a victory in the psychological battle it is waging against us.[32] The reluctance to name those who seek our destruction astonishes them as much as it assists them. Yes, astonishes them! Remember, they do not conceal their intentions toward us. Our refusal to acknowledge their true motivations renders us cowardly and foolish in their eyes.[33] To our enemy, might makes right; cowardice and stupidity are open invitations for attack.[34]

Are we so blinded by goodwill toward our enemy that we fail to see that its strategy for conquest is based on the zeal of the believer and the presumed reticence and timidity of the infidel? Our reluctance to offend the offenders denies us the clarity, understanding, and determination required to confront, oppose, and ultimately prevail against our enemies. To oppose our enemy, we must identify it by name. I hereby claim the right to do so.

We must confront the horror of those who represent the forces of chaos. And we must try, if it is not already too late, to put a dangerous genie back in its bottle—a genie that has been allowed far too much freedom, and has established itself as a prominent and dangerous element on the Western political landscape.

Islam has created and unleashed an uncontrollable wave of hatred and rage on the world, and we must brace ourselves for the consequences. Going forward we must realize that the portent behind the terrorist attacks is the purest form of what the Prophet

Mohammed created. It's not radical Islam. It's what Islam is at its core. A core that has been "peacefulized" over the past century as it became infused and diluted by the civilized and moderate norms of new adherents, by the strength of Western civilization, and by the historic weakness of the Muslim world. But Muslims are no longer weak and no longer poor. They have traded their swords for AK-47's, RPG's, TNT, and missiles. They are spreading their oil wealth around the world to bring Islam back. The time of moderation and watered-down religion is over, and the Islam of Mohammed is back. "Radical Islam" is Mohammed's Islam.

4

THE MUSLIM BROTHERHOOD "PROJECT" FOR NORTH AMERICA

One of the greatest challenges to people who monitor and follow developing terrorist activities is convincing the average Westerner that a totalitarian Islamic ideology is a threat to our way of life. Most people wish that Islamic radicalism were just a minor problem the world is dealing with and that somehow would be solved if we just pulled out of Iraq and brought the troops home. For those who believe our problem with Islam will be solved once we pull out of Iraq, please consider the following.

In November 2001—just a few short months after September 11—a detailed document was found in a villa in Switzerland by Swiss authorities. This document outlined a hundred-year plan for radical Islam to infiltrate and dominate the West and "establish an Islamic government on earth." In counterterrorism circles this document became known as "The Project."

This plan was conceived and written by the Muslim Brotherhood, the world's oldest and most sophisticated Islamic terrorist group. The Muslim Brotherhood was created in Egypt in 1928 by Hasan al-Banna and boasts seventy off-shoot terrorist organizations operating throughout the world. Its doctrine states: "Allah is our objective. The Prophet is our leader. Qur'an is our law. Jihad is our way. Dying in the way of Allah is our highest hope."[1]

In the documents that were seized many proposals and tactics were detailed in the fourteen-page plan, written in Arabic. Twenty-six of these points are listed below and identify strategies by which Islamists can gradually infiltrate nations and ultimately dominate the world with an Islamic political and religious ideology and Sharia law. Counterterrorism and radical Islam expert Patrick Poole has summarized these points:[2]

- Networking and coordinating actions between like-minded Islamist organizations
- Avoiding open alliances with known terrorist organizations and individuals to maintain the appearance of "moderation"
- Infiltrating and taking over existing Muslim organizations to realign them toward the Muslim Brotherhood's collective goals
- Using deception to mask the intended goals of Islamist actions, as long as it doesn't conflict with Sharia law
- Avoiding social conflicts with Westerners locally, nationally, or globally that might damage the long-term ability to expand the Islamist power base in the West or provoke a backlash against Muslims
- Establishing financial networks to fund the work of conversion of the West, including the support of full-time administrators and workers conducting surveillance, obtaining data, and establishing collection and data-storage capabilities
- Putting into place a watchdog system for monitoring Western media to warn Muslims of international plots fomented against them

- Cultivating an Islamist intellectual community, including the establishment of think tanks and advocacy groups, and publishing academic studies, to legitimize Islamist positions and to chronicle the history of Islamist movement
- Developing a comprehensive hundred-year plan to advance Islamist ideology throughout the world
- Balancing international objectives with local flexibility
- Building extensive social networks of schools, hospitals, and charitable organizations dedicated to Islamist ideals so that contact between the movement and Muslims in the West is constant
- Involving ideologically committed Muslims in democratically elected institutions on all levels in the West, including government, NGOs, private organizations, and labor unions
- Instrumentally using existing Western institutions until they can be converted and put into the service of Islam
- Drafting Islamic constitutions, laws, and policies for eventual implementation
- Avoiding conflict within the Islamist movements on all levels, including the development of processes for conflict resolution
- Instituting alliances with Western "progressive" organizations that share similar goal
- Creating autonomous security forces to protect Muslims in the West
- Inflaming violence and keeping Muslims living in the West in a jihad frame of mind
- Supporting jihad movements across the Muslim world through preaching, propaganda, personnel, funding, and technical and operational support
- Making the Palestinian cause a global wedge issue for Muslims
- Adopting the goals of the total liberation of Palestine from

Israel and the creation of an Islamic state as keystones in the plan for global Islamic domination

- Instigating a constant campaign to incite hatred by Muslims against Jews and rejecting any discussions of conciliation or coexistence with them
- Actively creating jihad terror cells within Palestine
- Linking the terrorist activities in Palestine with the global terror movement
- Collecting sufficient funds to indefinitely perpetuate and support jihad around the world[3]

The Muslim Brotherhood Project is unusual not because it outlines a strategic plan to establish a world Islamic caliphate but because it includes methods other than violence, to implement cultural jihad. This plan requires much patience from its administrators and relies on the non-Muslim population to unsuspectingly endorse and embrace it in the name of multiculturalism and freedom of religion. Some of the most alarming ideas outlined in the Project are: incitement to hate and commit violent acts against Jewish, Christian, and other non-Muslim entities; an acceptance of jihad as a necessary force in establishing a world Islamic caliphate; establishing a rapport with Western communities until trust is won and Islam is established; and the implementation of Sharia law throughout the world.[4]

The Project document was dated December 1, 1982, and its intentions have been implemented throughout the world since its creation. One of the hallmarks of the Muslim Brotherhood is the use of two principles: Taqiyya and Da'wa. The first is the Islamic practice of "concealing or disguising one's beliefs, convictions, ideas, feelings, opinions, and/or strategies at a time of eminent danger, whether now or later in time, to save oneself from physical and/or mental *injury*."[5] Taqiyya is also used as justification for lies and deceit to advance the cause of Islam. Da'wa is the act of inviting non-Muslims to accept the truth of Islam. Performing Da'wa involves both words and actions, and is frequently practiced in public schools in America and Western communities. Non-Muslim parents are invited to meetings in the homes of Muslim parents or teachers to learn about Islam as a docile religion. Conversion is the ultimate goal on the part of the Muslim initiating Da'wa.[6]

The practices of Taqiyya and Da'wa are encouraged by the Project's initiatives. Both manipulate Westerners to make them believe that Islam is a peaceful religion and its doctrines are written to help all mankind. In contrast to this Islamic principle, people raised in Judeo-Christian cultures are taught from childhood that lying is bad and honesty is good. It is not only a part of the foundation of our beliefs, but also a part of our culture. So when Westerners hear Muslim talking heads, either on television or in their communities, profess that Islam is a religion of peace, they believe them. Nothing disturbs me more than when I see ministers, priests, and rabbis who are involved in interfaith dialogue, listening to imams say that Islam is a peaceful religion that has been hijacked by radicals. They cannot imagine that someone can look them straight in the eye and lie. They accept what they hear at face value and are deceived. In their ignorance they support the spread of Islamic practices and culture in the West, and do so in the name of tolerance, understanding, and multiculturalism.

In February 2008 the Archbishop of Canterbury said, "The adoption of certain aspects of Sharia law in the United Kingdom seems unavoidable."[7]

We now have the head of the Church of England himself calling for the advancement of Islam in Britain. That's how successful Islam's cultural jihad in Europe has been. In America, George Bush himself calls Islam a religion of peace and has held Iftar dinners at the White House to tell imams how their religion has been hijacked by radicals. The FBI even invites CAIR, the Council on American Islamic Relations, when some of its leaders have been convicted on terrorism-related charges to one the country's largest airports, Chicago's O'Hare, and gives them a behind-the-scenes tour to demonstrate how security is conducted. CAIR is even giving sensitivity training to our FBI and government workers. Kansas City International Airport installed Muslim foot-washing benches in its bathrooms so Muslim cab drivers can wash their feet before prayers.[8] I lived in the Middle East for the first twenty-four years of my life. Never once did I see foot-washing benches in any public place, including airports, universities, public buildings, or hospitals. I can give hundreds of examples from around Western nations caving in to cultural Islam, enough to fill another book. Westerners are being taken for a ride in the name of tolerance, understanding, and multiculturalism.

· · ·

The Muslim Brotherhood is deploying its jihad as outlined in the Project throughout Europe as well. The French intifada and the Danish cartoon of Mohammed were the cause of two well-known incidents that sparked violent riots. These demonstrations were influenced and orchestrated by the Muslim Brotherhood in its attempt to rouse Muslim communities from their sleep and unite in the name of Islamic nationalism.[9] Remember, one of the points of the Project outlined above is: *Inflaming violence and keeping Muslims living in the West in a jihad frame of mind.*

Another document found in the home of a terrorist suspect in 1991 (and introduced into evidence by the U.S. Justice Department at the Holy Land Foundation trial in Texas in 2007) illustrates the

North American plan for the Project by "Ikhwan" ("Brothers"), the Muslim Brotherhood's American branch. This eighteen-page document is a comprehensive plan that charts the groundwork for the establishment of an Islamic government in North America and the implementation of Sharia law. The philosophy of the document is described below in a passage from Ikhwan's Plan for North America:

> The process of settlement [of Islam in the United States] is a "Civilization-Jihadist" process with all that the word means. The Ikhwan must understand that all their work in America is a kind of grand jihad in eliminating and destroying the Western civilization from within and "sabotaging" their miserable house by their hands and the hands of the believers so that it is eliminated and God's religion is made victorious over all religions. Without this level of understanding, we are not up to this challenge and have not prepared ourselves for jihad yet. It is a Muslim's destiny to perform jihad and work wherever he is and wherever he lands until the final hour comes, and there is no escape from that destiny except for those who choose to slack.[10]

The "Civilization Jihadist" process the Ikhwan are referring to is cultural jihad. Islamic practices are being pushed down the throats of American corporations and the public on many levels. Who would have thought that Sharia would come to Harvard University, which in 2007 regulated "women-only" gym hours.[11] An imam in Des Moines, Iowa, gave an opening prayer at the 2008 Iowa legislative session in which he called on Allah to "give us victory over those who disbelieve"—meaning victory over "infidels."[12] Muslim taxi drivers in Minnesota are refusing to pick up passengers carrying alcohol.[13] The first Islamic public school (Khalil Gibran Academy) in New York opened in 2007 and was funded by tax dollars.[14] Muslim radical compounds practicing Sharia law operate in many parts of the United States.[15] American colleges are designating Islamic prayer rooms on college campuses for use by Muslims only.[16] These are only a few examples of what I see as cultural jihad in America. Muslim radical groups are also using every opportunity available to them under democracy, including the use of charitable organizations, to advance their cause.

In August 2003, the U.S. Department of the Treasury's Office of Foreign Asset Control identified an American-based Islamic charitable organization, the Holy Land Foundation for Relief and Development, as the primary fund-raising branch of Hamas in the United States. The United States has labeled the Holy Land Foundation a Specially Designated Global Terrorist.[17] The Treasury Department has reported that since the foundation's creation in California in 1989 its funds have been used by Hamas to support schools that indoctrinate students to become suicide bombers.[18] The federal trial against The Holy Land Foundation in Dallas, Texas, was one of the most important events in the fight against radical Islam and the effort to expose its operation in the United States. During the trial Hamas was identified as the Palestinian branch of the international Muslim Brotherhood. Numerous published reports indicate that Hamas has set up fund-raising initiatives in the United States through supposedly respected and benevolent Muslim organizations and charities, including the Council on Islamic American Relations, the Islamic Society of North America, and the Muslim American Society.[19]

The Holy Land Foundation trial ended in a mistrial. The jury was made up of average citizens who, in my opinion, were overwhelmed with information and lacked the counterintelligence expertise to weigh the facts. I conclude that the jury couldn't tell the difference between Hamas, a terrorist organization, and Shin Bet, an Israeli intelligence agency. William Neal, the only juror who spoke publicly, is an art director who did not believe Hamas is a terrorist organization. He called it "a political movement. It's an uprising." The U.S. government said it would retry the case.[20]

. Richard A. Clarke, a former national security advisor to four presidents, told the U.S. Senate in 2003 that the Muslim Brotherhood serves to unite Islamic terrorist fund-raising initiatives.[21] The Brotherhood's long-term goal is to establish a pan-Islamic state that would unite the Muslim world under one political and religious leadership. As mentioned in the Project's documents that were seized, jihad does not necessarily need to "dominate by the sword." The Brotherhood's plan outlines behavior that works to systematically change the laws of the United States Constitution and the civil rights of its citizens through propaganda and economic control. Alluding to this plan, Dr. Yusuf al-Qarodawi, spiritual leader of the Muslim Brotherhood, has commented that jihad can be fought with the pen and the tongue, just as it can be fought with the sword and the spear.[22]

The Muslim Brotherhood can be described as an "insurgency." In fact, the United States counterinsurgency manual, FM 3-24, classifies the term as "an organized movement aimed at the overthrow of a constituted government through the use of subversion and armed conflict."[23] Surely, the documents of the Ikhwan branch of the Muslim Brotherhood presented in the Holy Land trial describe a powerful threat to the future survival of the United States and to the fabric of our society.

ISLAM FLOURISHES BEHIND BARS

Radical Islam is on the march in America, and the Muslim Brotherhood has embarked on a plan to recruit Americans to do their dirty work. Not just any Americans, but Americans who have been indicted on charges of murder, pedophilia, rape, burglary, and other violent crimes, residents of America's penal institutions. In a 2004 report by the U.S. Justice Department, it is noted that prisoners "remain vulnerable to infiltration to religious extremists." In addition, terrorist groups have trained Muslim prison chaplains to recruit and radicalize inmates.[24] A 2007 Justice Department report discusses Al Qaeda's recruitment of incarcerated African Americans for suicide missions in the United States.[25]

Fundamentalist Islam is targeting African Americans in an attempt to bypass security profiling that would normally draw attention to terrorist operations. This approach takes advantage of any resentment toward the white establishment and provides fundamentalist Islam with terrorists who do not fit the the the usual profiles. Dr. Ayman Al-Zawahiri, number-two man in Al Qaeda, has stated publically, "I want blacks in America to know that we are waging jihad to lift oppression from all mankind."[26] What Zawahiri doesn't say is that Mohammed disliked the black race immensely and referred to them as "raisin heads" several time in the Hadith (1:662; 9:256).[27] Throughout the Hadith blacks are also referred to as *abeds*, which means "black" in Arabic, and is also synonymous with the words "slave" or "filth." In fact, Arab Muslims have enslaved blacks for 1,400 years, and the black slave trade is still thriving in the Sudan and Mauritania.[28] In examining the relationship between blacks and Islam, readers will be surprised to find that throughout history, Islam has placed blacks on the same level as barn animals. Moreover, the barn is where most enslaved blacks are relegated after they are kidnapped and forced to convert to Islam or die.[29]

Al Qaeda and Islamic imams are able to convert felons in America's prison system because Islam appeals to the mentality of the aggressor. Imagine, for example, the following situation. An imam working in a federal prison approaches a felon incarcerated on rape charges. The imam explains to the prisoner that in Islam Allah created women to be the property of men, to do with them whatever they desire, at any time. And if the woman is disobedient he can beat her and it is his right to do so in the eyes of Allah.

> "You may have whomever you desire; there is no blame." (Koran 33:51)

> "Allah permits you to shut them in separate rooms and to beat them, but not severely. If they abstain, they have the right to food and clothing. Treat women well for they are like domestic animals and they possess nothing themselves. Allah has made the enjoyment of their bodies lawful in his." (Tabari IX:113)

Suddenly the prisoner is a good person in the eyes of Islam, although he is a rapist in the eyes of the West. Why wouldn't he convert if Islam feeds his deepest desire to rape?

Imagine another scenario. An Imam approaches an incarcerated murderer, a serial killer who thrives on the rush of complete power over his victims, and explains to him all the verses in the Koran that promote killing and jihad. Islam does not condemn him for killing; he is praised for it, and the more infidels he kills, the greater his reward in heaven. In fact, the Koran explains killing in such detail that it feeds his appetite for killing:

> "Your Lord inspired the angels with the message: 'I will terrorize the unbelievers. Therefore smite them on their necks and every joint and incapacitate them. Strike off their heads and cut off each of their fingers and toes." (Koran 8:12)

> "The punishment for those who wage war against Allah and His Prophet and make mischief in the land, is to murder

them, crucify them, or cut off a hand and foot on opposite sides . . . their doom is dreadful. They will not escape the fire, suffering constantly." (Koran 5:33)

There are plenty of places in the world today, from Afghanistan to the Philippines, where a Muslim jihadist can roam and kill unpersecuted.

Here is yet another scenario. An Islamic imam approaches a felon jailed for child molestation. The imam explains to him that Islam does not consider him a child molester; he is a good person. The Prophet Mohammed, whom Muslims consider the perfect man, married a six-year-old girl and consummated the marriage when she was nine. While in the eyes of the West he is a criminal, in the eyes of Islam he is not only a good person but is following in the footsteps of the Prophet. All of a sudden the prisoner considers himself justified if he becomes a Muslim. Why wouldn't he convert? His criminal appetites and resentment of the West are legitimized in one simple step.

Such scenarios give you an idea why Islam is spreading like wildfire through the prison system. Its appeal to the most violent and ruthless impulses of humanity makes it appealing to those who thrive on that dark side.

HAMAS

Hamas is one of the most violent and highly motivated terrorist groups to emerge from the Muslim Brotherhood. Sheikh Ahmed Yassin founded Hamas in 1987 as the political arm of the Muslim Brotherhood after the first Palestinian uprising against Israel for control of the West Bank and Gaza. Both Hamas and the Muslim

Brotherhood share an intense hatred for Israel and reject Western values.[30]

Although Hamas has dedicated itself to destroying the state of Israel and the Jewish people, Hamas is not only Israel's problem. Hamas has cells all over the world, including in the United States. In my previous book I discuss in detail Hamas' infiltration of America and name the cities in which they operate. In addition to the geographic location of cells, a financial paper trail has also been discovered. In September 2001, an official complaint to the Internal Revenue Service by Judicial Watch, Inc., a watchdog group, reported a list of American Islamic organizations that serve as fronts for terrorist operations in the United States and abroad. The report states that Hamas' political headquarters are located at the offices of the United Association for Studies and Research in Springfield, Virginia.[31] That report was updated in 2007 and now includes American Islamic associations that have been one way or another associated with Hamas and the Muslim Brotherhood, such as the Council for American Islamic Relations, Islamic Society of North America, Islamic Council for North America, North American Islamic Trust, Muslim American Society, United Association for Studies and Research, and Muslim American Youth Association.[32]

The Hamas Charter,[33] published in 1988, states Hamas' main mission: "Israel will exist and will continue to exist until Islam will obliterate it just as it obliterated others before it." Although Hamas' central objective is to destroy Israel and the Jewish people, Hamas has clearly become a problem on American soil as well. Cautiously and deviously creating cells throughout the United States, Hamas has partnered with American Islamic charitable and nonprofit organizations that serve as fronts for Hamas bank accounts. Its cells strategically positioned throughout the United States, Hamas thrives in Islamic communities big and small in both rural areas and major cities.

Article twenty-two in the Hamas charter, states:[34]

> The enemies have been scheming for a long time, and they have consolidated their schemes, in order to achieve what they have achieved. They took advantage of key elements in unfolding events, and accumulated a huge and influential material wealth which they put to the service of implementing their dream. This wealth [permitted them to] take over control of the world media such as news agencies, the press, publication houses, broadcasting and the like. [They also used this] wealth to stir revolutions in various parts of the globe in order to fulfill their interests and pick the fruits. They stood behind the French and the Communist Revolutions and behind most of the revolutions we hear about here and there. They also used the money to establish clandestine organizations which are spreading around the world, in order to destroy societies and carry out Zionist interests. Such organizations are: the Freemasons, Rotary Clubs, Lions Clubs, B'nai B'rith and the like. All of them are destructive spying organizations. They also used the money to take over control of the Imperialist states and made them colonize many countries in order to exploit the wealth of those countries and spread their corruption therein. As regards local and world wars, it has come to pass and no one objects, that they stood behind World War I, so as to wipe out the Islamic caliphate. They collected material gains and took control of many sources of wealth. They obtained the Balfour Declaration and established the League of Nations in order to rule the world by means of that organization. They also stood behind World War II, where they collected immense benefits from trading with war materials and prepared for the establishment of their state. They inspired the establishment of the United Nations and the Security Council to replace the League of Nations, in order to rule the world by their intermediary. There was no war that broke out anywhere without their

fingerprints on it: The forces of Imperialism in both the Capitalist West and the Communist East support the enemy with
all their might, in material and human terms, taking turns
between themselves. When Islam appears, all the forces of
Unbelief unite to confront it, because the Community of Unbelief is one.

Radical Islamists are telling us exactly where they stand and
what are their intentions. We are refusing to understand their simple words and how serious they are in their faith and its commandments. On American soil, Hamas uses American residents, laws,
and freedoms to sponsor its activities. It is implicating America in
its war against Israel, and using America to destabilize the Middle
East, which is only the starting point of radical Islam's quest to
dominate the world. Radical Islamists are posting their mission
and vision on the Internet for all to read. Unless we eradicate their
organizational fronts and cells, they will be here to stay . . . and we
won't!

5

MADRASSAS IN AMERICA
AND ABROAD

In *Because They Hate* I devoted a chapter to the infiltration of Islamic education and its influence into our universities. The chapter is titled "The Ivy-Covered Fifth Column: Islamic Influence Alive and Well on American Campuses." If you have a child or a grandchild in college, you will want to read it. You'll learn that universities such as Harvard and Georgetown receive federal funds as well as millions of dollars from the Saudis for Middle Eastern studies programs. In her study "The Stealth Curriculum," Sandra Stotsky, a former director of a professional development institute for teachers at Harvard, wrote about the material taught in Islamic studies through these centers: "Most of these materials have been prepared and/or funded by Islamic sources here and abroad, and are distributed or sold directly to schools or individual teachers, thereby bypassing public scrutiny."[1] But radical Islamic influence in America's educational system reaches beyond the university level into grade schools and high schools, both public and private.

Because of the rise of Muslim immigration to the United States in the last two decades the number of Islamic schools in the United

States has increased dramatically. It is estimated that now there are between two hundred and six hundred Islamic schools in America teaching almost fifty thousand students.[2] Many of these schools are breeding grounds for jihad in America and are financed with American taxpayers' money.

The Islamic Academy of Florida, a private school for grades one through twelve, is nestled deep in a neighborhood of Tampa Bay, Florida. In 2003 the academy received more than $350,000 worth of taxpayer-funded school vouchers to help underprivileged children attend their school.[3] In the same year a federal grand jury in Tampa issued a fifty-count indictment against the academy for being an affiliate of the Muslim Brotherhood organization Palestinian Islamic Jihad, which is headquartered in the Middle East and targets with suicide bombings Israeli civilians and other individuals it deems enemies. The indictment claimed the academy was helping support the Palestinian Islamic Jihad and its mission of murder and violence by raising funds through school vouchers and fund-raisers.

In charge of fund-raising at the academy was the Palestinian Islamic Jihad's former chairman, Sami al-Arian. Ramadan Abdallah Shallah, a former teacher there (and the current leader of Palestinian Islamic Jihad), and the academy's former director, Mazen al-Najjar, were both deported from the United States on separate terrorism-related charges. Furthermore, the school is owned by the North American Islamic Trust, an Islamic investment group[4] that manages the assets of the most dangerous and treacherous mosques in America and was named as an unindicted co-conspirator in the Holy Land trial.

Because of the charges brought against them, more than $350,000 of the academy's school tuition vouchers were revoked. During the same year, another Islamic private day school, the American Youth Academy, opened up next door to the Islamic Academy

of Florida. The schools share the same desks, books, teachers, and
telephone number. In 2005, $325,000 of taxpayer money was
awarded to American Youth Academy for its elementary/secondary
school program. In addition, $2,500 was awarded to the school for
each child enrolled in their pre-kindergarten programs.[5]

The Islamic Academy of Florida and the American Youth Academy are prime examples of Islamic terrorists and their associates
operating right under our noses. The amazing thing is that taxpayers were unintentionally funding the overseas murders of innocent
citizens, including Americans. Worried about the War on Terror
overseas? With 200-plus registered Islamic schools in the United
States, we'd better start scrutinizing these schools, their books, and
operations, as well as their leadership and their associations with
terrorist organizations.

On the West Coast, the New Horizons School in Pasadena, California, another Islamic private day school, won a Blue Ribbon
award for excellence from the United States Department of Education.[6] Excellence in what? The Bureau of Islamic and Arabic Education, which developed the school's program of study, has on its
website a new twist to the United States Pledge of Allegiance: "As
an American Muslim, I pledge alliance to Allah and his Prophet."[7]

The Islamic Society of North America (ISNA), which the United
States government named as another unindicted co-conspirator in
the Holy Land trial, is the initiator and architect of all the New
Horizons Schools in North America. Various reports state that
ISNA, which distributes Islamic educational material to mosques
and Islamic schools in the United States, is allegedly affiliated with
domestic terrorist groups and those abroad, and has invited Islamic
radical extremists to speak at its events.[8]

Imam Muzzamil Siddiqui, leader of the Islamic Center of Southern California (which also helped to develop the new Horizon's

school curriculum), and former president, gives sermons that emphasize the essence and importance of Da'wa (an Islamic tradition of converting non-Muslims to Islam). Da'wa is one of the main tools listed in the Muslim Brotherhood's plan to dominate America. The website www.DawaNet.com includes a section called "How to Make America an Islamic Nation." Another page entitled "Da'wa in Public Schools" describes the school environment as "fertile grounds where the seeds of Islam can be sowed inside the hearts of the non-Muslim student."[9] Da'wa directs Muslims to communicate with non-Muslims as if "every non-Muslim is a potential Muslim."

The United States Department of Education must learn about Islam before the U.S. Constitution and the Bill of Rights resemble Sharia doctrine. Private Islamic schools in the United States are not the only schools participating in the Muslim Brotherhood's plan of Islamic infiltration and dominance in America. Because of its ignorance, the United States government is a contributor as well.

In 2002, Excelsior Elementary School, a public school in Bryon, California, began teaching as part of its seventh-grade world history and geography classes, a three-week course that taught students to memorize and recite Islamic prayers and verses from the Koran. Students also adopted Muslim names, fasted for a day to experience Ramadan, the holiest of Islamic religious holidays, and wrote about their experience as a Muslim at the end of the program. Exercises during class included encouraging students to incorporate Arabic phrases such as *Allah Akbar* in their speeches, and for students to imagine that they were Muslim disciples on a pilgrimage to Mecca. Excelsior's principal, Nancie Castro, said in 2002 that "at no point do we teach or endorse religion; we teach about religion from an historical context. This is a state-approved curriculum, using state-adopted textbooks that have been part of

the instructional program in California for over a decade."[10] Ms.
Castro is living in fantasyland.

The Thomas Moore Law Center represented several Christian
families that filed suit against the Byron Union School District to dis-
continue use of the history textbooks and other material and activities that promote Islam at Excelsior Elementary. In a decision that
was ultimately upheld by the Ninth Circuit, in 2003, U.S. District
Court Judge Phyllis Hamilton dismissed the suit, stating that Excelsior is not indoctrinating their students in Islam, but rather teaching
them about the Muslim religion.[11] In addition, Judge Hamilton ruled
that the curriculum was absent of "devotional or religious intent, and
is therefore educational, not religious in nature."[12] This Islamic curriculum is still taught at Excelsior as of April 2008.

Am I missing something here or does the Excelsior Islamic curriculum sound like a course in "Steps to Take to Become a Muslim"?
I guess Judge Hamilton is not acquainted with the First Amendment[13] and the Establishment Clause,[14] which protect students from
religious indoctrination in the classroom. Where is the public outcry? If Christian, Jewish, or Hindu practices were taught and practiced in public schools, there would be a civic protest on an huge
scale. If the Lord's Prayer were being taught in school, or if students
were being given communion or being baptized, can you imagine
what would happen at school board meetings? Citizens of California
should be outraged that this type of education is happening in their
public school system.

• • •

Intentionally feeding misinformation to our school children is one
of the Muslim Brotherhood goals using Taqiyya (lying and deception). Susan Douglas, a convert to Islam and a well-known textbook
consultant in Islamic studies for American public schools, is

someone of interest, whose purpose, I believe, is to indoctrinate impressionable youth with false information about world history and to spread Islam in the United States.

Ms. Douglas taught social studies at the Islamic Saudi Academy (ISA) in Alexandra, Virginia, until 2003 (Usama Amer, Douglas's husband, also taught at the Islamic Saudi Academy).[15] Douglas now edits middle and high school world history textbooks and acts as an advisor to state education boards on curriculum standards concerning Islam in world religion studies. Douglas has also trained thousands of school teachers in classroom preparation of Islamic studies in elementary and high schools and universities. Now, there's a case of the fox guarding the henhouse.

Douglas has been accused by her critics of influencing publishers and teachers to skip over the negative and violent aspects of Islam and promote only the positive features of the religion to make it more attractive to young audiences, both Muslim and non-Muslim. The Council on Islamic Education, a California-based Muslim organization, has listed Douglas as a "principal researcher and writer."

The Islam Project, written by the Council on Islamic Education (CIE) and the Islamic Society of North America, is an initiative in the United States public middle and high schools that incorporates all aspects of Islam—religious, social, spiritual, and political.[16]

Shabbir Mansuri, director of the Council on Islamic Education, has participated in at least one Islamic Circle of North America and CAIR programs alongside Siraj Wahhaj, a radical imam of Al Taqwa mosque in New York, and Sheikh Abdur Rahman Al-Sudais, a radical imam at the Grand Mosque in Mecca. Mansuri stated in 2002 that "Muslims were here first on American soil since before this nation was founded."[17] Tell that to Captain John Smith and crew.

In fact, the Arab World History Notebook, a learning text that was developed by U.S. Islamic groups such as the Middle East

Policy Council and distributed to teachers across America, alleges that Muslims were in North America as early as 889 A.D.. The Notebook also states that Muslims married into the Algonquin tribe and became Algonquin chiefs. Peter DiGangi, Director of Canada's Algonquin Nation Secretariat in Quebec, said in an interview to the *Washington Times* that these claims were preposterous and outlandish, and that there was no evidence in Algonquin oral or written history to support such allegations.[18] The passages about the Algonquin tribe and their so-called relationship with Muslims eventually were removed from new editions of the Notebook. However, 1,200 teachers across America had been given the old editions of the Notebook over a five-year period.[19] By convincing Muslims and non-Muslims of all ages that the Americas were inhabited first by Muslims, radical Islamists can unite Muslims and sympathizers in the United States to fight for what they believe rightfully theirs.

The Council on Islamic Education is frequently consulted by major U.S. publishers of world history and geography school books for grades K to 12. Houghton Mifflin, McGraw-Hill, and Prentice Hall are the three main publishers of world history texts in the United States. Houghton Mifflin's seventh grade social studies textbook, *Across the Centuries*, has been a source of controversy among educators for years. A staple in the state of California (and used at Excelsior Elementary School), the textbook is, at best, an well of misinformation. *Across the Centuries* is 558 pages long and covers the 1,500 years between the fall of the Roman Empire and the French revolution. The text includes fifty-five pages devoted to Islam, seven pages noting the Middle Ages in Europe and six pages of Christian history. The chapter on the Byzantine empire receives only six pages. The chapter on Islam accounts for 10 percent of the text, while Christianity and Judaism are almost entirely absent.[20]

Although the text is full of wonderful illustrations and written in a manner that would attract an uninformed juvenile, *Across the Centuries* serves to mislead the reader about Islam. It paints a rosy picture of the tolerance of Islam without mentioning the massacres committed in its name over the centuries. It talks about jihad as a personal struggle instead of explaining that jihad is referred to throughout the Koran and its accompanying books as holy war. And here is a winner: women in Islam have "clear rights" not available in other societies. Huh? The right to be beaten, raped, married off at nine years of age, treated like barn animals? The Koran lowers a woman's worth to one half of a man's. Muslim women have fewer rights than any other women in the world.

Here is an example of a homework assignment described by Daniel Pipes in his review of the 2002 edition: "Form small groups of students to build a miniature mosque." Or: "You leave your home in Alexandria for the pilgrimage to Mecca. . . . Write a letter describing your route, the landscapes and peoples you see as you travel, and any incidents that happen along the way. Describe what you see in Mecca." And then there is this shocker: "Assume you are a Muslim soldier on your way to conquer Syria in the year 635 A.D. Write three journal entries that reveal your thoughts about Islam, fighting in battle, or life in the desert."[21]

Across the Centuries is just one example of textbooks that are sanctioned by state boards of education. William Bennetta, a journalist, fellow of the California Academy of Sciences, and editor of "The Textbook Letter," is well known for his writings on false science and history in schoolbooks. Bennetta's review of Prentice Hall's *World Cultures: A Global Mosaic* reveals what he sees as the true intentions of the author of the chapter on Islam, saying that *World Cultures* "serves as a vehicle for Muslim propaganda. Long passages . . . are devoted to promoting Islam, to making American students embrace Islamic religious beliefs, and to winning converts to Allah. In these passages, Muslim myths and superstitions are disguised as facts, and both the origin and the content of Islam are cloaked in seductive lies."[22] Gilbert Sewall, director of the American Textbook Council, a research organization dedicated to reviewing and improving the curriculum in history textbooks and other educational materials in primary and secondary schools, has also critiqued the chapters on Islam used in history classes in public schools. In his investigative report *Islam and the Textbooks,* he asserts: "Misrepresentation of Islam is a problem in today's world history textbooks. Much of it is deliberate, I believe. Sound scholarship is being ignored, and open review—the only way to reverse the problem—meets adamant resistance." He also added that *Islam and the Textbooks* found "repeated discrepancies between world history textbooks and exacting scholarship in the field. It explains how pressure groups, both Muslims and allied multiculturalists, manipulate nervous publishers who obey educational fashion and rely more heavily on diversity experts than on trustworthy scholarship."[23]

Sewall also mentions that American students are being offered opinions presented as facts. There is no mention in the textbooks of how Sharia law is dissimilar to the constitutional law and Bill of Rights. Nor do the textbooks discuss that under an Islamic government, many of an individual's basic human rights are severely limited or are nonexistent.[24]

KGIA, CAIR, AND HAMAS

Nestled deep in the heart of Brooklyn, New York, lies a cultural-themed public school that exposes its students to the tenets of

Islam . . . whether they like it or not. And the New York taxpayers are paying for this program, whether they like it or not. The Khalil Gibran International Academy (KGIA) began the 2007–08 school year with parental and community complaints. The KGIA is no ordinary public primary school. Its board of advisors included twelve clergy of several faiths. The three Islamic representatives are imams with radical Islamic ties: al-Hajj Talib'Abur, Rashid Sahmsi Ali, and Khalid Latif.[25][26] However, due to scrutiny and pressure by organizations opposed to the school, the board of advisors has been dismantled.

Islamic activists began working together on school programs in 2007. Lena al-Husseini, the director of the Arab American Family Support Center (AAFSC), joined forces with the KGIA to initiate Islamic programs to foster Islamic ideology and advance Islam in America.[27] The KGIA and AAFSC worked together to establish a curriculum for the school year 2007–08. The AAFSC's website has a link to the Council on Islamic Education as an educational resource for an Islamic school curriculum. In addition, lesson plans on the varieties of jihad are part of the core curriculum.[28] Some AAFSC board members are members of the American Arab Anti-Discrimination Committee, an Islamic organization funded by Prince Alwaleed bin Talal, the Saudi who financially supported families of suicide bombers and whose ten-million-dollar donation to a New York 9/11 victim fund was rejected by Mayor Rudolph Giuliani.[29]

KGIA was supported by the American Islamic charity, Council on American Islamic Relations. CAIR's New York chapter had publicly requested that New York Muslims and "other people of conscience" participate in a demonstration in support of the opening of the KGIA in September 2007.[30] Omar Mohammedi, the head of CAIR's New York chapter, is also president of the American Muslims

Arab Lawyers (AMAL) and served as counsel for the six imams who sued US Airways in November 2007 for being escorted off of the plane for suspicious behavior and intimidating fellow passengers. AMAL has been invited to be an integral part of the KGIA partnership program and will provide internships to students.[31, 32]

The irony of all of this is that the Khalil Gibran Academy is named after the Christian Lebanese writer and poet Khalil Gibran who came to America to escape the Islamic-dominated Middle East, just as I and hundreds of thousands of other Christians did. Gibran's ancestry was Phoenician, not Arabic.[33] Why would an Arab-dominated Middle Eastern studies program borrow a Christian's name to attract participants and teach Islamic ideology? I tell you why: because the Muslims know how to play gullible multiculturalist Westerners like a violin. They chose a very famous poet as a symbol of East and West coming together, something akin to naming a school, one hundred years from now, the Brigitte Gabriel Academy for Islamic studies.

READING, WRITING, AND JIHAD

The Muslim Brotherhood in America is creative and far reaching in its attempts to spread the word of Allah and hatred for infidels.

The Muslim Student Association (MSA), headquartered in Alexandria, Virginia, was founded by the Muslim Brotherhood in America in 1963, as part of their North American Project. MSA was founded to, according to its website, "serve Muslim students during their college and university careers by facilitating their efforts to establish, maintain, and develop local MSA chapters." And facilitating and developing they have done. On American college campuses, MSA students are more politically active than the Democrats and Republicans combined.

The Muslim Student Association has recently adopted a particularly offensive approach to its tactics of grooming Islamic youth to take an active role in United States politics. In a November 2006 press release on the MSA's website, its president, Mahdi Bray, who on numerous occasions openly supported Hamas and Hezbollah, describes a program that uses Muslim Boy and Girl Scouts of America to elicit votes in the 2006 Senate elections from the Muslim community during a phonathon in several states. The release states, "Through our MSA Youth department, Boy and Girl Scout Troops, we are training an upcoming generation that will be spiritually grounded and political [sic] savvy." Bray let his young scout phone-bank callers know that although these calls were nonpartisan, the Democratic candidate would be the best choice for the Muslim community.

After hearing about the MSA Dialing for Muslim Votes program, Boy Scouts of America executive scout Alan Lambert said: "We would expect that no organization would use children to play out their political desires." He continued: "From my perspective . . . we would sever our relationship with anyone who uses children to advance political agendas."[34] However, phone calls to Boy Scouts of America national area capital council in Bethesda, Maryland, produced no answers to whether the MSA scout phonathon would be discontinued in future elections.

If my children attended a scout meeting that emphasized warfare as a means to support my religion, I would be appalled as well as exceedingly angry. Yet, this is just what has been reported to be the scenario in effect at the Mosque of Islamic Brotherhood's (MIB) Boy Scout Program in Harlem, New York. The MIB was founded in 1964 by the Nation of Islam. On their Web site, MIB has posted the inspiration for Islamic suicide murderers world-wide, taken from Muslim Brotherhood's founder Hasan al-Banna's treatise "The Message of the Teaching":

> *Allah is our goal*
> *The Prophet Mohammed ibn 'Abdullah is our leader*
> *The Koran is our constitution*
>
> *Jihad is our way*
> *And death in the way of Allah is our promised end*

This particular mosque has employed imam Al-Hajj Talib Abdul-Rasheed, a disciple of Louis Farrakhan and the Nation of Islam, as a leader of its Boy Scout program. While rather atypical for American scouts, the MIB scouts have worn patches depicting the sword of Islam on their uniforms, a symbol of unified jihad. Pictures on their website also show older scouts as well as adults in combat fatigues. In addition, imam Abdul-Rasheed was on the board of advisors for the Khalil Gibran International Academy. The MIB website currently offers an article entitled, "The Pre-Columbian Presence of Muslim Africans in America is No Myth." This article gives the Islamist license to reclaim what they perceive as their God-given territory from the "modern inhabitants of North America."[35] This is the same reason given for reclaiming the land of the Israelites.

ISLAMIC JIHAD AND AMERICAN SUMMER CAMPS

The sounds of children's laughter and the sight of canoes on blue water that glisten with the sun's rays should conjure up visions of a pleasurable afternoon enjoyed by children at summer camp some-where in America. Unfortunately, at some summer camps children spend their afternoons sitting indoors, listening to speakers that preach "the way of jihad" for true believers of Islam. Filling the minds of impressionable youths with thoughts of taking their own life and the lives of nonbelievers, to fulfill an honorable bequest to Allah and preserve the tenets of Islam, is not what summer camp is about! So why are such camps knowingly allowed to flourish?

New Year's Eve is an enjoyable time of the year for people throughout the world to let their guard down, have a little fun, and commit themselves to a healthier lifestyle for the coming new year. A December 29, 2005, article on FrontPage Magazine.com, by Joe Kaufman, chairman of Americans Against Hate[36] and the founder of CAIR Watch,[37] reported that the Tampa chapter of the Muslim American Society was getting ready to host a New Year's Eve children's "jihad" retreat, from December 31, 2005, through January 2, 2006. MAS had invited two Islamic speakers who are well known in the field of radical Islam to instruct Muslim youth on the retreat's theme, "A Generation with a Mission."[38] Most of these speakers previous speeches had incorporated the mission of jihad.

The Young Muslims (YM) was created in the mid-1990s by the Islamic Circle of North America (ICNA). While it denies the asso-ciation, published reports indicate that ICNA's main goal was to model themselves after the Pakistani terrorist group Jamaat-e-Islami. Young Muslims holds youth retreats in summer and win-ter to teach young Muslims the ideology of political Islam and Sharia law, including Islamic world domination by the sword and martyrdom. In 2002, the theme of a Young Muslims retreat was "Planning for Our Akhira" (afterlife). Such themes appear to be a constant in every Muslim youth retreat sponsored by the Muslim

American Society, Muslim Student Association, and the Islamic Circle of North America.[39]

Chantal Carnes, a radical Islamist, a former president of the Chicago MAS and lecturer and radio talk-show host for the Islamic Broadcasting Network, was listed as a lecturer for the New Year's retreat. Ms. Carnes has publicly spouted praise for imam Hasan al-Banna, the creator of the Muslim Brotherhood. Carnes also extols the activities of al-Banna's grandson, Tariq Ramadan. Ramadan had his visa and work permit revoked in 2004 by the United States government on the grounds that he was a person who has "used a position of prominence within any country to endorse or espouse terrorist activity."[40]

Another charismatic speaker at the MAS retreat was Mazen Mokhtar. Mokhtar is director of the Youth division of MAS in New Jersey. Right before Mokhtar was to speak at another Islamic youth camp in Pennsylvania in August of 2004, the United States government accused him of assisting Al Qaeda through an Internet website he had created. The site, www.minna.com, was soliciting funds and recruiting mujahedeen for terrorist activities overseas. A video was found on Mokhtar's home computer's hard drive selling "terrorist operations," which told interested parties to contact Shammil Basayev, field commander of the Islamic army of the Caucasus. One month later, in September, Basayev claimed responsibility for the brutal slaughter of school children in Beslan, Russia.[41] (In 2007 Mokhtar was indicted for tax evasion.)

The Young Muslims youth camp in August 2006 included radical Islamic speakers with ties to terrorism. One of the more notorious was Siraj Wahhaj, who was named by the U. S. State Department as an unindicted co-conspirator in the Holy Land Foundation trial. Wahhaj has publicly said that Muslims need to elect a caliph to take over the United States and then establish a caliphate.[42] Another speaker was Nouman Ali Khan, a former member of the Muslim Student Association, who gave a lecture in 2005 at Hofstra University, sponsored by their MSA, called "Preparation for Death."[43] The speaker list also included Abdul Malik, chaplain of the New York City Metropolitan Transit Authority and former manager of CAIR New York, who stated in a speech titled "Service to Society: The Key to Reformation," "We don't want to democratize Islam, we want to Islamize democracy."[44]

Also in August 2006, Young Muslim Sisters (YMS), an auxiliary of the Islamic Circle of North America, held a summer camp session at Camp Bernie, a YMCA New Jersey facility. Three speakers at the August session also spoke at an ICNA-sponsored camp two weeks before 9/11. Before 9/11, administrators and campers would refer to the youth camps as "jihad camps." In the post-9/11 atmosphere, ICNA, MAS, MSA, YM, and YMS are much more cautious about making any references to jihad. The camps are now touted as retreats for Muslim children to learn about their heritage. Some speakers have prepared Muslim youth for their deaths with presentations such as "Preparation for Death" by Dr. Nouman Ali Khan, "The Life in the Grave," by Imam Badawi, and "Do You Want Paradise" by Br. Jawad Ahmad. Ahmad began his lecture with the words, "This should be our goal in life, I want to go to Jannah [paradise]."[45]

The list of speakers at the various summer camps sponsored by these organizations is extremely disturbing. What is going on behind closed doors in America provides an insight into the devastation and destruction that lies ahead for the people of our great nation. Children of Muslim descent in America are being trained to promote their religion at the cost of the lives of all other Americans.

American Islamic organizations have infiltrated public schools and universities to indoctrinate children with an Islamic ideology and teach hatred and intolerance for Jews, Israel, Christians, and others who do not embrace Islam's political and religious views. The Saudis are buying their way into the universities and public schools by donating millions of dollars to establish Middle Eastern studies programs run by professors who are Islamic militants. Lies are incorporated into ordinary history lessons. Hatred is alive and well and living on campuses throughout America.

THE MAKING OF AN ISLAMONAZI ARMY

During the Six-Day War between Israel and Arabs, an Israeli soldier who is now a friend of mine was one of the first soldiers in Gaza as Israel gained control of the territories. He walked into an Arab elementary school filled with Islamic scriptures and teaching materials that vilified Jews, and encouraged children to kill Jews for Allah's sake. Shocked at such hateful educational tools, he understood the determined ferocity that the Israelis face. He called his wife in northern Israel and told her, "We will be fighting this war for a long, long time." That was 1967. Can you imagine what is being taught to Arab children today?

The world now faces a new generation of students being indoctrinated into hate. Madrassas all over the world have paved the way and set the standards for such radical education.

"Madrassa" in Arabic means "school," and throughout the centuries it has come to mean an Islamic school. Madrassas are connected to their local mosque and incorporate secular subjects along with Islamic studies. Since 1973, wealth from oil revenues has allowed the Saudis to spread their totalitarian Sunni Wah-

habi beliefs throughout the world by financing Islamic madrassas in Pakistan and elsewhere.[46]

Pakistani Madrassas

During the 1979–89 Soviet/Afghanistan conflict, a new educational curriculum was created in the Pakistani madrassas, inciting
violence and hatred toward the Soviets and all other non-
Muslims. The majority of the Taliban were educated in Pakistani
madrassas and were specifically trained for warfare against Soviet
troops. Retired Pakistani police official and current Harvard University fellow Hassan Abbas estimates that 10 to 15 percent of all
madrassas in Pakistan support the Taliban, religious extremism,
and terrorism.

Mullah Abdul Rashid Ghazi ran some of the largest madrassas,
both for boys and girls, in Pakistan. He strongly identified with bin
Laden's philosophies and preached to his students that jihad is a
basic tenet of the Koran. He defied Pakistani government requests
to stop such teaching. The message sank into young, impressionable minds forced to recite Koranic verses from morning to eve-
ning. When the Pakistani government shut down his Red Mosque
in Islamabad July 2007, Ghazi died with almost 100 of his students
who had become well-armed radicals.[47]

Saudi Madrassas

Madrassas in Saudi Arabia teach a strict and literal interpretation of the Koran and Hadith. Students who are educated in these
madrassas must memorize all six thousand verses of the Koran.
Many secular-based curriculums, including basic English, math,
and science, are put on hold until the more crucial aspects of
Sharia law are taught.[48]

A report by the Middle East Media Research Institute highlights the Saudi philosophy on Islam in the schools in Saudi Arabia and around the world. As one educational document for Saudi Arabia's Higher Committee for Educational Policy dictates, "The purpose of education is to understand Islam in a proper and complete manner, to implement and spread the Muslim faith, to provide a student with Islamic values, and teachings." The same document emphasized the duty of every Muslim to spread the teachings of Islam throughout the world.[49]

Besides the teachings of the Koran and Hadith, Saudi madrassas notably teach hatred and condemnation of the West, non-Muslims, and Shiite Muslims as part of their history curriculum. World history textbooks in Saudi Arabia, are written, edited, and distributed by the Saudi government.[50]

The Ministry of Education committees in Saudi Arabia supervise the written material in all Saudi school textbooks for all subjects and grades.[51] The Saudi government also provides free textbooks to Islamic schools throughout the world. Many of the Saudi-issued textbooks contain wording that encourages hatred and intolerance for non-Muslims.[52] For example, in an eighth-grade text, a story of Mohammed's teachings describes the importance of jihad. Mohammed states in the Hadith: "Jihad for the sake of Allah." The textbook then interprets the Hadith to mean "the most important activity is jihad for the sake of Allah and the convocation of Allah's religion on this earth."[53]

The Saudi royal family and Saudi officials publicly support the religious intolerance taught in the country's educational system. Sheikh Mjed 'Abd al-Rahman al-Firian, Saudi Arabia's leading imam, stated in a sermon at the Suleiman Muqiran Mosque in Riyadh: "Muslims must . . . educate their children to jihad and to the hatred of the Jews, the Christians, and the infidels; educating the children to jihad and to revival of the embers of jihad in their souls.

This is what is needed now."[54] Saudi defense minister Prince Sultan Ibn Abd al-'Aziz's views on Saudi Arabia's educational curriculum also reflect a willingness to maintain a religious and political ideology of intolerance and hatred for non-Muslims: "We will never change our education system. . . . Our country has a policy . . . and above all religious curricula that must never be harmed."[55] In an interview in the *Al-Sharq al-Awast*, a Saudi-owned London newspaper, Prince Naif Ibn Abdul Aziz, Saudi minister of the interior, offered the following response to a question regarding changing malicious wording in Saudi textbooks that offends non-Muslims: "We strongly believe in the correctness of our education system and its objectives. We don't change our systems on the demands of others."

In 2004, the United States Commission on International Religious Freedom (USCIRF)—a nonprofit organization created in 1998 as an independent, bipartisan U.S. government agency "set up to monitor the status of freedom of thought, conscience and religion or belief abroad"[56]—named Saudi Arabia a "country of particular concern" for its use of textbooks to encourage intolerance and hatred. In 2006, the Saudi government stated that the books had been revised and the texts' wording had been reformed to eliminate text that promotes any intolerance and hatred of nonbelievers.

During a visit by a USCIRF delegation in the spring of 2007, the Saudi government refused to allow the delegation access to the new and reformed school textbooks. It had been a year since the government said that they had modified their textbooks. Why hide the books?

In 2006, there were two separate reports on the content of the revised editions of Saudi textbooks, issued by Freedom House in conjunction with the Institute for Gulf Affairs. Ali al-Ahmed, the director of IGA, is a Saudi Shiite, who has been working diligently for years to expose the hate ideology that the Saudi government imposes on its youth via media, textbooks, educational curriculum, and Sunni Wahhabi mosques. Freedom House was given twelve revised textbooks by the IGA to review. Below are several passages that were thought to have been revised but recently found in current Saudi textbooks.[57]

From a first-grade textbook: "Fill in the blanks with the appropriate words: Every religion other than _____ is false. Whoever dies outside of Islam enters _____." [Answers: Islam; hellfire.]

From a sixth-grade textbook: "Just as the Muslims were successful in the past when they came together in a sincere endeavor to evict the Christian crusaders from Palestine, so will the Arabs and Muslims emerge victorious, God willing, against the Jews and their allies if they stand together and fight a true jihad for God, for this is within God's power."

From an eighth-grade textbook: "As cited in Ibn Abbas: The apes are Jews, the people of the Sabbath; while the swine are the Christians, the infidels of the Communion of Jesus."

From a ninth-grade textbook: "The hour of judgment will not come until the Muslims fight the Jews and kill them."

From a tenth-grade textbook on jurisprudence: Life for a non-Muslim as well as Muslim women and slaves is worth a tiny proportion of that of a free Muslim male".

From a twelfth-grade textbook: "Jihad in the path of God—which consists of battling against unbelief, oppression, injustice, and those who perpetrate it—is the summit of Islam. The religion arose through jihad and through jihad was its banner raised high. It is one of the noblest acts, which brings one closer to God, and one of the most magnificent acts of obedience to God".[58][59]

This type of propaganda fosters an environment of hate, loathing, and resentment toward Western culture, Christians, Jews, Shiites, secular Muslims and non-Muslims. Saudi textbooks frequently quote verses from the Koran or Hadith that condemn non-Muslims, especially Christians and Jews. In many instances, the verse will direct the reader to commit murder in the name of Allah. There are approximately 25,000 public schools in Saudi Arabia, which accommodate 5 million youth. In addition, there are roughly 225 Islamic madrassas registered in the United States. There are also Islamic Madrassas in nineteen world capitals.[60]

A list of countries where the Saudis have established schools includes: the United States, Canada, Great Britain, France, Russia, Germany, Switzerland, Australia, Belgium, New Zealand, Spain, Austria, Scotland, Italy, Croatia, Bosnia, Hungary, Afghanistan, Pakistan, Egypt, Palestinian territories, Jordan, Lebanon, Yemen, Japan, Indonesia, South Korea, Thailand, Malaysia, Bangladesh, Burundi, Fiji, Azerbaijan, Kurdistan, Algeria, Nigeria, Chad, Kenya, Cameroon, Senegal, Uganda, Mali, Somalia, Sudan, Brazil, Eritrea, and Djibouti.[61][62]

Palestinian Authority Madrassas

Saudi Arabia is not the only Sunni region of the Middle East where hatred and violence toward others is taught in the classrooms. Here is the update on what began in the 1960s in Gaza. It appears that the Fatah government (yes, the Fatah government that America calls "moderate," not Hamas) of the Palestinian Authority (PA) is expanding its hate curriculum. It has issued textbooks that not only cultivate hate against the Jewish people but also against the United States. They are bolstering their position of animosity by rewriting history.

In February 2007, the organization Palestinian Media Watch (PMW) came out with an extensive report on textbooks issued by the Palestinian Authority to be used in Gaza and the West Bank. Itamar Marcus and Barbara Cook of PMW conducted the study that focused on schoolbooks issued by the Palestinian Authority and written by its Palestinian Curriculum Department (PCD). The PCD is comprised of educators who are selected by the Fatah Movement of the Palestinian Liberation Organization. In their report, "From Nationalist Battle to Religious Conflict: New Twelfth-grade Palestinian Textbooks Present 'A World Without Israel,'" Marcus and Cook examined eight books assigned by the Palestinian School System in 2006 that literally present a world without Israel.

From 2000 to 2005, the Palestinian Authority was criticized for its textbooks' theme of the destruction of Israel. Under pressure from world opinion, the PA promised to remove its radical and intolerant content toward Israel and the Jews from its textbooks. Not surprisingly, the report found that the new and "reformed" 2006 books still contained language that portrayed Israel and the West as enemies of Islam that must be destroyed. The textbooks also deny Israel's right to exist and literally erase Israel from all geography maps. On maps of the Middle East Israel is now labeled "Palestine" and defined as *dawla*, the Arabic word for state.[63]

This attempt to inculcate their youth with the notion that Israel does not exist as a state, is also illustrated in other ways. Textbooks routinely eradicate any mention of the Holocaust or of Jews. Without any mention of the Jewish people and Hitler's final solution, the texts refer to the territorial impact of World War II, and Hitler's views on racism.[64] The texts also allude to the fact that there will never be peace with Israel (the occupier), and Israel's annihilation will be the only way for the Palestinian people to effectively live in the region.[65]

The United States and the West are also presented in twelfth-grade textbooks as the enemies of the Palestinian people and as human rights abusers. The United States is labeled in a derogatory way as an economic provider of Israel, without any mention of how much monetary support, in the millions of dollars, that is given to the PA by the United States government. In addition, the texts *Contemporary Problems* and *History of the Arabs and the World in the 20th Century* call suicide bombers in Iraq who have murdered U.S. and British soldiers "brave resisters." In fact, suicide bombers are described as revered and the textbooks define acts of "resistance" as "acts of most glorious heroism and sacrifice."[66]

The concepts of jihad *shahada*, death for Allah, are continually mentioned in the Palestinian curriculum. Jihad is even emphasized in grammar exercises! One twelfth-grade textbook underlines the importance of a *shahid* (martyr) in Islam and a believer's role in sacrificing his own life on earth for Allah's eternal love.

The textbook *Islamic Education* emphasizes that martyrs are with their god, and are filled with happiness and the benevolence that Allah gave them. The verse from the Koran used to support this point reads: "Even if we do not sense these lives, and we do not know their truthfulness, and therefore [the Koran] forbade us to refer to them as 'dead.'"

The following verse is an example of what is used to indoctrinate school-aged children into the ideology of martyrdom. It appears in the 2002 edition of *Reading and Text Part II*, for the eighth grade:

"O heroes . . . do not talk yourselves into fight. Your enemies seek life while you seek death. These drops of blood
that gush from your bodies will be transformed tomorrow
into blazing red meteors that will fall down upon the heads
of your enemies."[67]

If you think the eighth grade is pretty young, then textbook indoctrination has nothing on the PA's efforts via television. The use
of television is a relatively new method to communicate *shahada* to
its young viewers but Hamas has extended its reach to its infant
population. In May of 2007, Al-Aqsa, a Hamas-affiliated television
station, launched a new children's television show aimed at indoctrinating Palestinian youth into an Islamic ideology of violence,
murder, and hatred for Israel and the United States. The main
character is a Mickey Mouse lookalike named Farfur, who directs
children to pray until there is "world leadership under Islamic
rule." Farfur also encouraged children to fight Israel, which is defined as "the oppressive invading Zionist occupiers." June 29, 2007,
was Farfur's last day on camera. After world pressure and wide
publicity about the hateful character, Hamas decided to terminate
him. The glory of dying for Islam was emphasized in the final
episode as Farfur was beaten to death by an Israeli and instantly
became a martyr for Allah and his people,[68] thus further reinforcing the hatred Palestinian children have for Israel.

The Hamas-led Palestinian Authority has created an environment for its youth to feel good about the idea of prematurely and
violently ending their life for a future in the afterlife. The code of
belief that dominates political Islam's violent ideology and pen-
chant for suicide bombing is instilled in the minds of the Muslim
Palestinian children since birth. It becomes their life's goal and a
national duty to become a soldier of Allah and give up their lives

and that of innocent people worldwide for the preservation and conquest of Islam.

U.S.-Funded Saudi Madrassas

In 2004, then secretary of state Colin Powell, called madrassas breeding grounds for "fundamentalists and terrorists."[69] Consider the Islamic Saudi Academy (ISA), founded in 1984; its two campuses are in Alexandria and McLean, Virginia. Approximately a thousand students are enrolled in grades one through twelve. ISA is funded by private donors, the core of its operating budget paid for by the Saudi government. The chairman of its board is none other than the Saudi ambassador to the United States. Because ISA is funded by the Saudi government, it is considered an appendage of the Saudi government and is subject to U.S. regulations and restrictions to activities of nondiplomatic actions of foreign governments in the United States.[70] With the ISA, the Saudi embassy overstepped its authority, and in October 2007, the United States Commission on International Religious Freedom ruled that the embassy was in violation of federal law. *USA Today* reported: "The U.S. Commission on International Religious Freedom singled out the Saudi-supported Islamic Saudi Academy . . . in a broader report that accused Saudi Arabia of promoting Muslim extremism and religious intolerance six years after the Sept. 11 attacks."[71] Failed past requests by USCIRF that the Saudi embassy examine the revised Saudi-issued nonviolent textbooks used by ISA influenced the Commission's decision to close the school until the new revised textbooks were turned over to the Commission for examination.[72] In 2002, the Association of Independent Schools terminated ISA's accreditation after learning how the academy was funded and about reports that the ISA was teaching hatred and violence in their curriculum.[73]

Wahhabism, a Saudi sect of Sunni Islam founded by the eighteenth-century sheikh Muhammad ibn Abd al-Wahhab, follows the strict observance of Sharia law and teaches that nonbelievers of Islam shall die by the sword.[74][75] This interpretation of Sharia law apparently was being taught at the ISA and was sanctioned by the Saudi government. The U.S. Commission on International Religious Freedom, the Center for Religious Freedom, and the Institute for Gulf Affairs thoroughly examined two of the Saudi texts used by the ISA and concluded that the texts are tools that teach hatred, blatant lies, and incitement to commit violent acts against Christians, Jews, and Shiite Muslims.[76]

These are the same textbooks the Saudi government has authorized for use in Saudi schools or madrassas around the world, including the United States.[77] Consequently, it is no surprise that Ahmed Omar Abu Ali, the young Muslim who in 2005 was found guilty of a 2003 assassination plot to murder President Bush, was the ISA's 1999 valedictorian. Abu Ali admitted that he created forged documents and trained in weaponry with Al Qaeda cells to fight U.S. servicemen in Afghanistan. Two other graduates of the Islamic Saudi Academy, Mohammad Osman Idris and Mohammad el-Yacoubi, both of Fairfax, Virginia, were stopped by the Israeli government from carrying out a suicide mission in 2002.[78] With graduates like these from schools located within the United States, who needs to worry about border control and immigration and people sneaking in to harm us!

Saudi Arabia is one of the leading financial contributors to Islamic terrorism worldwide. Part of that contribution is made by funding madrassas throughout the world and the brainwashing Muslim children with intolerant teaching toward anything and anyone non-Muslim. The United States has had an amicable relationship with Saudi Arabia for almost seventy-five years, but this relationship is in a precarious state. The United State has two main political motives for this friendship—oil supply and support of anti-Communist policy with regard to Russia. There is a constant fear on the part of the United States that Russian influence in Saudi Arabia might result in the withholding of oil supplies. The Saudis have proven throughout the years that they are strongly opposed to Communist politics and have made several proclamations to that effects. They have spent billions of dollars for foreign aid to countries that were at war with the former Soviet Union.[79] Accordingly, the United States has refrained from putting pressure on the Saudis to reform their policies in order to remain amicable and maintain an unlimited supply of crude oil.

The Saudis' devotion to spreading Islam and the literal interpretation of Sharia law is made possible by their oil wealth. The United States must apply pressure on the Saudis to reform their madrassas' textbooks, values, and attitudes toward non-Muslims and Shiites. We cannot afford to look the other way while our enemy is planning our destruction from within.

6

REVIVING THE CALIPHATE:
ONE WORLD NATION UNDER ALLAH;
SUPERSIZING THE MUSLIM WORLD

Having lost my once Christian-majority country of Lebanon to an Islamic takeover, I have a very personal response to the word "caliphate." It worries me. Radical Muslims are honest and forthcoming about their goals and intentions. On television and the Internet, in newspapers and on the radio, they issue their warnings, and when they speak about their vision for the future, they talk about the establishment of a caliphate. So what is a caliphate?

It is a Muslim imperial state that evolved after Mohammed's death to carry on his dream of a Islamic government ruling over all Muslims regardless of nationality or ethnicity. The Islamic caliphate existed from 632 to 1924, when its last remnant was abolished in Turkey by Mustafa Kemal Ataturk.[1] The caliphate takes its authority and direction from the Koran and Sharia law. Relatively speaking, it is the authority over the body of all Muslims throughout the world—literally, one nation under Allah. A caliphate would be ruled by a caliph (analogous to the pope, in the Catholic Church) who is appointed or elected by a parliamentary-styled *shura* (council), which represents the will of the people. That is, the will of the people according to Allah.

Abu Abdullah, a senior member of the Hizb ut-Tahrir al-Islami (Islamic Party of Liberation), which is uniting hundreds of thousands of Muslims around the goal of creating a modern caliphate, puts the re-creation of the caliphate this way: "We want to free all people from being slaves of men and make them slaves of Allah."[2]

Abdullah's is not the only voice sounding the call for a return of the caliphate. From the Gaza Strip and the West Bank to Thailand and Turkey, from Khomeini to Ahmadinejad, Muslims yearning for the glory days of Islam are looking for a modern-day caliph to lead them toward, as Ayman Al-Zawahiri puts it, "the glory of this world and the prize of the hereafter."[3] That vision of glory, according to Abdullah, is to abolish all national boundaries of present Islamic nations and establish a single state. This Islamic state, ruled by a supreme leader, would stretch from "Indonesia to Morocco and contain more than 1.5 billion people."[4] It's a concept that has caught the attention of many and the support of radical Islam's leaders.

Purists like bin Laden see the attainment of a caliphate as the reward for reverting to the deepest spiritual form of Islam and interpretation of the Koran, and for following Allah's will and drawing closer to him and his favor. They believe that the corruption of Muslim values and spiritual integrity has cost them Allah's favor, which lead to the decline of the caliphate that once ruled the world from the Atlantic to the Indian Ocean. In an Al Qaeda training manual, bin Laden attributed the loss of the caliphate to a malaise in the Muslim world:

> The bitter situation that the nation has reached is a result of its divergence from Allah's course and his righteous law for all

places and times. That [situation] came about as a result of its children's love for the world, their loathing of death, and their abandonment of jihad.[5]

Bin Laden reveals his final goal for Al Qaeda in his closing words to his warriors: "I present this humble effort to these young Muslim men who are pure, believing, and fighting for the cause of Allah. It is my contribution toward paving the road that leads to majestic Allah and establishes a caliphate according to the prophecy."[6]

And he means business. More from his manual:

> Islamic governments have never and will never be established through peaceful solutions and cooperative councils. They are established as they [always] have been, by pen and gun, by word and bullet, by tongue and teeth.[7]

For nations he wants to conquer, including those already Muslim which he deems insufficiently observant, his methods of attack are clear:

> The confrontation that Islam calls for with these godless and apostate regimes does not know Socratic debates, Platonic ideals, nor Aristotelian diplomacy. But it knows the dialogue of bullets, the ideals of assassination, bombing, and destruction, and the diplomacy of the cannon and machine gun.[8]

Baitullah Mehsud, a Taliban leader in Afghanistan, supports bin Laden. "Allah on four hundred eighty occasions in the holy Koran extols Muslims to wage jihad. We only fulfill God's orders. Only jihad can bring peace to the world," he says. "We will continue our struggle until foreign troops are thrown out. Then we will attack them in the U.S. and Britain until they either accept Islam or agree to pay jizyah. jizyh."[9] Radical Islamists have a clear mission and a vision. They are articulating their goals and recruiting thousands of faithful to join the holy fight to reestablish the caliphate and the return of Islamic pride. In a sermon that aired on Hamas' Al-Aksa TV on April 11, 2008, Yunis Al-Astal, Hamas MP and cleric, told worshipers that Rome, "the capital of the Catholics, or the Crusader capital," would soon be conquered by Islam, just as Constantinople was. It then, he said, would become "an advance post for the Islamic conquests, which will spread through Europe in its entirety, and then will turn to the two Americas, and even Eastern Europe."[10]

Prior to September 11, 2001, world leaders and intelligence agencies discounted those crazy extremists' vision of reviving the caliphate, and brushed them aside as irrelevant zealots and fundamentalists. Fewer and fewer leaders and intelligence agencies are laughing now, as the cry for unity and the push for the return of the caliphate echoes louder among extremists around the world. "A few years ago people laughed at them," says Zeyno Baran, a senior fellow at the Hudson Institute and the leading expert on Hizb ut-Tahrir al-Islami. "But now that bin Laden, Zarqawi, and other Islamic groups are saying they want to recreate the caliphate, people are taking them seriously."[11]

The call for reviving the caliphate is drowning out the voices of Islamic moderates who favor a move toward a Western model of democracy and tolerance for all religions. The concept of a caliphate is becoming a common rallying point for the Islamic world. Momentum builds with every perceived success in overcoming Western civilization's ideals, values, traditions, or governments. Muhammad Abdel-El, a spokesman and leader for the Popular Resistance Committee, a terror group in Gaza, stated in an interview with Aaron Klein in his book *Schmoozing with Terrorists*, "America will be overthrown. We are seeing more and more signs that prove that the process had already started."[12] One seemingly simple sign, dwarfed by the territorial expansions taking place in Africa and the Far East, is the election of Keith Ellison, a Muslim, to the U.S. House of Representatives. Klein's interview with Sheikh Yasser Hamad, a leader of Hamas, reveals that Ellison's election means a lot in fueling other radicals' optimism. Sheikh Yasser Hamad said: "This is proof of the spread of Islam and that Islam will one day dominate. We believe that this process will become bigger, stronger, and larger."[13]

Some insight as to the importance of the caliphate is useful here. Whereas in the West, elected officials and administrations change every few years, Islamists revere and honor the institution of caliphate as being from Allah as handed down by Mohammed. "The idea of a government based on the caliphate has a historical pedigree and Islamic legitimacy that Western systems of government by their very nature do not have," notes senior fellow at the Jamestown Foundation, Stephen Ulph.[14]

The caliphate originated in the city of Medina and grew as Islamic armies invaded and conquered surrounding cities, and then countries inhabited by Jews, Christians, and pagans. These armies were dutifully following what Mohammed had established as a normal modus operandi: "So, fight them till all opposition ends and the only religion is Islam" (Koran 8:39). For Islam to become the only religion, they invaded, enslaved, and killed people and forced them to convert or pay the jizyah. They took this fight all the way across northern Africa and throughout Spain. In France they captured Avignon, Lyons, and Marseilles. Their fleets captured most of the islands in the Mediterranean, including Crete and Sicily, portions of Italy, the Balkans, Greece, and Turkey. To the east they conquered everything to the Indus River in present-day Pakistan. And of course all of Arabia. Their farthest incursion into Europe took them to the outskirts of Vienna.

While most of the post-caliphate area today remains Muslim, it is the loss of Spain and the other northern Mediterranean territorries that invokes a goading shame. This shame inhabits a large part of the Islamic mind-set, and is a constant reminder that Islam has lost its supremacy. However, these territories weren't theirs in the first place. They killed a lot of people conquering them the first time between 711 to 751. Many more were killed again when the original owners tried to take it back during the Crusades from the eleventh to the sixteenth centuries. The catch is that in the Muslims' minds, once they conquer a land it belongs to them. If they lose it, they will fight passionately till they get it back. The Koran allows for no alternative.

While the Islamic Party of Liberation hopes to usher in the caliphate peacefully through cultural jihad accomplished by manipulating Western freedoms (freedom of religion, of the press, and of speech), and capitalizing on the tolerance, multiculturalism, and open-mindedness of the West, it holds to the position that it is every Muslim's duty to Allah to bring about Islamic rule by any means. While Abu Abdullah and his Islamic Party of Liberation are offering a less violent path than Al Qaeda to achieve their goals, Abdullah confuses his ends with the means. His primary methodology is to force Muslims to hold to their duty to reestablish the caliphate, and then invite them to stage military coups once they are strong enough in number and the host society has appeased them. After countries are under Islamic control, the Islamic Party of Liberation will then link the countries together to form a powerful, united Islamic state. It is just this kind of thinking by Hizb ut-Tahrir, the largest radical Islamic group in Europe and Africa dedicated to bringing back the caliphate, that became too troublesome in the

United Kingdom. The government outlawed them following the London bombings because their unrelenting agenda was to "replace the secular government with an Islamic caliphate, or super state run according to Sharia law."[15]

Despite its censure in the United Kingdom, Hizb ut-Tahrir remains strong in Central Asia where it is believed by many that the group takes steps to quickly establish the caliphate. With estimated tens of thousands of active followers, Hizb ut-Tahrir continues with efforts to mobilize the grass roots and the power players. One follower, Nur Mohammad, lives in the mountains of Kyrgyzstan and says that Hizb ut-Tahrir is working in his village "because people trust us, not the authorities." Even though Hizb ut-Tahrir is banned in Kyrgyzstan, it is aiming for support beyond villagers. As the official spokesman for the Islamic Party of Liberation in southern Kyrgystan, Nur Mohammad has no doubt that the movement to revive the caliphate will be successful: "All Muslims in the world already want to live in a caliphate under Sharia law. . . . It will be a huge state, a very powerful state. Even now you are all afraid of us—America, Israel, you in the United Kingdom, too."[16]

Hizb ut-Tahrir also has a strong following in Europe and the Middle East. Appealing to the geographic and political differences of its host countries, the Party of Liberation tells "Muslims that they have to create parallel societies and that they should not follow European laws," according to terrorism expert Zeyno Baran. "They're stronger in places where people know less about Islam and can't read the Koran in Arabic."

But Abu Mohammad disagrees with Ms. Baran. He comments:

> Islam obliges Muslims to possess power so that they can intimidate—I would not say terrorize—the enemies of Is-

lam. . . . In the beginning, the caliphate would strengthen itself internally and it wouldn't initiate jihad. . . . But after that
we would carry Islam as an intellectual call to all the
world. . . . and we will make people bordering the caliphate
believe in Islam. Or if they refuse then we'll ask them to be
ruled by Islam.[17]

Osama bin Laden, Ayman Al-Zawahiri, and others are equally
convinced that the caliphate will be restored. Jihadists the world
over echo the mandate of bin Laden: "The establishment of a
caliphate in the manner of the Prophet will not be achieved except
through jihad against the apostate rulers and their removal."[18]

This is a theme that continues to be prominent in bin Laden's
audio and video messages. He demands that Muslims fulfill their
religious and political duty: "The Umma and its youth, women, el-
derly, must offer themselves, their expertise, and all sort of financial support enough to raise jihad in the battlefields of jihad. Jihad
today is a duty to every Muslim."[19]

Bin Laden's words are being taken seriously by thousands
across the world who are fueled by the belief that the promised
messiah (the twelfth imam) is soon to appear. Only jihad can
usher him in, and only absolute dedication to the cause of Islam
around the world can bring him to his place of glory. Sheikh
Ahmed Yassin, a spiritual leader of Hamas, made these provocative
statements before he was killed in an Israeli strike in 2004:

The era preceding the end [of days] has begun—the era of the
military rule, the era of revolutionary rule. Allah willing, we
are at the end of this era and, Allah willing, the caliphate will
return, in accordance with the prophecy, and I pray that we
will be among its soldiers. Had He wanted, He would have
beaten them. But He tested you in suffering. We must prepare
the ground for the army of Allah that is coming according to

the [divine] predetermination. We must prepare a foothold
for them. Allah willing, this unjust state will be erased—Israel
will be erased; this unjust state, the United States, will be
erased; this unjust state, Britain, will be erased.[20]

It is the intensity of that jihad that will create the right Islamic
spiritual atmosphere for the twelfth imam—the Mahdi, the Islamic messiah—and the caliphate. Sheikh Abdel Rahman, who
planned the first attack on the World Trade Center, funneled these
words to his fellow faithful, smuggled from a U.S. prison:

> Oh, you Muslims everywhere, sever the ties of their nation,
> tear them apart, ruin their economy, instigate against their
> corporations, destroy their embassies, attack their interests,
> sink their ships, and shoot down these airplanes. Kill them in
> land, at sea, and in the air; kill them wherever you find them.[21]

This is exactly what radical Islamists have done. Not only have
they attacked us militarily on the land and the sea, but they are attacking us culturally and economically, acquiring ownership and
holding power in major American corporations. In a move reminiscent of the famous Trojan horse, Abu Dhabi Investment Authority, a
sovereign wealth consortium of oil-rich Middle Eastern countries,
bailed out Citigroup in November 2007 to the tune of $7.5 billion.
(Earlier that month, Charles Prince, CEO of Citigroup, had resigned
in the midst of a furor over $11 billion in losses.) The agreement
with Abu Dhabi Investment Authority makes them the single largest
shareholder within Citigroup. Other wealthy countries in the Middle East have been on a buying spree lately. Sheikh Mohammed bin
Rashid Al Maktoum, the ruler of Dubai and the prime minister and
vice president of the United Arab Emirates, bought a large stake in
Sony Corporation.[22] But what else did the huge Arabic conglomerate

and the sheikh have in mind? Extending a gift in one hand, and the sword of Islam in the other, to begin the takeover of American corporations? To deal a blow to the troubled U.S. economy? Instead of the suicide bomber or terrorist attack, jihad has invented an inside job of devastating proportions. Make no mistake, the attack of radical Islam will continue on all available fronts as jihad steps up a notch to bring in the caliphate and the Mahdi—the promised one, the Islamic messiah.

So anticipated is this Mahdi that official Iranian radio has completed a series of broadcasts on the imminent appearance of this Islamic messiah, who will defeat all of Islam's enemies and impose global Islamic rule. A direct descendant of Mohammed, the Madhi will bring peace, justice, and security. Iran's president Ahmadinejad has a preoccupation with the coming of the Mahdi. His mystical obsession with the promised one has many in the intelligence and counterterrorism community concerned that he might use a nuclear attack against Israel to trigger events leading up to the Mahdi's appearance. Here is Ahmedinejad speaking about his spiritual experience at the UN:

> In a videotaped meeting with Ayatollah Javadi-Amoli in Tehran, Ahmadinejad discussed candidly a strange, paranormal experience he had while addressing the United Nations in New York last September. He recounts how he found himself bathed in light throughout the speech. But this wasn't the light directed at the podium by the U.N. and television cameras. It was, he said, a light from heaven. The Iranian president recalled being told about it by one of his delegation: "When you began with the words 'in the name of Allah,' I saw a light coming, surrounding you and protecting you to the end." Ahmadinejad's "vision" at the U.N. is strangely reminiscent and alarmingly similar to statements he has made about his personal role in ushering in the return of the Shiite Muslim messiah.[23]

Radical Muslims are so intent at restoring the caliphate that Hizb ut-Tahrir uses their extreme anguish to exhort party warriors to action. Hizb ut-Tahrir reminds them that it was Kemal Ataturk, the "English agent," as Islamists derogatorily refer to the first president of the Turkish Republic, who ended the caliphate in 1924, adopting democracy, giving rights to women, banning Islamic dress outside of places of worship, and instituting a secular Turkish government. This memory rallies jihadists, and reminds them that they should never allow anyone to quash their dreams of a caliphate. Hizb ut-Tahrir declares that only the reestablishment of the caliphate will rescue the Islamic nations from their current state of humiliation in the world.[24] When jihad fighters converged on Iraq in 2003 to face off with American troops, Mullah Mustapha Kreikar, the leader of Ansar al-Islam, a radical terrorist group, described to the jihadists the big picture: "The resistance is not only a reaction to the American invasion, it is part of the continuous Islamic struggle since the collapse of the caliphate. All Islamic struggles since then are part of one organized effort to bring back the caliphate."[25]

If jihadists need more motivation, they need only look to the father of all modern-day Muslim jihadists Hasan al-Banna, the founder of the Muslim Brotherhood. He died in 1949, but his words still stand today as a rallying call to extremists ready to bring on the Madhi and the rule of Sharia. He saw the end of the caliphate in Turkey as a "Western invasion which was armed and equipped with all [the] destructive influences of money, wealth, prestige, ostentation, power, and means of propaganda."[26]

Thanks to their wealth of petrodollars, Islamists are mounting their own "re-invasion" of the Western world. Even more forceful in his declarations was Imam Abu Hamza Masri: "Islam needs the sword. . . . Whoever has the sword, he will have the earth."[27]

And those who have the sword are ready for battle, from Iraq to the West Bank, from Pakistan and Turkey to Dallas and West Virginia. In 2004, Muslims in northern Texas extolled the virtues and legacy of Khomeini in a conference titled "Tribute to the Great Islamic Visionary." Remember, it was Khomeini who established the Republic of Iran, called America the "great Satan," and declared that "Islam makes it incumbent on all adult males, provided they are not disabled or incapacitated, to prepare themselves for the conquest of countries so that the writ of Islam is obeyed in every country in the world."[28] Yes, the fight to restore the caliphate has come to Texas.

Muslims are responding to Khomeini's vision to establish not just a new Republic of Iran but an Islamic global government. For radical Islamofascists, nothing else will do. For many of them, Iraq is the test case, rallying the faithful to join together in establishing Iraq as the base of the new caliphate, and testing the world's resistance to such an endeavor. The jihadists hope that Iraq will be the first to fall in a global domino effect. Al-Zarqawi makes this point explicitly:

> We now move on to the occupied land, to the land of the caliphate, the glorious land of Iraq. The American wolves, and behind them the Rafidite Shiite dogs, have desecrated our [women's] honor in Tel'afar and other Sunni cities, while the Muslims and the scholars of the sultans keep silent."[29]

For years, terrorists have made their intentions clear. Daniel Pipes, founder of Middle East Forum, writes in the *New York Sun*: "The Islamists who assassinated Anwar el-Sadat in 1981 decorated their holding cages with banners proclaiming 'caliphate or death.' "[30] One of the most influential thinkers in Islam, Abdullah Azzam, said that for him life "revolved around a single goal, namely the establishment of Allah's rule on earth" and restoring the caliphate.[31] (Azzam has been a primary mentor to Osama bin Laden.) Another Al Qaeda leader, Fazlur Rehman Khalil, declared, "Due to the blessings of jihad, America's countdown has begun. It will declare defeat soon, to be followed by the creation of a caliphate."[32]

The radicals of Islam have been telling us all along what they want. They want to rule, and they are finding democracy to be useful to legitimize their rise to power when the demographic numbers swing their way. For example, 40 percent of British Muslims said in a poll that they would rather live under Sharia law.[33]

In America we believe that "Congress shall make no law respecting the establishment of religion, or prohibiting the free exercise thereof." That's a tenet of our democracy and a signpost of a free society. In Islam, the opposite is true. The Koran includes a comprehensive code of law, and regulates everything that involves daily life for Muslims. Mohammad Elachmi Hamdi, editor in chief of *Al-Mustakillah*, observed:

> The heart of the matter is that no Islamic state can be legitimate in the eyes of its subjects without obeying the main teachings of the Sharia. A secular government might coerce obedience, but Muslims will not abandon their belief that state affairs should be supervised by the just teachings of the holy law."[34]

As Americans, and other freedom-loving people around the world, we simply don't grasp the idea of Islamic rule of Sharia law. We're too used to freedom. But that freedom is going to be a thing of the past if we don't stop the jihadists' intent upon putting the world under the rule of the revived caliphate, where Sharia trumps all.

7

THE ISLAMIZATION OF EUROPE

Over the last fifty years, European governmental policies, immigration policies, and political correctness have changed the hearts and minds of those who courageously fought alongside America against the scourges of Nazism and Communism. They have moved from being valiant allies to complacent or hostile onlookers of the war against Islamofascism. At the same time they are becoming helpless victims of their own shortsighted making. Western European civilization is under cultural and often physical attack by forces of Islam that are eroding Europe's political, social, spiritual and cultural core. Scholars who closely track the results of this transformation have labeled this phenomenon the "Islamization" of Europe. World-renowned author Bat Ye'or has taken to referring to Europe as "Eurabia" in her book *Eurabia, the Euro-Arab Axis.* I present here my points on the issue with some supporting comments from her voluminous work, which is a must-read.

What Europe lost in World War II provides us with an interesting study of how economic pressure and needs can lead to social and cultural changes for societies. Europe lost not only her infrastructure—homes, schools, businesses, and public works—but also a huge source of manpower because of a war that cost some 50 million lives in total.[1] While decimating Europe, the war brought about major changes of alliances in the geopolitical land-scape and a decolonization movement, both of which resulted in a loss of foreign resources. Sharing a postwar yearning for peace and prosperity, the leaders of Europe needed goods, services, and stable markets for their exchange. In order for Europe to rebuild physi-cally, economically, and politically, the United States provided funding for recovery under the Marshall Plan, while planning and direction was up to the Europeans. As their economies improved European nations created policies that resulted in the creation of the European Economic Community. The plan of bringing nations together to work on a common economic goal worked so well in Europe that it eventually lead to the creation of the European (EU) Union. This coalition will serve its member nations well if every-one involved is equally committed to the common good. The key is: everyone in every country.

The EU was built on the premise that all countries have values and goals in common, which are bigger than their individual na-tional dreams and aspirations. These common goals and values, however, did not lessen the obstacles of limited energy and man-power still facing Europe. In fact, in the changing face of postwar Europe nations moved from monarchies and colonial powers to democracies. Lost colonies meant lost resources for energy needs. Prompted by fears of oil and manpower shortages, the logical step for the European Economic Community was to reach out to Mediterranean countries where both energy and manpower were plentiful. An alliance was formed between the European Economic Community and Mediterranean countries including Turkey, Mo-rocco, Libya, Algeria, Spain, and Tunisia, based on economic treaties and policies to mutually benefit all countries. It's a plan that is looking more like a disaster each day as it creates a besieged "Eurabia" rather than a stronger Europe.

It was an easy and understandable error on the part of European leaders who were idealistic in their vision for the future. However, what they lacked was a knowledge and understanding of the culture of the Middle East, and, in particular, Islam. Europe neglected to understand that the values and ideals common to Europeans were not shared by Muslims.

Europeans share Western values built on Judeo-Christian traditions, morals, and secular humanism. These values include a love of democracy, tolerance, decency, and respect for life. These values are summed up in the Charter of European Identity drafted by the European Union to offer a comprehensive statement on Europeans:[2]

> Europe is above all a community of values. The aim of unification is to realize, test, develop, and safeguard these values. They are rooted in common legal principles acknowledging the freedom of the individual and social responsibility. Fundamental European values are based on tolerance, humanity, and fraternity. Building on its historical roots in classical antiquity and Christianity, Europe further developed these values during the course of the Renaissance, the Humanist movement, and the Enlightenment, which led in turn to the development of democracy, the recognition of fundamental and human rights, and the rule of law.[3]

These communal values caused Europe to rise up against Nazism in the 1940s and stand against Communism in subsequent decades.

As is often the case in political plans and strategies, more is going on than meets the eye. EU leaders had more than European redevelopment in mind when they turned to the Middle East. Efforts to turn the Middle East into an economic ally was not only for the purpose of obtaining energy, resources, and manpower but was "also a deliberate strategy that was foolishly set in motion by French Gaullists who wanted to create a means of attaining a European-Arab counterweight to the United States."[4]

Little did those who negotiated treaties and policies for Europe realize that these strategies would mean the loss of their own identity. Nor did they realize that economic alliances and shifting the job burden to other ethnic and religious cultures would cost them their soul. In an effort to counter the rising economic power of the United States, our European NATO allies relinquished their identity.

Their economic plan and alliances to strengthen Europe have become the source of Europe's demise and the birth of Eurabia.

The EEC, and later the EU, increased their alignment with Arab policy which strongly opposes Israel and its defender, the United States. Most Arab countries refuse to have diplomatic relations with Israel and some don't even acknowledge its existence. In aligning itself with the Arab League, Europe has ruptured its traditional transatlantic solidarity with the United States. The overriding lust for material, economic, and political power supplied Europe with incentive to drive a wedge between itself and human decency. Old habits are hard to break. As Bat Ye'or put it in a speech at the Counter Jihad Conference in Brussels in 2007: "For forty years, Eurabia has built its networks, its finance, its hegemonous power, its totalitarian control over the media, the universities, the culture and the mind of the people. If one wants to reverse this system, one must reverse decades of policy."[5] Arab League objectives of establishing closer unity between members, and coordinated political actions concerning Arab interests demanded—and Europe has granted—a European political commitment against Israel and an alignment with the Arab League. This overall economic alliance between Arabs and Europeans gave way to an anti-Israel and anti-American animosity expressed through Europe's political, diplomatic, economic, cultural, educational, technological, and media institutions. Europe thus accords the League a multitude of platforms from which to attack Israel and the United States. But the price Europe must pay is higher still. The League has initiated an irreversible process of cultural, religious, and political infiltration that has undermined European sovereignty and is transforming the overwhelmingly Christian continent into an Islamic one. The kinship that should naturally exist between Europe, Israel, and the United States as outposts and protectors of Western civilization has been torn asunder.

After creating informal alliances with Arab countries and loose affiliations through the European Economic Community in 1974, Europe was ready, willing, and able to accept the presence of "guest workers." Unskilled laborers poured into Western Europe from Southern Europe, Turkey, and the Mahgreb region of Northern Africa (Tunisia, Morocco, and Algeria). Though unskilled, they "contributed significantly to the reconstruction of Western Europe . . . and to the creation of economic prosperity."[6]

After the initial rebuilding and redevelopment, the workers remained in Europe to fill other unskilled industrial positions. Around this time, the birth rate of Europeans, which had been falling since 1945, continued its downward trend while Muslim communities had higher birth rates. For the Europeans, economic development meant more leisure time and discretionary income. For some Muslims it meant more money and social services to take care of more children. (There is hope that the high birth rate among Muslims in Europe is beginning to decline. "The longer immigrant women live in France, the fewer the children they have;

their fertility rate approaches that of native born French women.["]7)
The erosion of Europe had begun.

Long-term residency did not necessarily equate with assimilation. It was more or less understood that guest workers who would be staying in their host country for only a year or two, would keep to themselves. The fact is, for those Muslims adhering closely to their faith, not assimilating with Judeo-Christian European culture was the plan from the beginning, straight from the Koran: "Believers, take not Jews and Christians for your friends. They are but friends and protectors to each other." (Koran 5:51)

So, from the Western viewpoint there was no need for them to learn the culture or the language of their host country since their stay was intended to be temporary. And for the Muslim guest, there was the language barrier and the cultural barrier: Muslim dress, Muslim prayer times, Muslim dietary practices, Muslim family practices, and social dynamics to be held to and observed. It was only natural, a Westerner would think, that these new migrants would choose to live in culturally homogenous communities within the host countries.[8]

Yet despite the cultural differences, the temporary guest-worker situation became permanent. The situation is similar to the attraction of Arabs to the Holy Land because of economic opportunity being created by the Jews in Israel. They came. They worked. They stayed. And now they are posing a threat to Israel's long-term stability as a Jewish state through their birth rate and the democratic process. Same with illegal immigration to the United States. They come. They work. And they stay. They get welfare services and possibly soon Social Security. Muslim guest workers in Europe eventually were joined by their family members through unification programs introduced by the European Union. Muslim families grew in size, and a continuous stream of legal immigrants contributed to the population growth of Muslim workers. On top of that was illegal immigration. The unforeseen effects of the influx of Muslim guest workers moved the issue of Islamic immigration from economic recovery to a clash of cultures. The cultural issues of a growing Muslim population has serious implications because immigration, says Bat Ye'or, "is part of the whole strategy, which is an ambition to create a new civilizational concept based on multi-culturalism, on the dissolution of people's typical characteristics."[9]

Evidence of this Islamic growth is seen all over Europe where multiculturalism has gone amuck. Some examples are just plain silly to the Western mind; others, while appearing trite, can be potentially life threatening. One such case occurred in a Belgian hospital where a pregnant Muslim woman was about to receive an emergency caesarian section. When the male anesthetist arrived to assist the patient's female gynecologist in the operating room, the patient's outraged husband blocked the operating room door and demanded a female anesthetist; none could be found. A two-hour discussion ensued, with no results. Finally "an imam was summoned. The imam permitted the doctor to apply an epidural injection, but only if the woman was fully covered with only a small area of skin showing. During the surgery itself, performed by a female gynecologist, the anesthetist was to remain in the hallway. Through a door that was slightly ajar, he shouted instructions to a nurse who was monitoring the anesthesia."[10] Although the mother's life and that of her baby were on the line, radical Islam called the shots. In a way, this episode is a metaphor for Europe—religion is more important than health, and the woman's safety—like Europe's—registering as secondary.

Every time Europeans accommodate Islamic demands to conform to Islamic law, culture, or tradition, a chip of European culture is eroded—there is a bit less democracy, freedom, enlightenment, and Judeo-Christian values. Europe is losing its soul to compromise and appeasement, and it is no different from the appeasement of Germany prior to World War II. It only delays the inevitable.

Compromising freedom of speech and freedom of expression is the first dagger in the heart of Western societies. Appeasement is the result of accommodating a Muslim society that refuses to assimilate and prefers domination over assimilation. Europe is committing social suicide using the rope of political correctness. In his analysis "Europe's Angry Muslims" in *Foreign Affairs*, Robert Leiken writes:

> Today, Muslims constitute the majority of immigrants in most Western European countries, including Belgium, France, Germany, and the Netherlands, and are the largest single component of the immigrant population in the United Kingdom. Exact numbers are hard to come by because Western censuses rarely ask respondents about their faith.[11]

Through population growth, citizenship, and the passage of time, Muslim guest workers are coming of age. Those who entered as strangers in a strange land are becoming leaders—in schools, universities, communities, and society at large. These leaders have not adopted European ways but instead are intent on converting Europe to Islamic laws and ways. In his article "The Muslim Brotherhood's Conquest of Europe," Lorenzo Vidino writes:

> Europe has become an incubator for Islamist thought and political development. Since the early 1960s, Muslim Brotherhood members and sympathizers have moved to Europe and slowly but steadily established a wide and well-organized network of mosques, charities, and Islamic organizations. Unlike the larger Islamic community, the Muslim Brotherhood's ultimate goal may not be simply "to help Muslims be the best

citizens they can be," but rather to extend Islamic law throughout Europe and the United States.

Four decades of teaching and cultivation have paid off. The student refugees who migrated from the Middle East forty years ago and their descendants now lead organizations that represent the local Muslim communities in their engagement with Europe's political elite. Funded by generous contributors from the Persian Gulf, they preside over a centralized network that spans nearly every European country.[12]

As a consequence of years of ignorance and apathy mixed with Islamic demography, ideology, and culture, Europe now has become a home to millions of Muslim youth who may hold European citizenship but have no connection to European culture, identity, society, or values.

Instead, a complicated vision presents itself. On the one hand, Muslims position themselves as victims and on the other, they present themselves to their fellow Arabs as victors who are carefully and masterfully using the West's liberal-mindedness and inability to stand up for itself to overthrow it.

According to Muslims, they are the victims of Judeo-Christian values, of discrimination, of xenophobia and, worse still, of Islamophobia. They create and perpetuate their victimhood by using the Western legal, political, and social systems to plead and "prove" their case. At the same time, they erase from history their own display of aggression, and get upset when people like the Pope happen to point out their past transgressions. This denial is absolutely necessary to further the purposes of Islam.

It is incumbent upon us to keep history alive and communicate it without apology from one generation to the next. Without faithful representation of history, the truth is lost. It would be like saying to the holocaust survivor whose arm bears a tattoo,

"Concentration camps were but your imagination, you are just being Nazi-phobic." It would be like telling me that I did not live in a bomb shelter in Lebanon or that the scars on my arm are from shrapnel that did not hit me because Muslims did not bomb my home. History proves that the conflict between Islam and the rest of the world goes back to Mecca! Islamic aggression could not be reasoned with then and it cannot be reasoned with now. Western culture believes that with enlightenment through reason we can grow in wisdom. With reason, we are better equipped to handle deep ideological, religious, and political issues. But when reason does not work, then what?

We all remember the incident of the cartoons published in a Danish newspaper, which allegedly insulted Prophet Mohammed. In response to the cartoons, a letter was sent to Danish prime minister Anders Fogh Rasmussen by ambassadors from eleven Islamic countries to demand that he take the "necessary steps" to avert an offense to Islam.[13] When Rasmussen refused,

> the Egyptian foreign minister got the Arab League and the Organization of the Islamic Conference (OIC) involved soon after. The OIC had already made clear what it wanted in its "Declaration of Human Rights in Islam" in 1990: "All have the right to freely express their opinions in a manner that does not run counter to Sharia law." In essence, what the OIC wanted was to compel Western nations to bring their form of freedom of expression into conformity with Sharia law.[14]

Prime Minister Rasmussen reasoned it was not his responsibility to discipline journalists in a country that values freedom of speech, and declined to meet with the incensed ambassadors. This was not what the world of Islam wanted to hear. The conflict immediately went to the next level. *Spiegel International* reported:

> "On Feb. 3, 2006, a "Day of Anger" was proclaimed. Across the Muslim world, the Mohammed cartoons were the focus of Friday prayers. Millions of Muslims who couldn't even locate Denmark on a map demonstrated against these insults to the Prophet, incited by their imams. The embassies of Denmark and Norway were set on fire in Damascus, the Danish embassy was torched in Beirut, firebombs were hurled at the Danish consulate in Tehran, and Danish and Norwegian flags were burned in Nigeria and Algeria.[15]

Is there anything reasonable about such a response to someone's freedom of speech? Reason does not always triumph over evil and when it doesn't, evil must simply be stopped.

Europe has fallen into a trap by persisting in reasoning with people who use Europe's rational response to manipulate and control situations. As they long for continued peace, Europeans are continually trying to figure out what can be done differently and better. To promote equality, Europeans allowed Muslims the right to develop madrassas, Islamic cultural centers, Koranic colleges and institutions, and even to implement Sharia law.

In the back of one of these sanctioned madrassas in Britain is a court, a Sharia court. According to an investigation by Paul Jeeves of the *Daily Express*, the Sharia court system, called the Sharee Council, has been set up in the heart of Dewsbury, West Yorkshire. It "is a model for others across the countries which are operating outside the British legal process. The council operates as a Muslim judiciary making decisions by which attendees must abide. Non-Muslims are excluded from the secretive court, which is registered as a charity to receive British tax benefits. In many countries, hard-line interpretations of the Islamic law allow people to be stoned to death, beheaded, or have their limbs amputated."[16] Is this really something enlightened Westerners want to condone? Esther Pan, staff writer for the Council on Foreign Relations, writes in her analysis: "Europe: Integrating Islam":

> The continent has been deluged with hundreds of documen-
> taries, news stories, films, and editorials about Islam in the
> last few years, part of a lively debate about the religion's in-
> fluence. Some British banks now advertise their compliance
> with rules governing Islamic banking. The German province
> of Saxony-Anhalt became the first in Europe to issue a *sukuk,*
> or Islamic bond, which complies with Quranic rules barring
> the payment or collection of interest. In Denmark, one of the
> most secular countries in Europe, the Quran is required
> reading for high school students; the Bible is not. But experts
> say the new efforts do not necessarily change countries' gen-
> erally assimilationist policies, or the attitudes of many of
> their people.[17]

The consolidation of Muslim immigrants in their own commu-nities, out of motives of self-segregation and cultural segregation, creates mini incubators for the Islamists. Robert S. Leiken, director of the Immigration and National Security Program at the Nixon Center says: "To make matters worse, the very isolation of these di-aspora communities obscures their inner workings, allowing muja-hedeen to fundraise, prepare, and recruit for jihad with a freedom available in few Muslim countries."[18]

One thing the West can be thankful for is the Arabic tendency to brag openly about terrorist operations. Here is an example. Re-sponding to criticism that Saudi Arabia has served as a conduit to fund international terrorist organizations, Prince Saud al Faisal pointed an accusing finger at the West. "There is more money reaching these terrorist organizations from Western countries, including the U.S., than comes from sources in the Middle East or Islamic countries. The infrastructure of personnel who work for recruiting and propagating the ideas, for promoting the interests, they exist more in the capitals of Europe than they exist in the capitals of the Middle East."[19]

While Saudi Arabia does not deserve to be exonerated for promoting Islamic terrorism, Prince Saud al Faisal was correct to declare the capitals of Western Europe hotbeds of radical activity. We must recognize that radical Islam's seeds have been planted in Europe's heart. The roots are spreading in creative and persistent ways and will undermine and kill the culture and tradition Europe once embodied.

So who's all that worried about a few bits of culture and traditions, you might say? While not directly a compliance issue with Islamic banking, British banks have skewered one tradition with political correctness taken to an extreme. Their acquiescence is as revealing of behind-the-scenes cultural assault as it is humorous and ludicrous. Remember the piggy bank? For most children in Western cultures, the piggy bank is their first savings plan. Scratch that for the children of England, thanks to Salim Mulla, secretary of the Lancashire Council of Mosques. "Muslims do not eat pork, as Islamic culture deems the pig to be an impure animal."[20] In an effort not to offend Muslims the Bank of Halifax and NatWest were the first to ban piggy banks from their premises. Mulla went on to say, "This is a sensitive issue and I think the banks are simply being courteous to their customers."[21]

As if this weren't enough, the political correctness don't-hurt-the-Islamics'-feelings, police take it to a whole other level by banning toy pigs, novelty pig calendars and all pig-related items, even

Winnie the Pooh and Piglet in Dudley Metropolitan Borough, in West Midlands, England. Workers there were told "to remove or cover up all pig-related items, including toys, porcelain figures, calendars and even a tissue box featuring Winnie the Pooh and Piglet. The pigs were offensive to Muslims during Ramadan."[22]

Mark up another success story for cultural jihadists who by invoking political correctness are reshaping Western culture as the West willingly surrenders. Rather than through headline-grabbing acts of terror, bin Laden's tactics of pen and sword are being played out as cultural jihad in Europe is fought one skirmish at a time.

For years, Great Britain and other countries of Western Europe have bent over backward to accommodate the growing Muslim population within their borders. It has been nearly an article of faith that multicultural tolerance of Muslims, even militant Muslims, would promote peace and interfaith dialogue, and diminish the possibility of terrorist attacks.

That "article of faith" is proving to be an illusion.

In January 2007, Britain's *Daily Mail* ran an article entitled "Multiculturalism Drives Young Muslims to Shun British Values."[23] The article noted that a study had found that "Multiculturalism has alienated an entire generation of young Muslims and made them increasingly radical. . . . In stark contrast with their parents, growing numbers sympathize with extreme teachings of Islam, with almost four in ten wanting to live under Sharia law in Britain. . . . 13% said they 'admired' organizations such as al Qaida . . ."

Any student of history and the doctrines of Islam understands these attitudes. What we in the West regard as a virtue (tolerance and accommodation) Islam regards as weakness and an implicit if not explicit acknowledgement that Islam is superior and we are inferior. The harder the West tries to accommodate Islam, the more it is seen by Muslims as weak. This is why, in spite of everything Great Britain has done to accommodate Islam, Islamic militancy in Britain grows and the threat of terror increases.

Contrary to the hopes and best intentions of those seeking to accommodate Islam, the tolerance of Islamic intolerance will simply promote more Islamic intolerance. It is something the West in general and America in particular must come to acknowledge.

When I travel, I often tell the workers at security checkpoints in airports that I appreciate their work and diligence in preventing terrorism and our submission to terrorists and their ideology. But the real threat of Islamists, the ones who hold up signs in England saying "Dominate the World," comes from the bedrooms of the Muslim world. Although there are no accurate statistics on the Muslim population of the EU countries,

> it is estimated that between 15 and 20 million Muslims now call Europe home and make up four to five percent of its total population. . . . France has the largest proportion of Muslims (seven to ten percent of its total population), followed by the Netherlands, Germany, Denmark, Sweden, the United Kingdom, and Italy. Given continued immigration and Muslim fertility rates, the National Intelligence Council projects that Europe's Muslim population will double by 2025.[24]

In a few years, if the Islamic population growth continues at this rate, Muslims will constitute almost 20 percent of the European workforce and therefore have the ability to influence policies and decision-making.[25] As the population has grown so has its determination to remain separate from of society until society itself is transformed into an Islamic one. Analyst Nabil Shabee writes in Islamoline.com,

During the past few decades there has been a religious revival amongst European Muslims. Their assimilation into Western society has thus slowed, and the number of practicing Muslims has increased. This is reflected in the increased observance of the hijab among women, and in the increase in the number of mosques and prayer facilities.[26]

According to Western values, everyone has freedom of expression in speech, dress, and religion, so the wearing of the *hijab* on the part of Muslim women does not offend Westerners. Most Westerners, though they have the freedom to speak, dress, and hold their own belief systems, do not force others to change their habits when visiting or working in other countries, but will conform to what is appropriate. Take for example the workplace. If you work in a restaurant there is an expected code of dress. If you work in a bank, there is a different expected way of dress. It all depends on the work environment and the demands of the job.

Imagine the shock of a British hair salon owner when she was sued by a Muslim teen for religious discrimination. The salon is located in London and caters to those who desire the "urban, funky, punky" look. The first rule of marketing for a salon is that the stylist is your best marketing tool. A stylist's hair would attract customers, and so to wear a *hijab* in that job culture would not be appropriate. The teen who insisted on wearing her *hijab* was not hired; this seems logical, at least according to Western thinking.

The teen who brought suit, however, did not see the logic. She claimed religious discrimination and sued the salon owner for lost wages and damages to "her feelings." The shop owner denies any form of discrimination: "It has nothing to do with religion. It is just unfortunate that for her, covering her hair symbolizes religion. I now feel like I have been branded a racist. My name is being dragged through the mud and I feel victimized.' "[27] Europeans are waking up to the new reality. They no longer live in Europe. They live in Eurabia where Muslims are getting the upper hand:

> Europe, in the words of Felice Dassetto and Albert Bastenier, is the new frontier of Islam. The term "frontier" describes better the ongoing processes of Islam's growing presence in Europe. Now, one increasingly speaks of Islam in the West and, eventually through the role of second- and third-generation immigrants and converts, of an Islam of Europe, if not yet of a European Islam. Islam is no longer a transitory phenomenon that can eventually be sent back "home."[28]

The Islamists are becoming emboldened as Europe cowers to Islamic demands.

The leading Muslim cleric Yusuf al-Qarodawi heralds Islam's conquest of Europe. He posts fatwas of this nature on his Web site, www.islamonline.net:

> The Prophet Mohammed was asked: "What city will be conquered first, Constantinople or Romiyya?' He answered: "The city of Hirqil [the Byzantine emperor Heraclius] will be conquered first"—that is, Constantinople. . . . Romiyya is the city called today Rome. [Constantinople] was conquered by the young 23-year-old Ottoman Muhammad bin Morad, known in history as Muhammad the Conqueror, in 1453. The other city, Romiyya, remains, and we hope and believe [that it too will be conquered].
>
> This means that Islam will return to Europe as a conqueror and victor, after being expelled from it twice—once from the South, from Andalusia [Spain] and a second time from the East, when it knocked several times on the door of Athens. . . . I maintain that the conquest this time will not be by the sword but by preaching and ideology. . . . We want an army of preachers and teachers who will present Islam in all languages and in all dialects."[29]

The nonviolent conquest of the West continues apace as mosques are constructed all over America and Europe, but woe be it to anyone who wants to construct a church in Saudi Arabia, Iran, or Egypt. Muslims are using multiculturalism to present Islam as an alternative to the Christian West. Muslims believe the West lacks spiritual commitment and political honor. They look at Western families torn by divorce, children raised without parental supervision, gay pride parades, murder, drugs, alcohol, and depression plaguing Western societies. They offer Islam to many who are lost in a society that doesn't have strong family ties and structure. Islam offers a community, which embraces the individual and offers spiritual dignity and meaning to life.

Islam's numbers in Europe are at the tipping point. France has one of the largest numbers of people of Muslim origin, estimated between 3.5 and 6 million. The presence of a significant Muslim population is due in part to the fact that France colonized and then governed Algeria, Tunisia, and Morocco. For many years, inhabitants of those countries freely moved in and out of France. Michel Gurfinkiel, editor in chief of *Valeurs Actuelles,* France's leading conservative weekly newsmagazine, writes:

> Perhaps more important than exact numbers is the spectacular rate of growth since World War II. Muslims in France in 1945 numbered some 100,000 souls; fifty years later, the population has increased by thirty or forty times. It continues to grow at a rapid clip, through further immigration (illegal but until now poorly suppressed), natural increase (immigrant Muslim families retain a comparatively high birthrate), or conversion (either as the result of intermarriage or out of a personal religious quest).[30]

As is consistent elsewhere in Europe, Muslims in France have not become assimilated into the general population.

You can change the country, but the story remains the same. In Holland, the integration, or lack thereof, of Muslims is a concern for the Dutch government, particularly after a filmmaker critical of Islam, Theo Van Gogh, was murdered in 2004 by a Dutch radical Islamist originally from Morocco. Further tensions have mounted because Muslim youth in Holland, especially Moroccans, account for the second-highest rate of crimes and have a problem with unemployment.

Holland has one of the most liberal cultures in Europe. Some would label the culture as decadent, given its permissiveness and acceptance of just about everyone and everything. Holland's general social tolerance and liberal policies regarding prostitution, drugs, women, abortion, and gays are renowned. It is hard to imagine anyone in Holland being offended by such matters, yet Ahmed Salam, a radical imam from the city of Tilburg, was. In 2004 he refused to shake the hand of then minister of immigration and integration Rita Verdonk on camera. His ideas are not limited to shaking the hand of a woman. In fact, he "caused a sensation in 2002 in Tilburg. He preached that men should treat their wives with physical violence."[31]

Imam Salam refuses to assimilate into the culture of his adopted country. He came to the Netherlands from Syria in 1989 but does not speak Dutch well; he brings his son with him to translate whenever they are in public. At a recent public meeting, they "demanded that no alcohol (i.e., wine) be drunk by anyone at the table, since *their belief* does not allow it."[32] Those in charge complied with their demands. The imposition of Sharia doesn't stop here for the imam. He is also credited with telling his followers "not to pay taxes so as to do harm to the Dutch State."[33]

In September 2006, Dutch justice minister Piet Hein Donner was reported as saying the Netherlands should give Muslims more freedom to behave according to their traditions. "For me it is clear: if two-thirds of the Dutch population should want to introduce the Sharia tomorrow, then the possibility should exist," according to Donner. "It would be a disgrace to say: 'That is not allowed!' "[34]

This is outrageous! Justice Minister Donner would allow Sharia to be democratically introduced to Holland! Once it is introduced, Sharia will shut down the democratic process! The Muslim population in Holland is only 10 percent as of 2007. If they have already influenced the larger Dutch society, through intimidation and pressure, to the point of introducing Sharia law, the rest of Europe is doomed.

The problem of Islamic infiltration and growth is also plaguing Russia. It is estimated that Muslims account for up to 16 percent of the population. Fifteen years ago Russia had about three-hundred mosques. Today there are at least eight-thousand. Some predict that Russia will never be Islamized but will halt the spread of Islam. Others are less confident. Concerns surround not only birth rate, but also the increasing number of practicing Muslims and the ongoing and deepening "friendship" between Russia and Iran. And on these points both Paul Goble, an expert on Islam in Russia and the imam agree: "Across Russia, Islam is thriving. Experts say the country is undergoing a startling change and that if current trends continue, more than half of Russia's population will be Muslim by mid-century. . . . 'They [Muslims] are embracing their faith again,' said Ildar Alyautdinov, an imam at the Sobornaya Mosque."[35]

However, there are those Muslims who do not fit the mold. Some Muslims in Europe have assimilated, and are successful members of their communities and countries. Others have remained separate but practice their faith in a nominal manner, keeping their traditions but not necessarily their faith; they are secular Muslims similar to secular Jews or secular Christians. These secular Muslims either have no concerns about how Islam is being perceived or are not voicing those that they have. In either case they are marginalized by the more outspoken, hardcore Islamists, many of whom remain totally segregated from the country and culture in which they reside. Although it is difficult to assess exactly how many Muslims are spread across Europe and across the globe, all sources indicate the number is growing. We will find out how many there are only when it's too late, when mosques have replaced cathedrals and the call of the muezzin replaces the peal of church bells.

8

THE SUBTLE ISLAMIZATION AGENDA: BOILING THE WEST ALIVE

Radical Islam has found itself homes throughout the western hemisphere. Canada, Mexico, the countries of South America, as well as the United States are all infested with the spreading cancer of Islamic fundamentalism—and vulnerable to the terrorists who are inseparable from its ideology of hatred and conquest.[1] The United States and Canada in particular have attracted thousands of Islamists because of their welfare systems and democratic laws, and an open society where radical Islamists can operate within communities protected from scrutiny in the name of multiculturalism. And even if agents of law enforcement began investigating them, there would be a line of attorneys lined up to defend those terrorists in the name of "innocent until proven guilty." This democratic formula is fertilizer for Islamists plotting terrorist operations By the time an Islamist has committed his terrorist act and became a martyr, any guilty verdict will be as ineffective as the tears shed by thousands of people mourning their dead loved ones.

SOUTH AMERICA

South America has the very real potential to become an alternate center of operations for Islamic terrorist activity—which will threaten the stability of North America as well.

To international police and American diplomats, "the communities on the triple border of Paraguay, Brazil, and Argentina are hideouts for terrorists who are poised to wreak havoc on South America and the rest of the world."[2] Despite Brazilian government denials, American and Paraguayan officials are gravely concerned that this triple border region has become a haven for Islamic extremists, allowing them to conceal themselves within a large, growing, and prosperous Islamic community.[3]

U.S. officials say that the area's porous borders and lack of adequate policing make it a safe haven for Islamic terrorist organizations. In May 2002, the State Department issued a report noting that Hezbollah and other terrorist groups were using bases in Latin America to "raise millions of dollars annually via criminal enterprises."[4] Other radical Muslim groups also reportedly had operatives there—possibly including Al Qaeda.[5] Some radical Islamic terror suspects had been apprehended, but others remain at large.[6]

Asa Hutchinson of the U.S. Drug Enforcement Administration remarked that "the two major terrorist organizations in the tri-border area are Hezbollah and the Islamic resistance movement known as Hamas. . . . [T]heir [suspected] illegal activities range from producing counterfeit U.S. currency to smuggling illegal substances through the tri-border area."[7] Testifying before the House International Relations Committee, Hutchinson stated that Hamas and Hezbollah activities remain unhindered. He pointed out "the ease with which terrorist organizations can infiltrate and assimilate in other countries and go relatively undetected for an extended period of time."[8] While not widely known as such, the area remains a "hot zone" for terror groups.[9]

In 2002 and 2003, Miguel Angel Toma, an agent of SIDE, Argentina's intelligence service, visited Washington, Berlin, London, and Paris, to warn officials there of the growing threat posed by Islamic terrorists in the triple border region and detailing terrorists' partnerships with drug lords, smugglers, and counterfeiters. As pressure on Middle and Central Asian jihadi rings mounted, Toma maintained, the jihadists shifted operations to the southern hemisphere.[10]

The triple border region has spawned successful and attempted terrorist attacks in the past, including the 1992 and 1994 bombings of the Israeli embassy and the Jewish cultural center in Buenos Aires.[11] In October 1998, Lebanese national Sobhi Mahmoud Fayad was arrested for allegedly planning to bomb the U.S. embassy in Asuncion, Paraguay,[12] but was released and remained at large until November 8, 2001, when he was arrested for sending thousands of dollars to Hezbollah and recruiting members for the organization.[13] He later went to prison for tax evasion. In February 1999, authorities arrested Al-Said Hassan Hussein Mokhles and Mohammed Ibrahim Soleiman in Chui, Uruguay. Mokhles had trained with Al Qaeda and established terror cells in Foz, the area's central town.[14] Cairo accused him of complicity in a 1997 assault that murdered fifty-eight tourists in Luxor.[15]

In December 2000, counterterrorism agents in Asuncion arrested Salah Yassin, a Lebanese national and nephew of the Hezbollah leader Sheikh Yassin, who was later killed by Israeli forces on March 22, 2004. Salah Yassin was on his way to bomb Israeli targets.[16] After September 11, authorities arrested sixteen Lebanese nationals who had entered Paraguay illegally. In an October 2001 raid on a wholesale electronics store in Ciudad del Este, Paraguay, two radical Muslims were arrested, and agents found documents definitively linking owner Ahmed Assad Barakat with Hezbollah. A letter from Hezbollah Secretary-General Hassan Nasrallah was thankful "for the contributions Assad Ahmad Barakat has sent from the triple border." Evidence uncovered later showed that Barakat had sent some $50 million to Hezbollah since 1995.[17] Barakat's cell had planned the Buenos Aires bombings. He was finally apprehended in Brazil and extradited to Paraguay in November 2003.[18]

Evidence has clearly established connections between the triple border region and terrorist attacks on three continents.[19] Officials warn that the region's highly successful Arab entrepreneurs continue to provide financial backing for Muslim radicals.[20]

In June 2002, the Organization of American States adopted the Inter-American Convention against Terrorism. But even the ratification of this binding legal instrument, the first international treaty against terrorism since September 11,[21] left the United States largely tilting at windmills. Brazil remained reluctant to act.[22] In December 2003, Brazilian president Luiz Inacio Lula da Silva met with Syrian president Bashar al-Assad in Damascus at the beginning of a tour of five Arab nations. He sought increased Brazilian "economic ties in the region," support for a Brazilian seat on the U.N. Security Council, and an Arab/Latin American summit. He also opposed the U.S. sanctions outlined in the Syria Accountability and Lebanese Sovereignty Restoration Act,[23] which President Bush signed on May 11, 2004.[24] And he visited Syrian-occupied Lebanon, the United Arab Emirates, Egypt, and Libya—countries not known for their devotion to defeating terrorism.[25]

Radical Islam seems to have spread to Bolivia as well. On December 4, 2003, ABI, the Bolivian state news agency, reported that the government had arrested sixteen Bangladeshi Muslims at the southern Viru Viru airport, based on a tip-off from French authorities. Apparently, they planned to hijack a plane to attack U.S. targets.[26]

MEXICO

A congressional report on homeland security by the subcommittee on investigations of the House Homeland Security Committee acknowledged the threat of terrorist organizations sneaking into the United States through the Mexican border.[27] "We apprehended five Pakistanis on the U.S.–Mexico border with fraudulent Venezuelan documents," said Representative Michael McCaul, who chaired the subcommittee.[28]

In this same report (titled "A Line in the Sand: Confronting the Threat at the Southwest Border") the case is made as to the number of aliens other than Mexican, known as OTM, crossing the border at an alarming rate. Those OTMs are nationals of Iran, Syria, Pakistan, Afghanistan, and Iraq.[29] In my earlier book, I detailed the collaborative efforts of the MS 13 gang and terrorist organizations such as Al Qaeda and Hezbollah in smuggling terrorists into the United States. Drug cartels also have figured out a way to make money working with terrorist organizations such as Al Qaeda, which has the financial ability to provide between $25,000 to $50,000 per terrorist they need smuggled into the United States through Mexico.[30]

In June 2001, Mexican national security adviser Adolpho Aguilar Zinser announced that Islamic terrorist organizations were represented along the U.S.–Mexico border.[31] He said that these groups might be developing relationships with Mexican guerrilla organizations.

Joseph Farah, founder of the *G2 Bulletin*, an online intelligence report, noted that the Mexican government has even provided "survival kits to those intending to cross the Rio Grande and make their way to the 'Promised Land.' "[32] He noted the "horror and anguish that Americans will experience when the first truck bomber makes it across the border and delivers his load at a vulnerable U.S. target . . . when the first airliner is blown out of the sky by hand-held, guided, American-made Stinger missiles from south of the border or north . . . when Katyusha rockets start hitting American cities the way they routinely hit Israeli towns in Galilee."[33]

Farah made these observations before September 11. In October 2004, authorities investigated evidence that as many as twenty-five jihadists from Chechnya had entered the United States illegally through Mexico.[34] American officials did not consider this a unique incident, and were investigating the possibility that the next major terrorist attack could come from jihadists who crossed our southern border.[35]

What's more, American media are now beginning to consider the threat posed to American aircraft by Stinger-wielding Islamic terrorists already positioned in the United States.[36] The U.S. intelligence community's biggest fear regarding the U.S.–Mexican border now is the potential for a nuclear or biological bomb to be smuggled into the United States.

CANADA

On May 3, 2002, the *Wall Street Journal Europe* reported that law enforcement officials were investigating a possible Canadian link to a deadly April explosion at a Tunisian synagogue, the suspected work of Islamic extremists. A Royal Canadian Mounted Police spokesman said investigators were looking into reports that Tunisian citizen

Nizar Nawar, the alleged driver of the truck that carried the bomb that destroyed the synagogue, "previously resided and may have studied in Canada."[37] Al Qaeda claimed responsibility for the blast.[38]

Canada, liké the United States, is home to a vast terrorist infrastructure.[39] Jamaat ul-Fuqra (JF) first mention, a group linked to terrorist activities in the U.S., also has communities in Canada. The *Ottawa Citizen* described Jamaat ul-Fuqra as "a cloistered Islamic community west of Ottawa, whose plans to build a mosque recently sparked an uproar among its neighbors." The paper said that the group "was inspired by a violent Pakistani sheikh in the 1980s and was embroiled in a sensational criminal case in the early 1990s over a plot to blow up a Hindu temple near Toronto. . . . Questions have also been raised about the connection between this Muslim community and the U.S.-based Muslims of the Americas network that operates almost identical rural compounds in the States. Muslims of the Americas is widely viewed by U.S. and Canadian law enforcement agencies as a thinly disguised front for Jamaat ul-Fuqra—a militant, Pakistani-based Islamic organization with a history of violence in North America."[40] An e-mail sent out by Muslims of the Americas in January 2002 calls for commitment and sacrifice:

> The Ummah cannot afford to sit back complacently as an idle observer witnessing his own destruction. Along with a return to Allah, Muslims are required to sacrifice and aid those who are in the forefront in the field to guard the Ummah and Islam. Rasulullah (Sallallahu-'Alayhi-Wa-Sallam) said that there will always remain a small devoted band of his followers who will remain ever vigilant, holding aloft the Standard of Islam . . . exposing themselves to dangers and sacrificing their all for the love of Allah . . . Muslims who are unable to enter into this field of effort and sacrifice are at least required to aid this holy task with their *Du'as* [prayers] and financial resources and with whatever other means they possess. If the

Muslims fail in this duty, they will most assuredly be apprehended by the punishment of Allah.[41]

Canada is the major conduit of terrorists into the United States
after the Mexican border. The conspirators who sought to bomb
the Seattle Space Needle and Los Angeles International Airport
during the millennium celebrations entered the United States from
Canada, and had lived there while they planned the attacks.[42]

More ominously still, the September 11 attacks had a Canadian
connection. Nabil al-Marabh, arrested in Burbank, Illinois, on September 19, 2001, was suspected of playing a major role in coordinating the attacks. He was alleged to have provided the actual
perpetrators with cash, along with phony passports and driver's li-
censes. He communicated by phone with at least two of the hijackers.[43] He had shared a Boston apartment with another alleged Al
Qaeda operative, Raed Hijazi, who was later imprisoned in Jordan
for allegedly plotting to bomb a Jordan hotel in December 2000.[44]
The two had both worked for the same Boston cab company. Moreover, authorities found drawings of an airport flight line, which included aircraft and runways, at an apartment in Detroit that
al-Marabh had shared with three other Middle Easterners who were
also arrested.[45]

Al-Marabh, a Kuwaiti, according to Insight magazine, "had
been in custody less than three months before his Sept. 19 arrest.
On June 27, 2001, a U.S. border guard in Niagara Falls, N.Y., found
al-Marabh in the back of a tractor-trailer trying to sneak across the
border with a fake Canadian passport."[46]

The al-Marabh incident had Canadians concerned that their
country had become a hub for terrorists. According to an October
2003 report by the Canadian Security Intelligence Service, "Terrorism of foreign origin continues to be a major concern in regard to

the safety of Canadians at home and abroad. Canada is viewed by some terrorist groups as a place to try to seek refuge, raise funds, procure materials and/or conduct other support activities. . . . Virtually all of the most notorious international terrorist organizations are known to maintain a network presence in Canada."[47]

According to David Harris, a former strategic planning chief for the Canadian Security Intelligence Service, "We've got a lot of blood on our hands worldwide. If some can say the Americans were asleep at the switch prior to the eleventh of September, we've been in a coma."[48]

Canada's 2001 Anti-Terrorism Act dealt a serious legal challenge to terrorist groups raising funds there, according to a U.S. Library of Congress interagency study.[49] But as the U.S. State Department reported in April 2003, Canada's privacy laws and porous borders of over 5,500 miles, and its insufficient funding for investigation agencies, continue to conspire to the advantage of global terrorists.[50] By July 2003, moreover, Canada had banned only sixteen terror groups—fewer than half the number listed by the State Department.[51]

Meanwhile, Canada's terrorist problem has grown increasingly urgent. In 2006 agents of Canadian law enforcement arrested seventeen Muslim men in Toronto who, inspired by Al Qaeda, tried to acquire three tons of ammonium nitrate and bomb-making components. The group was "planning to commit a series of terrorist attacks against solely Canadian targets in southern Ontario," Royal Canadian Mounted Police Assistant Commissioner Mike McDonell said at a news conference.[52]

Threats notwithstanding, Canada seems willing to yield politically as the country's Muslims demand implementation of Sharia-based personal arbitration courts. (In a most welcome development, the foremost opposition to these arbitration boards has come from a group of Muslim women.)[53] For now, Canada's Sharia courts are voluntary. But many Muslims seek full and formal implementation of Sharia as the law of the land the moment Muslims obtain a majority in any nation. Indeed, the Canadian Muslim convention included Sunni and Shiite imams, led by Canadian barrister Syed Mumtaz Ali, who began his campaign for Canadian recognition of Islamic law in 1962. "It's shocking to see the seeds of an Islamic republic being sown here in Canada," said one opponent of the arbitration courts. "Sharia doesn't work anywhere else in the world. Why does the government believe it will work here?"[54]

It is likely that terrorist organizations will continue to use Canada to enter and launch attacks against the United States. Well-financed and highly motivated terrorists find our long coastlines and shared borders all too easy to penetrate.

Hamas, Hezbollah, and Al Qaeda: our new neighbors. Are we ready for this?

THE CULTURAL INVASION

A seditious culture is advancing worldwide. Its seeds have been implanted in the fabric of countries all over the globe. It is creating a crisis and laying a foundation that has the potential to change the future of people and cultures worldwide. No nation is exempt. Big or small, powerful or weak, countries around the world know first-hand the effects of Islam's growing agenda. Its push to alter cultures is evident throughout the world, especially in the West. These radical extremist proponents of a cultural coup d'etat are making progress, and these inroads are just the tip of the iceberg of the war for Islamic cultural dominance.

Universities in the United States and Europe are extending olive branches to our enemies in the name of education and intellectual exchange, while refusing to allow others to express their opinions on campuses.[55] Fortune 500 companies are setting aside their standing policies in order to accommodate Muslim prayer schedules and religious observances,[56] while refusing the same privileges to those of other faiths. Retail giants are trying to rake in higher profits by devising new strategies to add Muslim markets to their demographics. While Americans accept and accommodate *niqabs*, *burqas*, and foot-washing basins,[57] all in the spirit of political correctness, our culture escalates into crisis.

Europe couldn't imagine what would happen to them when they opened up their borders to Muslims three generations ago. But today, third-generation radicals are overtaking Western Europe with a militant, extremist agenda. And they are doing it with riots, rape, murder, beatings, and burnings, and running native citizens out of their homes.[58]

But Europe was just a blueprint for the eventual cultural collision planned for America, and it's already arrived at a city near you. Make no mistake about it, terrorists, cleverly disguised behind the freedoms they enjoy, are living among us.

The true agenda of radical Isamofascists is hidden beneath the slick, deceptive illusion of inclusion and assimilation. While mosques and madrassas spring up across the United States, Muslims are courted by American marketing machines. U.S. companies trying to cash in on the untapped demographic of American Muslims, have now provided American Muslims with their own brand of essentials. Soon the Middle Eastern version of the Barbie doll will line the shelves of toy stores throughout America. *TD Monthly*, a trade magazine for the toy, hobby, game, and gift industry, published an article stating:

"This isn't just about putting a *hijab* on a Barbie Doll," explained Fawaz Abidin, vice president in charge of the Fulla line for the doll's manufacturer, Syrian company New Boy Design Studio. There has been a Moroccan Barbie, and veiled dolls like Sara in Iran, and Razanne in Britain, but Fulla is a phenomenon based on a character that "Muslim parents and children will want to relate to. She has Muslim values.[59]

A big hit throughout the Middle East,[60] some of the dolls have made their way to America, sent as gifts to girls here as early as 2003.

Food companies are also catering to Muslim customers. McDonald's first auditioned halal chicken in their Britain venues. A variation of the American favorite, Chicken McNuggets, halal chicken is made according to Islamic dietary laws. Because of its success, the menu item was introduced in Australia last December, and then appeared in Detroit, where American Muslims traveled all the way from New York City to sample it.[61] McDonald's response to customers who protested the menu change—simply go somewhere halal food is not offered.[62]

Don't be too surprised if other fast-food giants like Pizza Hut, KFC, and Burger King, who have long been serving halal meats in Western Europe,[63] soon accommodate Muslims' Islamic preferences by offering hand-slaughtered meats here in America. And it won't just be the fast-food giants either. Outback Steakhouse has already announced it will add halal lamb to their menu. And the pressure is mounting on other restaurants to comply. Muslims recently have enlisted the help of the Council on American-Islamic Relations and the American Civil Liberties Union (ACLU) and are threatening to take to court businesses that refuse to add halal items to their menus. Even the inmates of an east New Jersey state prison have their own complaints about halal not being offered in the cafeteria. The ACLU is on tap to begin that fight on behalf of the prisoners.[64] And so it goes, as long as Americans continue to look the other way, satisfied that their favorite meat is still on the menu.

Starbucks, the coffee magnate, prepared a treat for Muslims to celebrate Ramadan. It launched the Date Frappuccino created especially for their customers in the Middle East. Said to be designed to suit Arab taste, the beverage is flavored with the juice of dates. "We are committed to surprising and delighting our customers through innovative products. The new Date Frappuccino reflects a beverage that has been created for the first time specifically for our Middle East customers and we hope it is enjoyed throughout Ramadan," said Antoun Abou Jaoude, marketing manager for Starbucks Coffee Middle East.[65] Don't be surprised if that same beverage comes to America to celebrate Ramadan next year. Wake up and smell the coffee of political correctness!

While Muslims, both moderate and radical, participate in the conspicuous consumption they have so decried as part of the evil web of the Great Satan, the terrorist underground grows almost undetected in cities across North America. While Muslims accuse American companies of discrimination and tie them up in court cases over human rights and freedom of expression, most Americans go about their daily grind oblivious to what is really happening. Preoccupied with the life that could so easily disappear because of their inaction, many Americans are oblivious to the accommodations occurring everywhere for Muslims who demand their "freedoms," such as diversity classes at Disney World led by Muslims.[66] Managers at Disney World receive training on how to juggle schedules and prayer times and the company provides prayer rooms for Muslim employees. (I wonder how many rooms they have on the premises for their evangelical and Catholic employees who wish to pray.) Kansas City Airport and the University of

Michigan campus have installed foot-washing basins for Muslims to prepare for their five daily prayers.[67] If footbaths are so important to Muslims, how come they don't have them in Syria, Egypt, Jordan, or Lebanon?

What about the sensitivity training the FBI conducts for its agents and employees, funded in part by George Soros and his Open Society Foundation in partnership with the Whiting Foundation?[68] Or the rehiring, under pressure, of seven Muslim women by Argenbright Security Inc. after these women filed a religious-bias complaint with the Equal Employment Opportunity Commission. The EEOC, which also mandates Muslim sensitivity training to security employees, forced the security company to rehire these Muslim women. Argenbright was contracted by United Airlines to operate screening posts at Dulles Airport in Washington, D.C., and Liberty International Airport in Newark, New Jersey.[69] Or the lawsuits filed in state after state alleging unfair dismissals because employees Muslim refused to remove their *hijab* or shave their beard?

All of this tolerance and accommodation of religious practices in public places seems a smokescreen, a distraction to divert attention from what's actually happening—that while America and the West promote diversity, tolerance, and freedom, radical Muslims, hiding within our culture, are inserting their ways into Western daily life. We are in peril and we don't even know it.

An old Arabian proverb says: "If the camel gets his nose in the tent, his body will soon follow."[70] Each of the above examples is nothing more than one more inch of the camel in the tent, as we say in the Middle East.

• • •

In September 2007, Columbia University extended an invitation to Iran's president Mahmoud Ahmadinejad.[71] The university said it did so to promote an open exchange of ideas.[72] But how is it possible to have a productive conversation, never mind an exchange of ideas, with a man who openly calls for the destruction of a nation (Israel)? Who by his own admission supports international terrorism and targets innocent people around the world? A man who has openly declared that he intends to use nuclear weapons to blow Israel off the face of the earth? Not to mention that this man and his government refuse to allow free speech and regularly imprison those who try to express themselves freely.[73]

Look at the sensitivity classes that the United States government is conducting for its 45,000 Transportation and Safety Administration (TSA) security personnel. The classes developed and taught by the Council on American-Islamic Relations outline how Muslims should be treated by TSA and airline personnel. A press release quoted CAIR communications director Ibrahim Hooper as saying that meetings with TSA, Homeland Security, the Immigration and Naturalization Service, and Border Patrol officials have focused on "issues related to cultural sensitivity and national security."

CAIR's agenda from the start has been to Islamize America. Its cofounder and chairman, Omar Ahmad, a Palestinian American, told a Muslim audience in Fremont, California, in 1998: "Islam isn't in America to be equal to any other faith, but to become dominant. The Koran should be the highest authority in America, and Islam the only accepted religion on earth." Ibrahim Hooper, national spokesman, is on record stating: "I wouldn't want to create the impression that I wouldn't like the government of the United States to be Islamic."[74]

CAIR, which is financially supported by both the Saudis and the United Arab Emirates, is also offering training to the U.S. military. In June, three-hundred military personnel were trained at the marine corps air station located in Yuma, Arizona. By invitation of the Pentagon, CAIR dedicated an Islamic center at the Quantico Marine Corps headquarters, outside Washington, D.C. It is the first of its kind in the history of the U.S. Marine Corps. CAIR also regularly meets with the FBI, whose Case agents rarely deal with the Muslim community without first consulting CAIR. In fact, the organization is on the Justice Department's advisory board.[75] We have knowingly given what some see as our most treacherous and deceitful enemies access to the agencies created to protect us and our freedoms.

• • •

As a commander of the Muslim Brotherhood stood powerful and determined, with a Hamas flag in one hand and his Koran in the other, the crowd chanted, "*Allahu akbar walillahi'l-hamd!*" (Allah is great and to Allah we give praise!). He provided the passionate crowd with further inspiration as he shared the report of a successful suicide bombing in the streets of Jerusalem that killed sixteen Jewish soldiers. And then, to almost deafening cheers, he said, "I call upon my brothers to take up arms with us!" This speaker was not in Palestine. He was not in Iraq. He was not in Iran. He was in Kansas City. And this was in 1989.[76] Groups like his have been flying under the radar, sheltered by the openness of U.S. society and the rights and freedoms we afford. They have been here for decades, and they aren't leaving anytime soon.

Islamic groups have their own compounds spread throughout the country, where they live and practice military training with live ammunition. Jamaat ul-Fuqra is the leading group in the United States. Since the founding of Jamaat ul-Fuqra (meaning "community of the impoverished") by Sheikh Mubarak Ali Gilani in 1980, a network of forty-five paramilitary training camps in North

America have been created. Gilani is a radical Islamist who has rubbed shoulders with terrorist organizations such as Hamas and Hezbollah, and leaders such as Osama bin Laden. Gilani also trained jihadists for fighting in Kashmir, Chechnya, and Bosnia. Gilani refers to himself as the "sixth Sultan Ul Faqr" and considers himself a direct descendent of Mohammed. Jamaat ul-Fuqra seeks to "purify Islam" through violence. In the United States, the group has committed attacks, staged robberies, acquired contraband arms, engaged in counterfeiting, and proselytized effectively among African-American prison inmates. Its members participated in the 1993 bombing of the World Trade Center.[77]

Although federal and state law enforcement authorities have investigated and monitored Jamaat ul-Fuqra, it is—incredibly—not considered a terrorist organization, and the IRS has not taken away its tax-exempt status. Nevertheless, Jamaat ul-Fuqra's objective, as revealed in a 1991 investigation of its Open Quranic University, is "their foremost duty was to wage jihad against the oppressors of Muslims."[78] As an organization of Islamist extremists, it is more virulent in some ways than the Muslim Brotherhood branches in this country and abroad.[79] It has found fertile ground in American prisons, attracting Muslim converts, and estimates of its U.S. membership range as high as six-thousand.

The American headquarters of JF is located in Hancock, New York. Other locations include: Hagerstown, Maryland; Falls Church, Virginia; York, South Carolina; Dover, Tennessee; Buena Vista, Colorado; Talihina, Oklahoma; Tulare County and Squaw Valley, California. Large complexes have been established in Red House, Virginia, and Commerce, Georgia. In Canada JF has two basic training facilities in the greater Toronto area.[80]

JF's activities in the United States, as laid out by Dr. Paul

Williams in an article entitled "In the Belly of the Beast: Jamaat ul-Fuqra," published in the *New Media Journal,* is mind-boggling:

- Jamaat ul-Fuqra has close ties to Al Qaeda. In December 1993, founder Sheikh Mubarek Ali Gilani was an honored guest at an international gathering of Islamic terrorists at the residence of Hassan al-Turabi, in Khartoum. There, Gilani and Osama bin Laden were caught on film chanting, "Down, down with the USA!" "Down, down with the CIA," and "Death to the Jews." The film now remains in the "Alec File"—the CIA dossier on bin Laden.
- Members of the group have been arrested for trafficking in firearms, including AK-47s. A recent report prepared by the Center for Policing Terrorism maintains that Jamaat ul-Fuqra "may be the best positioned group to launch an attack on the United States, or, more likely, help Al Qaeda to do so."
- Since the time of its establishment at a radical mosque in Brooklyn, New York, Jamaat ul-Fuqra has been responsible for more terror attacks on America soil (thirty and counting) than all other terrorist groups combined. It has spawned and sponsored assassinations, kidnappings, mass murder, grand theft, and fraud.
- Some noted associates of Jamaat ul-Fuqra include Richard Reid, the shoe bomber, and John Allen Muhammad, the Beltway sniper.
- Members of the group, including Clement Rodney Hampton-El, took part in the 1993 bombing of the World Trade Center.

JF's pattern of violence stretches back to the 1980s. More recently, JF was caught in a counterfeit clothing scheme uncovered by federal authorities at the organization's Red House, Virginia, complex.[81]

The JF mosque in Brooklyn, a beehive of Islamist radicals, may have spawned several of the Fort Dix Six plot perpetrators. Six Muslim men were caught and charged with plotting to attack and massacre members of the military in Fort Dix, New Jersey. They were also planning to attack the Dover, Delaware, Air Force base, Coast Guard and Navy facilities, and the federal office building in Philadelphia.[82] Three of the Fort Dix Six acknowledged attending services at the JF mosque in Brooklyn. These jihadis were caught by a sharp-eyed Circuit City clerk who contacted the FBI. The suspects have been incarcerated since June 2007, have been denied bail, and are awaiting federal trial in New Jersey.[83]

Cases of homegrown Islamic radicals are popping up all over America. The case of the Folsom, California, prison Jihadis has all the hallmarks of a JF terror cell. On December 14, 2007, a Los Angeles Federal District Court convicted members of a gang of jailhouse Muslim converts. They plead guilty to conspiracy to attack Los Angeles area synagogues and military installations as well as to armed robbery charges in connection with a string of gas station holdups.[84] The four suspects were part of a radical Muslim group Jamiyyat Ul-Islam (JIS), founded by Kevin James while he was an inmate at the California State Prison in Sacramento.

• • •

Islamofascists are making maximum use of the civil, religious, and political freedoms that Americans treat so cavalierly. They plan to make an end-run around America by using our freedoms, and it seems to be working. Their assumption that Americans will remain oblivious, complacent, preoccupied, ignorant, and uninvolved is proving accurate—at least for now. The Australian writer

Warner MacKenzie has the American mind-set nailed. In his article "It's the Ideology, Stupid!!" he states:

> The West's propensity for ignorance is nothing short of astounding when one considers that, in this first decade of the 21st century, a veritable gold mine of information, on any topic, is available at one's fingertips via the Internet. Never before have books on the subject of Islamic history and terrorism been so prolific, yet the same old dangerously erroneous opinions on the causes of Islamic violence remain as popular, uniformed and widespread as ever."[85]

It's this kind of ignorance that gives radical extremists the time and the opportunity to move one step closer to realizing their jihadist objectives of a global Islamic state. Somehow, too many Americans are still closing their ears to statements like the following, from Sayeed Abdul A'la Maududi, founder of the Jamaat-e-Islami:

> Islam is a revolutionary faith that comes to destroy any government made by man. Islam doesn't look for a nation to be in a better condition than another nation. Islam doesn't care about the land or who owns the land. The goal of Islam is to rule the entire world and submit all of mankind to the faith of Islam. Any nation or power that gets in the way of that goal, Islam will fight and destroy. In order to fulfill that goal, Islam can use every power available every way it can be used to bring worldwide revolution. This is jihad."[86]

9

ISLAM'S CONTEMPT
FOR WOMEN AND MINORITIES

One of the major hallmarks of a modern, mature culture is equal-ity under law the guaranteeing that individuals—including women, minorities, and the poor—have the right to personal lib-erty and freedom of choice. As long as citizens act within the law, the individual should be permitted to live his life according to his own set of rules. Regretably, it took hundreds of years for the West, from Europe to the Americas, to give equal rights to women, abol-ish slavery, allow freedom of religion, and establish programs to ensure that the poor have access to food, shelter, and medical care. Now, with radical Islam thrusting itself upon the world stage, and as the veil of mystery is pulled off its ideology, precepts, and cul-ture, we are discovering Islam's morally deficient character and are at risk of being pulled back into its seventh-century way of life.

The moral strength and character of a culture is demonstrated by its capacity for compassion and respect for the weak. There is no greater lack of compassion than in the world of devout Muslims. What sets the Islamic world apart from the West is its so-called

God-given teachings concerning the abuse and even murder of minorities and women.

ISLAM AND THE MISTREATMENT OF WOMEN

Islam's oppressive treatment of women has been in place since Mohammed began receiving revelations from the angel Gabriel. The Koran and Hadith are filled with verses that are orders on how Muslim men must conduct themselves when dealing with women and nonbelievers. Regrettably, Islam's ancient mind-set has not advanced in fourteen hundred years. Control of behavior and disregard for human life are key elements in Islamic ideology.

The following Hadith passage exemplifies Islam's treatment of women. Tabari, a collection of Koran verses and Hadith quotes, illustrates how Allah allows the abusive treatment of women, likening them to animals and sex objects.

> "Allah permits you to shut them in separate rooms and to beat them, but not severely. If they abstain, they have the right to food and clothing. Treat women well for they are like domestic animals and they possess nothing themselves. Allah has made the enjoyment of their bodies lawful in his Koran." (Tabari IX:113)[1]

Can you imagine the outrage if the Pope made a declaration like that about women? By definition, women in Islam will never be equal to men, and thus always subjugated unless moderate Muslims reform their religion and bring it up to twenty-first-century standards. The shocking reality is that most Muslim men, including those educated in the West, have no objection to honor killings and the degradation of women in their countries. Across the Muslim world, even in moderate Islamic countries, women's rights are almost nonexistent.

Women in the Muslim world are hidden away, confined to their homes, and sometimes to their rooms, when visitors arrive. They are hidden away as if they are foreign, not quite human. When they need to go out in public they must cover their shame, their very existence, behind black veils. If you've ever wondered why Muslim women dress modestly, covering their heads and/or bodies, consider the following verse:

> "Prophet! Tell your wives and daughters and all Muslim women to draw cloaks and veils all over their bodies (screening themselves completely except for one or two eyes to see the way). That will be better." (Koran 33:59)[2]

Woman in Islam are considered unclean, deemed inferior even to dirt:

> "Believers, approach not prayers with a mind befogged or intoxicated until you understand what you utter. Nor when you are polluted, until after you have bathed. If you are ill, or on a journey, or come from answering the call of nature, or you have touched a woman, and you find no water, then take for yourselves clean dirt, and rub your faces and hands. Lo! Allah is Benign, Forgiving." (Koran: 4:43)[3]

And the Western world wonders why Muslim men treat Muslim women in such a subservient manner? The Prophet Mohammed set forward numerous examples defining how Muslim men should behave toward Muslim women. The following are two more examples of Islam's narrow-mindedness toward women.

"The Prophet said, 'Isn't the witness of a woman equal to half of that of a man?' The women said, "Yes." He said, "This is because of the deficiency of a woman's mind."[4]

The Prophet said, "I looked at Paradise and found poor people forming the majority of its inhabitants; and I looked at Hell and saw that the majority of its inhabitants were women."[5]

ISLAM AND MARRIAGE

Women living in Islamic countries face a grim prospect when it comes to whom they will marry. The dark situation often worsens after they marry. The whole deal is tilted to favor the husband. The teachings of the Koran give husbands the right and responsibility to beat their wives should they misbehave. In chapter 4, verse 34, the Koran states: "If you fear high-handedness from your wives, remind them [of the teaching of God], then ignore them when you go to bed, then hit them. If they obey you, you have no right to act against them. God is most high and great."[6]

It is important to remember that the Koran is considered the word of Allah. That this holy book gives directives to Muslim men to beat their wives, and emphasizes that this action is a duty, is an indication that the outlook for the rights of Muslim women is dismal.

Wife-beating in Islamic nations is more prevalent than one can imagine. In Pakistan, it has been reported by the Institute of Medical Sciences that 90 percent of its female population has been beaten for such wrongdoings as giving birth to a daughter or cooking an unsatisfactory meal.[7] After the African country of Chad attempted to outlaw wife-beating, Islamic clerics in that nation deemed the bill "un-Islamic."[8]

There is contention within Islamic schools of thought as to

whether verse 4:34 in the Koran, instructing men to beat their wives, truly says "beat" or "leave" or something less demeaning toward women. The argument apologists offer up is that some Arabic words have different meanings and leave the interpretation up to the reader. This is a red herring.

As someone whose native language is Arabic and who can read the Koran in the language in which it was written, here is a transliteration of the word in verse 4:34: "Tad-ru-bu-hu-nna." It means "beat them." There is no other translation. But don't take my word for it. Here are six different translations of the section in verse 4:34 from the Koran that address the beating issue:

Ali translation: . . . refuse to share their beds, (and last) beat them (lightly)[9]

Pickthall translation: . . . admonish them and banish them to beds apart, and scourge them[10]

Dawood translation: . . . admonish them and send them to beds apart and beat them[11]

Shakir translation: . . . and leave them alone in their sleeping places and beat them[12]

Arberry translation: . . . banish them to their couches, and beat them[13]

You're the reader. You decide.

Clearly Islam's systematic oppression and humiliation of women denigrates the integrity and social position of females in the eyes of devout Islamic cultures and societies. Let me sum up what is being taught in the Koran and Hadith:

Females can be shut in separate rooms.
They can be beaten.

They are to be treated like domestic animals.

They possess nothing.

They need to hide themselves behind cloaks and veils.

They are unclean in the sight of Allah.

You can't pray if you have touched a woman and not washed your hands.

The witness of a woman in court is equal to half that of a man.

Women have deficient minds compared to a man's.

The majority of the inhabitants of hell are women.

Feeding on this poisonous thinking from childhood to adulthood programs both men and women in Islamic culture. It creates an elitist attitude in men toward women and gives women a feeling of inferiority in society. Sadly, these principles are the reason devout Muslim men can perform the ultimate crime against a woman or young girl if she is deemed to have brought shame or dishonor to her family.

ISLAM AND HONOR KILLINGS

The contempt Islam holds toward women is best illustrated through its time-honored practice of honor killings. Any woman's or girl's perceived transgression against the teachings of Islam or against a man's wishes, or behavior that insults a man, permits a male member of a family (father, brother, uncle, nephew, or husband) to murder the female to avenge and restore honor to the family in the eyes of society. Honor killings are executed by slitting the victim's throat, hatcheting them, stabbing, burning them to death, decapitation, bullets to the head and chest, or by any other means imaginable. In addition, it is also customary to cut off the victim's left hand or index finger to prove to tribal elders that the deed has been accomplished and the family honor can now be restored.[14] [15] Even moderate Jordan withdrew a referendum to tighten laws on honor killing after devout Muslims said that the law would eradicate Islamic values and traditions.[16] Furthermore, Article 341 of Jordanian law stipulates that murder is a legal act of defense when "the act of killing another or harming another was committed as an act in defense of his life, or his honor, or somebody else's life or honor."[17] Honor killings are performed throughout the Muslim world. In 1997, an attorney general in the Palestinian Authority told an audience of women that, in his opinion, the honor killings of Palestinian women in Gaza and the West Bank were close to 70 percent of all female deaths.[18] The independent Human Rights Commission of Pakistan, citing government figures, said in a 2006 report that about a thousand women die annually in honor killings.[19]

The problem is not limited to Islamic countries. In 2004 European police met at The Hague to compare notes and come up with ways to handle the new European phenomenon known as honor killings. Police are reopening murder files going back ten years to investigate murders in European Muslim homes.[20] The British police alone have reopened more than 100 cases for investigation. Honor killings have also come to the West thanks to the rise of Islamic immigration. In December of 2007 in Toronto, Canada, Aqsa Parvez, a sixteen-year-old Muslim immigrant from Pakistan, was strangled by her father. Aqsa wanted to dress like other Canadian teenagers and refused to wear a *hijab,* the Muslin head covering. She even went so far as to move out of the family home.[21] More recently, in January of 2008, two sisters were brutally murdered by their Egyptian father in an honor killing in Dallas, Texas. Their crime was wanting to adopt a more typically American teenage lifestyle.[22] Many argue that honor killings are a cultural practice only in the Middle East and that it has nothing to do with Islam. If this is the case, why don't we see Christian Arabs and Jewish Arabs murdering their daughters? Why does it occur only in Muslim families? Honor killing has become a trend in almost every Islamic community in Europe. What kind of a culture would sanction killing one's own flesh and blood? Parents raised in other cultures—religious or not—would give their own lives for their children's. If Westerners analyzed how can a father kill his own flesh and blood without remorse or conscience, they would be forced to realize that if Muslim people kill their own children they would kill the infidel with even more ease.

ISLAM AND CHILD ABUSE

Mohammed was forty-nine years of age when he became betrothed to Aisha, the daughter of one of his closest friends. At the time, she was six years of age. Three years later, after she completed her first menstrual cycle, Aisha and Muhammad consummated their union. At the time, Mohammed was fifty-two and Aisha was nine.[23] Unfortunately, the Islamic practice of marrying a child bride of the age of nine is still practiced today. It occurs so often, that in 2001, Iran passed a law lowering the legal marrying age for females from twelve to nine years of age.[24]

The motivation behind the early marrying age stems from the precedent of Mohammed. Because he married and consummated his union with a nine-year-old girl during his years of prophesying, Muslim men believe that it is a symbol of their devoutness to do the same. Mohammed's advice is being followed by Muslim families around the world. The United Nations Children Fund surveyed the children in an Afghan refugee camp and found that two-thirds of second-grade girls were either married or engaged, and most girls who were past second grade were already married."[25] Although marring underage girls is legal in conservative Islamic circles, in the United States, we would label the type of man who does so a pedophile and incarcerate him.

One of the most devastating practices to young girls of the Islamic world is female genital mutilation. Young girls have their clitoris removed without anesthesia to eliminate their sexual drive and preserve them for a life of sinlessness and purity in.[26] As so much rides on a woman's honor, including the livelihood and community standing of every member of her extended family, the practice is a kind of insurance policy. Female genital mutilation ensures that honor will be preserved because the girl will not have any sexual attraction to boys. It also will ensure that the girl, who is considered a financial burden to the family, will be prime property on the marriage market as a virgin.

In Bandung, Indonesia, a free female circumcision event is held every spring by the Assalaam Foundation, an Islamic educational and social services organization. A 2003 survey by the Population Council shows that 96 percent of respondents acknowledged that their daughters had been mutilated by the age of fourteen.[27]

UNLIMITED HUMILIATION AND ABUSE

The handling of sexual politics in Islam is heavily weighted in men's favor. Whereas women are held on a tight rein, one Islamic cultural practice allows men to marry temporarily (for as little as one night) in order to have sex outside the marriage without the baggage of divorce. This practice is known as *m'uta* (pleasure) marriage and is practiced primarily among the Shia Muslims.[28] A Muslim woman married for more than one night is nothing more than a disposable commodity that can be tossed out of her home by her husband by saying: "You are divorced. You are divorced. You are divorced." The husband is usually awarded custody of the children and the wife is given no financial help. She is now used property, without any prospect of remarriage, forced to work as a servant to feed herself. Considering how young Muslim girls are forced to marry, many find themselves divorced by their twenties, sentenced to a life of humiliation, depression, and hardship.

Rape in Iran is punishable by death . . . for the victim, that is. Atefeh Rajabi, fifteen, was hanged in a public square in Iran after being charged with "adultery."[29] Many charges of adultery in Islamic nations really mean that the woman was raped. Punitive actions are almost always taken against the female victim who is usually looked down upon in Islamic culture as "perpetrator of all crimes."

One of the most devastating stories involving the mistreatment of women occurred in Saudi Arabia in 2007 and captured the world's attention. A nineteen-year-old woman was ordered to receive ninety lashes after being repeatedly raped by a gang of seven men, to the point where she was mutilated by the ferocity and extent of the attack. The court reasoned that this was justly deserved because the poor lady was found meeting with an unrelated male friend when the men attacked her. When she appealed the court order and went to the media for sympathetic publicity her punishment was raised to two-hundred lashes, because the victim attempted to "aggravate and influence the judiciary through the media." The courts did not stop there. The woman's attorney was also punished—he was banned from defending his client and his law license was revoked. In addition, the victim's lawyer is required to attend a disciplinary hearing at the Ministry of Justice, where further punishments may be handed out. After world outrage and a realization on the part of the Saudis that the story was not going to disappear from the world media, the king reconsidered the two-hundred lashes.[30] (The men in the case were also punished, and each was sentenced to two to nine years in prison.)[31]

Women are discriminated against and belittled in Saudi Arabia and many other Islamic countries by the court systems. As archaic as it seems, today in Saudi Arabia and elsewhere it takes the testimony of two women to equal the testimony of one man. Furthermore, in divorce cases, which are rare, women are not allowed to speak on their own behalf. They must deputize a male relative to speak for them.[32]

In Islam, women as sexual beings pose a danger to a man's leadership. Women living under the literal interpretation of Islamic law are not allowed any authority in society other than in their capacity of serving and becoming extensions of men as wives or mothers. Islam's prophet says: "There is no salvation for a man or a nation who allows women to rule over them."[33] Islamic culture also dictates that the *hijab* separate men from women, and thus protect society from any possible moral and social risks or damage.

In the Koran, 4:34, Allah makes clear his views on a woman's place in society: "Men have authority over women, for that God has preferred in bounty one of them over another, and for that they have expended of their property. Righteous women are therefore obedient . . . and those you fear may be rebellious, admonish them to their couches, and beat them."[34] The symbol of the veil is so important that in 2002 in Mecca, religious officials allowed fifteen schoolgirls to perish in a fire rather than let them seek refuge outside without their head coverings. Female students are allowed to remove the coverings only when indoors, where there is no male student population.[35]

ISLAM AND SEX SLAVES

Prostitution and the sex slave trade is one of the most profitable businesses in Iran.[36] Donna Hughes, a professor at the University of Rhode Island, reports that the numbers of girls who are subjected to this type of abuse has grown astronomically in recent years. "Exact numbers of victims are impossible to obtain, but according to an official source in Tehran, there has been a 635 percent increase in the number of teenage girls forced into prostitution. The magnitude of this statistic conveys how rapidly this form of abuse has grown. In Tehran, there are an estimated 84,000 women and girls in prostitution; many of them are on the streets, others are in the 250 brothels that reportedly operate in the city. The trade is also international: thousands of Iranian women and girls have been sold into sexual slavery abroad."[37] The girls are also bought and sold at early ages, some as young as eight.[38]

If the girls manage to escape the slavery into which they are sold, the situation they face when they return home can be equally dire. Dr. Hughes gives on to say, "Upon their return to Iran, the Islamic fundamentalists blame the victims, and often physically punish and imprison them. The women are examined to determine if they have engaged in "immoral activity." In other words, girls are examined to see if they lost their virginity. Based on the findings, officials can ban them from leaving the country again."[39]

When Islamic fundamentalists campaign to recruit new members for their fold, they invoke the alleged immorality in Western countries to attract listeners. However, what is not discussed is the horrific treatment of women who are sold into sexual slavery by their own families. Women are not viewed as equals in Islamic countries, they are thought of as property. Dr. Hughes explains this point more thoroughly when she explains that "exploitation and repression of women are closely associated. Both exist where women, individually or collectively, are denied freedom and rights. Second, the Islamic fundamentalists in Iran are not simply conservative Muslims. Islamic fundamentalism is a political movement with a political ideology that considers women inherently inferior in intellectual and moral capacity. Fundamentalists hate women's minds and bodies. Selling women and girls for prostitution is just the dehumanizing complement to forcing women and girls to cover their bodies and hair with the veil."[40]

Unfortunately, young girls and women are not the only people who are sold into slavery in Islamic countries. Young male children between the age of three and fifteen are sold into slavery as camel jockeys. When not competing, they are often beaten, raped, and forced to sleep with the animals they serve. *Sports Illustrated* writer Andrew Lawrence described the life of a typical camel jockey: "The child camel jockey is between three and fifteen years old and ideally weighs fifty pounds. Each day he rises at 3 A.M. to train, often flogged awake with his camel whip in a flout of Islamic law. He fills his days doting over his steed from head to hoof. At night, he retreats to a camp encircled in barbed wire. Here, abuse is just a part of life. Give in, or go home, in a box."[41]

SLAVERY AND ISLAM

Slavery has existed since antiquity. Forced labor was part of the ancient civilizations of Mesopotamia, Egypt, the Indus Valley of India, and China.[42] The Code of Hammurabi (named for the sixth king of the Amorite Dynasty of Old Babylon), the earliest known set of laws, acknowledged slavery,[43][44] but Islam was the catalyst that established its institutionalization.[45] This is the reason slavery in Islamic cultures has survived when it has been eradicated elsewhere.

Mohammed himself owned dozens of slaves. His followers throughout the centuries have kept slaves and continue to do so today. The Koran defines the fundamental inequality between the slave and owner as well as the rights an owner has over his slave.[46] Not surprisingly, the Hadith also justifies slavery and gives instruction in several chapters concerning ownership.[47][48] The Koran specifically asserts the right of Muslims to own slaves, either by purchasing them or acquiring them through the bounty of war.[49] Since Muslims believe the Koran to be the word of Allah and is unchangeable, slavery will always exist in Islam. This mentality allows Muslim governments and followers of the Koran to declare jihad on neighboring villages of non-Muslims and force them into the bonds of slavery. Although most of the men captured are killed, the women are used as sex slaves or laborers. This criminal behavior is alive and well and flourishing in many Allah-fearing nations today.[50]

The Atlantic slave trade that ended by the middle of the nineteth century is a sad period in the history of America. But the truth is that Muslims were enslaving black Africans (Muslims and non-Muslims) thirteen centuries before the slave ships brought black Africans to the New World. Most interesting, though, is that even though black slavery by Muslims began long ago,[51] almost no descendents of those slaves are alive today in the Muslim world. Why is there no black culture in the Middle East? Most slaves were either killed or died from being worked to death.[52][53] Islamic racism is so entrenched in Muslim society that the Arabic word for black is *abed* (slave) or *abeeds* (slaves). There is no other respectable word in the Arabic language that describes a black person as equal or even human. Blacks are also referred to as filth. As a child, I remember when we used to play and get dirty, the saying was: "You look filthy like an *abed*."[54][55] In contrast, Mohammed described the Muslim people as "the nobles of all races" and reassured them that they were immune from slavery.[56]

Today, the African nations of Sudan and Mauritania preserve brutal, racist, and corrupt Muslim governments that rightfully have been accused of the most heinous crimes against its non-Muslim citizens. There is evidence of the enslavement in Mauritania of four hundred thousand black Africans throughout the centuries.[57] The practice of using slaves as soldiers is now being revived. Thousands of black Africans called Haratines have been kidnapped from their homes and forced to raid the black communities in the southern part of the country, their mission to massacre residents and take over the villages. The brutality Mauritanian Muslims inflict upon their slaves is endless. Many slaves are burned on their genitals or hung on a post for days as a form of punishment.[58] The Mauritanian government refuses to take action to stop these atrocities, even though slavery has been abolished several times since the country's independence from French colonial rule in 1960.[59][60] It has been established recently that one hundred thousand black Africans in Mauritania are enslaved today.[61]

The situation in the Sudan is worse. Since 1983, the dominant Muslim-controlled government has enforced rigid Sharia law throughout the country. Then, in 1989, Sudan's Islamic regime declared jihad on the black Christians and non-Muslims in the western and southern areas of Darfur, Sudan's western region. Brutal raids to slaughter and kidnap non-Muslims and black Muslims are being carried out by the Janjaweed, the government-supported

Muslim militia, whose members are recruited from local Arab tribes.[62][63] Countless innocent victims are from the Dinka tribe, the largest ethnic group in the Sudan, many of whom are black Christians.[64] To date, nearly 2 million villagers have been executed, and tens of thousands have been enslaved by Muslim communities. More than 4 million have been displaced.[65]

For a vivid and moving account of modern day slavery by Muslims, I highly recommend Francis Bok's memoir, *Escape from Slavery*. Bok was seven years old when he was kidnapped from the local marketplace by Muslim militia. Miles away, smoke filled the sky as his family's farm and neighboring villages were burned, and villagers slaughtered, including his family. While the Muslims struck down the traders and patrons at the marketplace, selected woman and children were marched along the road with a rope tied around their neck, or mounted on a horse and trekked through the Islamic-dominated north. Bok was taken to the farm of a Muslim family. When the children ran out of the house toward him, he thought that they were eager to meet him. Instead, they picked up sticks that were lying on the ground and began to beat him while yelling, "Abed, Abed, Abed!" Francis's life was a living hell. His days consisted of beatings, rotten food, living in the barn with the animals he attended, exhaustion from being overworked and constant threats of killing him or mutilating his body parts if he was disobedient. But Francis was one of the fortunate ones. He was able to escape ten years later, at the age of seventeen. Others whom he had met while he lived in captivity had either been killed or had a leg cut off so they could not escape.[66]

In his article, "Slavery Lives in the Sudan," Michael Coren depicts the agony of the ill-fated children and women who become slaves. One former slave remembers "the rape of girls and boys alike, the forced circumcision of boys and girls, often with them fully conscious and screaming and having to be held down by many people. . . . Sodomy and sadistic torture are common." Another ex-slave reflects how "families were broken up, with children sometimes murdered in front of their mothers as a warning and because they were too much trouble. We cried out to the West, to the countries who said they believed in human rights, but they were indifferent to our agony."[67]

Antislavery groups around the world have heard the cries of the victims of the blood-splattered southern and western Sudan. They have petitioned the United Nations to take action and stop the genocide. In July of 2005, a Comprehensive Peace Agreement between the government of Sudan and two rebel groups, the Sudan Liberation Movement and the Justice Equality Movement, was signed.[68] Although the three sides agreed on matters of wealth sharing (oil profits), humanitarian rights, and assistance for the people of the Sudan, slavery still continues to this day despite the agreement. Racism, slavery, and tribal conquest is imbedded so deeply into Islamic culture, religion, and traditions, that it may take more than several lifetimes to free Islam from its rigid and intolerant societal laws.

If you think non-Muslim slaves exist only in Africa, think again! In his article "The Problem with Slavery," Daniel Pipes, director of Middle East Forum, a think tank that promotes American interests in the Middle East, reports that slavery is flourishing in the United States, among the Saudis. Homaidan Ali Al-Turki, thirty-six, an immigrant from Saudi Arabia and a graduate student at the University of Colorado, and his wife were accused of enslaving an Indonesian woman who cared for their four children. She was forced to cook, clean, and serve as nanny, among other tasks, with no pay. The woman said that she feared that she would suffer at the hands of her captors if she were disobedient.

Pipes names four Saudi royals who also live in the United States and have been accused of and/or charged with holding their housekeepers against their will and threatening them with "serious harm" if they were not compliant. There have also been an abundant number of reported cases of Saudi royals and dignitaries living in the United States who have held their servants hostage.[69]

These Very Important People must think they're at home. Even though slavery was abolished in 1962 in Saudi Arabia, it is still practiced there today.[70] Not only is the government aware that it still exists, but religious and influential clerics sanction it. Sheikh Saleh Al-Fawzan, an opponent to Saudi antislavery laws and member of the Senior Council of Clerics, Saudi Arabia's highest religious body, says, "Slavery is a part of Islam and whoever wants it abolished is an infidel."[71]

ISLAM AND THE PERSECUTION OF OTHER FAITHS

The oppression of non-Muslims by Islamic governments occurs across the globe. This oppression and discrimination could not be more obvious than in the Muslim Middle East, where Christians and Jews are treated like second-class citizens. The government of Egypt has decreed that its citizens be allowed to choose and practice their own religions. However, Human Rights Watch has observed: "Although Egypt's constitution provides for equal rights without regard to religion, discrimination against Egyptian Christians (Copts), and intolerance of the Baha'i sect of Islam and minority Muslim sects remains a problem. Egyptian law recognizes conversions to Islam but not from Islam to other religions. There are credible reports that Muslims who convert to Christianity sometimes face harassment. Difficulties in getting new identity papers have resulted in the arrest of converts to Christianity for allegedly forging such documents. Baha'i institutions and community activities are prohibited by law."[72]

Paul Marshall, an expert on global religious intolerance, writes in his article "Islam: From Toleration to Terror": "The Saudi restriction on the expression of any religion besides Islam means, quite simply, that Christian worship is banned. It is illegal to wear a cross or to utter a Christian prayer. Christians cannot even worship privately in their own homes."[73] Marshall also describes how Egyptian Coptic Christians are inhumanely treated in Egypt and throughout the world in his book, *Their Blood Cries Out: The Untold Story of Persecution Against Christians in the Modern World*.[74] The author gives an account of a young Egyptian girl who was kidnapped, tortured, and raped by terrorists from Gamat Islamiya, Egypt's largest militant group.[75] She was forced to go without food while praying and memorizing verses from the Koran. The militants burned a tattoo, a symbol of her Christian faith, from the girl's wrist. Fortunately, the girl escaped but is forced to live a lifetime of suffering while reliving the horrors of her experience.[76] Today, there are approximately 6 million Coptic Christians in Egypt who face a lifetime of religious persecution from their Islamic government. The Egyptian government has imposed the jizya on Christians only, and as a result many Coptic Christians have been forced to renounce their faith and become Muslims because they could not afford to pay such a high tax.[77] Not only do women living in Islamic nations face religious persecution, but they also face kidnapping, rape, and the forced conversion to the Islamic faith by their Muslim countrymen.

Jews are another group that radical Muslims target for hate. Jews are considered Muslims' archenemies, based on the teachings and instructions of Prophet Mohammed. With the increase of the Muslim population in Europe, anti-Semitism is at an all-time high. However, the hatred is coming not from Christian Europeans but from Muslim immigrants.

In Denmark in 2002, Hizb ut-Tahrir, the leading Islamic pro-caliphate group, distributed leaflets demanding that Jews be killed. Assaults and harassment followed, and the word *Juden* appeared persistently on cars, walls, and traffic signs. Likewise, Sweden has had its share of anti-Semitic expression. In Stockholm, anti-Israel rallies organized by Muslim immigrants have attracted large groups, and have been marked by violence and inflammatory cries of "Kill the Jews." Britain has also been the setting for anti-Semitic attacks, including an assault upon a Finsbury Park synagogue located near a highly recognizable mosque. The attackers smashed windows, spread excrement over the floor, and painted swastikas near a Star of David. Radical Muslims from the nearby mosque were suspected.[78]

Christians and Jews aren't the only religions to face persecution from Islamic fundamentalists. According to esteemed Belgium historian Koenraad Elst, the Hindu population in Western and Central Asia was conquered by Muslims in 1399 and forced to covert or face death. Elst explains that 80 million Hindus have been slaughtered by Islamic forces since the year 1000, around the time Afghanistan was dominated by Islamic rule.[79]

The world is at a crossroad. Having learned lessons from World War II about the price of intolerance and apathy, are we going to sit by idly and allow Islamic bigotry and hatred to drag the world into another war? We must strengthen our determination to unite and fight to protect our ideological heritage based on liberty, freedom, equality, and respect for one another.

10

TOLERANCE: A ONE-WAY STREET

Isn't it interesting that we are always hearing from Islamic apologists and organizations like CAIR that Islam is a "tolerant and loving religion"? Yet, the all-pervasive racism, bigotry, and intolerance of Islam clearly reveals itself in the hypersensitivity of its leaders and their followers to every sleight against Islam, however unintended or insignificant. The Islamic world is shameless in its demands for redress for these perceived grievances, and their boisterous and often deadly outbursts of anger are proving effective in making media, organizations, and governments kowtow and submit to their demands. If the aggressive advance of the Muslim agenda is not impeded, the world will be remade in Islam's image.

The application of Muslim religious criteria to non-Muslims should make us "infidels" shudder. The fact that cartoons published in a European country, Denmark, could set off acts of violence throughout the world should be a wake-up call to the West. The fact is that the white flag of surrender is hanging from the buildings of the *New York Times,* the *Los Angeles Times,* and many other prominent publications that refused to publish these cartoons.

It's a testament to the fact that Muslim bullying works. But who could criticize these major publications for concluding that prudence was called for when thousands of Muslims were willing to rampage, destroy property, and shut down civic life in order to express their fury at yet another "insult to Islam"? When the followers of a religion are willing to go that far because of a cartoon they find offensive, when emotions can be raised to such a pitch of fury and hysteria as to justify the burning of cars, looting of shops, killing of civilians, and invasion of embassies, what else are they capable of in defense of the honor of Islam?

Jyllands-Posten, the Danish newspaper that published the Mohammed cartoons, certainly has learned its lesson. The lesson, my fellow infidels, is that Islamic violence is self-justifying. Again and again the international community has taken the position that it is the victim's, or the potential victim's, responsibility to modify his conduct. The offices of *Jyllands-Posten* are now protected by security guards and the cartoonists have gone into hiding because of death threats. This occurred in the aftermath of the murder of Theo van Gogh in the Netherlands: in Britain, Germany, and Denmark itself, public officials called for various accommodations for Muslims in order to prevent more such incidents. The forty-seven European countries that are part of the Council of Europe criticized the Danish government for insulting the Prophet Mohammed and hiding behind freedom of the press.[1] The infidel West fails to learn its lesson the first time, so it must be punished again and again until the lesson is learned. In this way the whole world can be brought into submission under Dar Al Islam.

The state of Israel is being punished for not learning the lesson that Muslims want the Jews to learn: Jews are the enemy of Islam, they are inferior, and therefore do not have a right to a Jewish state, let alone a state that occupies what used to be Islamic land. Israel's offense against Islam is its very existence. How could the Jews who rejected Mohammed make a homeland right in the middle of what used to be the Islamic caliphate? Such a slap in the face to Islam has brought much self-perceived shame on the Muslim world, to the point that Muslim society glorifies the suicide bombers who give their lives to avenge Islam's wounded honor. The phenomenon of suicide bombers for Allah has been authored and perfected by the Palestinians against the Jews and exported around the world. And Allah, according to Muslim preachers around the world, justly rewards mass murderers who kill in his name and take the lives of Jews and infidels with them.

You will find that Islamic leaders who cry prejudice and claim that Muslims are being unfairly labeled as terrorists also venerate the principles and values of Hamas, Al Qaeda, Hezbollah, and the Muslim Brotherhood. While they cry wolf, they simultaneously define themselves as devotees of the cult of the suicide bomber. The desirability of martyrdom is a subject of lectures and sermons throughout the Muslim world. The issue of martyrdom takes center stage in mosques, at conferences and symposia, and even on children's television broadcasts. Purveyors of the ideology of pure Islam proudly display photographs and video of toddlers and kindergarten children wearing bombs strapped to their bodies or pointing guns to their heads. These children are the heroes of the "Islamic nation" of the Hamas charter, of the Al Qaeda manual, of the Muslim Brotherhood Project, and the like.

Many of those who detonated bombs to kill themselves and scores of innocent Israelis in the early 2000s have been teenagers—mere children, and as such often invisible to their victims. Israel has no defense against them. It is a civilized country that is being savaged by an alien society that has turned its children into killers—

killers who are strangers to guilt, remorse, and empathy, and whose culture defines them simultaneously as heroes and victims.

Israel is the prototype of the battlefield of the future. Suicide bombers are worshipped by Muslims as heroes not only in Gaza, Cairo, Riyadh, Baghdad, and Mecca, but in London and Paris, New York and Los Angeles. The cult of the suicide bomber has become virtually universal in the Muslim world, and massive, unchecked immigration is this cult's emissary to the land of the infidel.

Nonetheless, as lofty as it considers its mission to be, pure Islam (what the majority in the West defines as radical Islam) is not above asserting its "rights" in insignificant matters whenever it perceives a stain on the honor of Allah. The Mohammed cartoons published in Denmark; the British teacher in Sudan who was arrested for "insulting faith and religion" because she allowed her class of seven-year-olds to name a teddy bear Mohammed as she was teaching them about democracy and voting; the pope quoting a fourteenth century emperor during an academic lecture about the violence in Islam, which sent hundreds of thousands of Muslims into the streets in Islamic countries killing, burning, and destroying—all these events illustrate the bizarre and irrational reactions that have become customary responses to the ubiquitous "insult to Islam." Hundreds of similar occurrences are never brought to our attention.

Organizations such as CAIR and Muslim Public Affairs Council have been interfering with film productions for years, inserting themselves into the creative process and managing to exert leverage over film companies, producers, directors, and actors because of the perception that a film may contain an insult to Islam. CAIR, for example, pressured Paramount Pictures to alter their adaptation of the Tom Clancy novel *The Sum of All Fears* to change the Muslim terrorists in the book to neo-Nazis in the movie. The film's director, Phil Alden Robinson, had to write an apology to CAIR, telling them he had "no intention of promoting negative images of Muslims or Arabs, and I wish you the best in your continuing efforts to combat discrimination."[2] But what if a film is produced not to insult Islam but to tell the truth about it? It wouldn't matter: if the creator's vision does not conform to that of the American Muslim leadership, a campaign of intimidation will begin and never let up. American Muslim leaders are attempting to control the manner in which Islam is discussed and debated—as if they were part of a totalitarian government with the power and authority to approve every word uttered in public. If the agents of devout Islam take or are accorded the right to censor writing about Islam in the United States, and silence radio talk-show hosts and news broadcasts, the truth about Islam may never be heard in this land. WMAL-AM radio, the Washington, talk-show station, fired Michael Graham in July of 2005 for his remark criticizing Islam as an instigator of terror. CAIR launched an attack against the station as well as its advertisers, which led to Graham's firing.[3] If this is the way we are going to surrender our freedoms of speech and of the press— to appease organizations linked to terror—when and where are we going to draw the line to defend the pillars of our democracy and values?

Already discussion in colleges and universities has been stifled when deemed insensitive to Muslim feelings. Speakers who aren't friendly to Islam (such as myself) require a full security staff, including bodyguards and K9 units, to ensure that our lives will be protected when giving a lecture on a university campus. When I spoke at the University of Detroit at Ann Arbor in 2006, I was accompanied by security details fit for a president. This was the result of a Palestinian group in California sending an e-mail to their Detroit friends urging that "Muslims, Arabs, their friends, and allies to show up and give Brigitte Gabriel the proper welcome," That is, disrupt my lecture just as they did with two other speakers in the weeks before mine. Professors have been reprimanded all across the country for stating what is deemed politically incorrect according to the standards established by Islamic apologists. Professor Thomas Klocek, an adjunct professor at Chicago's DePaul University for fourteen years, was one of those fired for offending Muslim students with his views.[4]

The problem extends even to the Pentagon, the seat of military power of the United States. Under the Muslim Outreach Program, which was instituted after September 11, Muslims were hired in every military branch of our government. The United States government thought that by including Muslim Americans in military and government branches that they would be an asset to our government in fighting "the war on terror." Some of those hires have access to high-level classified documents dealing with the war on terror and the terrorists' ideology. Political correctness in the Pentagon is deceiving our military leaders, halting any criticism of Islam as well as any education about its tenets of hatred and bigotry toward infidels. This situation has reached such a level that Stephen Coughlin, the most authoritative Pentagon specialist on Islamic law and extremism, was fired in January of 2008. The reason he was fired? Pentagon officials said he had become "too hot" within the circles of the Pentagon. Hasham Islam, a key Muslim aide in the office of Deputy Defense Secretary Gordon England, was offended by Coughlin's writings about militant Islam and confronted him to soften his views on Islamist extremism. Coughlin was one of the few people within our government who possessed the moral clarity to identify the enemy, analyze its strategy, and devise a plan to defeat it.

Coughlin had written a memorandum a few months earlier

about the Muslim Brotherhood Project for North America, which was discussed at the Holy Land Foundation trial in Texas. One of the group identified during the trial was the Islamic Society of North America, whose members had been hosted by England at the Pentagon.[5]

When news of his firing was made public, support for Coughlin came roaring to his side, especially from members of the military, who deal with terrorists firsthand and understand their true mentality. In a letter to the editor of the *Washington Times*, Lt. Col. Lance Landeche from the Marine Corps, had this to say:

> Though I cannot assess the value of Mr. Coughlin to those inside the Beltway, outside the Beltway and on the front lines of this struggle, his understanding of the relationship between Islamic law and Islamist jihad doctrine is invaluable. Mr. Coughlin's thesis, written for the National Defense Intelligence College, "To Our Great Detriment: Ignoring What Extremists Say About Jihad," is quickly becoming a must-read among my peers. Unfortunately, soon Mr. Coughlin will no longer be available to help us understand Islamic jihad, and we will again find ourselves at a severe disadvantage in this ideological struggle. I only wish more of my taxpayer dollars could be spent on such invaluable contracts that directly support those out in front."[6]

Is it any wonder why an Islamist inside the Pentagon and his gullible friends want to get rid of a national treasure such as Stephen Coughlin at a time in history when we are trying to protect our national security?

In 1995, terrorist expert Steven Emerson produced the film *Jihad in America*, which exposed the worldwide network of Islamic terrorist organizations and their presence in the United States. Emerson did not employ actors. He simply presented the phenomenon of devout Islam as it exists, with actual video footage of terrorists at conferences and symposia that are held in the United States. He showed what Muslim leaders were doing and saying. They declared openly that they intended to be "a dagger in the heart of their [our] civilization," and "butcher the Jews" and "destroy the skyscrapers" that "Americans are so proud of."

No one took Emerson or his film seriously. No one wanted to believe that terrorist cells operate in America and hold conferences espousing hatred and bigotry toward infidels and calling for jihad. No one wanted to believe this is really happening in America. A friend of mine who was an executive in a Jewish Federation had invited Steve Emerson to be a keynote speaker two days before September 11. Members of the community, including the board of directors of the federation, were very upset with her for inviting "Mr. Gloom and Doom" to their event. The person who threw the biggest fit was shaking two days later as his daughter who worked in the World Trade Center barely escaped with her life. Does it have to take such a tragedy to knock us out of our apathy? To make us listen to those who are warning us ahead of time while we can still make a change?

For his pains, Emerson became the target of a vicious vilification campaign instigated by American Muslim leaders. He is now one of the most hated men in the Islamic world. Al Qaeda mentioned him by name in one of their videos. He is frequently the subject of defamatory articles on Islamic Internet sites and in Arabic publications in the Middle East. He lives under the constant threat of assassination.

Islamic tolerance is a one-way street that demands that the infidel West accommodate Islamic imperatives and sensitivities. But Islam feels no obligation to regard with any level of respect or sympathy the social, religious, or political norms of the West, nor do they grant any concessions—even when residing in the West. The treatment of Christians in Muslim countries vividly illustrates this. The media finds persecutions, enslavement, and massacres of Christians, to say nothing of the day-to-day intimidation and harassment, such as in Egypt or Kosovo, hardly worthy of comment. It seems that Islamic influence in the West has rendered politically incorrect any criticism of Muslim countries for their abuse of Christians.

When will Christians living in the West rise to the occasion and speak out on behalf of their suffering brethren living under Muslim tyranny? I lived in a bomb shelter for almost all my teenage years, praying every night that the Christians in the West would save us from ruthless and brutal murderers. No one came except the Israelis. My hope was shattered slowly at the feet of the small cross hanging over my shrapnel-bruised bed.

Mordechai Nisan, the author of *Minorities in the Middle East: A History of Struggle and Self-Expression,* writes:

> The West's opening of the gates to Muslim penetration is a surrealistic replay of the Christians' opening of the gates to Muslim conquest in the Middle East during the first few years of post-Mohammedian history. The towns of Syria and Egypt, part of the Byzantine empire in the East, opened their gates and accepted Muslim rule by consent. Islamic conquest was in some ways more of a political assault than a military attack. And so it seemed in the late twentieth-century as the Christian West opened its gates and peacefully capitulated to the assault of Islam. Various forms of tribute followed suit: releasing convicted Arab terrorists from European jails, canceling Arab debts to Western governments, recognizing the Palestine Liberation Organization, and supporting Arab demands against besieged Israel, providing weaponry for Arab warfare (while Europe itself was being targeted by Libyan and Iranian long-range missiles)."[7]

Is the West even conscious of its rush to capitulate anew to Islam?

For the most part, the answer is no. Yet devout Muslims have made no secret of their intention to Islamize the United States. As Abdurahman Alamoudi, former head of the American Muslim Council, has observed, whether it takes "ten years or a hundred years," the United States will become a Muslim country.[8]

Since the late 1980s, the devout Islamists' presence on American soil has expanded, creating dozens of interconnected groups that advance the purists' agenda while adopting a pleasant façade that simulates respect for American values, pluralism, and religious freedom. Islamic activists, including members of the Council on American Islamic Relations and other Islamic groups, are using this strategy to place themselves at the very center of American power by attaining high-level security jobs within our government, while continuing to sympathize with the enemies of the United States.

Even worse, virtually all the Islamic organizations mentioned in this book have adopted some variant of the position advanced by the Saudi prince Waleed bin Talal—that America's foreign policy was responsible for the attacks of September 11. The freedom of movement, freedom of association, freedoms that Muslims enjoy in this country have not tempted them to renounce their dreams of destroying the United States. Instead, these freedoms afford them free passage on their journey to promote murder and mayhem worldwide in the name of their cause. Organizations such as the Muslim Brotherhood, Hamas, and Hezbollah have found the United States hospitable terrain to raise money, sponsor conferences and symposia, create front organizations, and disseminate anti-Semitic and anti-Zionist propaganda. Their pseudo-moderate connected organizations successfully wield influence in local, state, and national politics. They have even established themselves on American college and university campuses through the Muslim Student Association.

And until 9/11, they had been inconvenienced by very few political and legal restraints. How else can one explain the fact that Arab American professors at the University of South Florida were able to function effectively as agents for Palestinian Islamic Jihad, and that one of them, Ramadan Abdallah Shallah, assumed the leadership of that group?[9] Another student at the University of South Florida who entered the United States in 1974 and remained for fifteen years, Musa Abu Marzook, rose to the top levels of Hamas.

Islamic organizations agitate politically within the United States and are reaping huge successes. The American Muslim Alliance is determined to bring Islam's influence into the highest circles of American power. The organization promotes candidates, registers voters, and places interns (whom it has trained for advocacy) on Capitol Hill.

Islamists have already made inroads into American government. We have seen the election of the first Muslim congressman from Minnesota, Keith Ellison, who chose to swear his oath of office on a Koran. Ironically, it was the same copy of the Koran acquired by Thomas Jefferson in the 1700s so he could study and understand the religion and principles of the Islamic pirates who were terrorizing ships at sea, and learn how to defeat them. We have seen highly sensitive positions at the Pentagon and other branches of government filled with Muslims about whose background and loyalties we know nothing. The shocker to many Americans was the illegal Lebanese immigrant FBI agent who had access to top-secret and sensitive information, which she passed to her relatives and friends at Hezbollah in Lebanon. We Christians and Jews who came to the United States from the Middle East look on with utter amazement and disgust at the gullibility and stupidity of those who allow Muslims to work in such sensitive areas of government.

In June 2001, a delegation of Muslim organizations was received at the White House to discuss President Bush's faith-based initiative. Abdullah al-Arian, a twenty-year-old student, was present, but was soon ejected by the Secret Service without explanation. This prompted the entire group to walk out of the meeting. The American Muslim Council issued a statement that attributed the incident to suspicion arising from the political activities of al-Arian's father, Samial-Arian. The *Middle East Times* reported that "the Secret Service denied any political motive behind its action. 'We regret the error and any inconvenience the individual or the group experienced,' said Marc Connolly, a spokesman for the Secret Service, but he would not elaborate. He said after White House security officials realized a mistake had been made, they attempted to invite the group back, but the invitation was rebuffed."[10]

Abdullah al-Arian charged that he was a victim of racial profiling. A joint statement issued by the delegation, which included CAIR, MPAC, AMA, AMC, and other devout pseudo-moderate groups, further communicated a sense of victimization: "This incident is the latest in an unfortunate pattern of exclusion by the Bush administration. American Muslim organizations reject the notion that community members must pass a litmus test. A meaningful dialogue must be based on equity, accessibility, and fairness and not exclusion, discrimination or exploitation by special interest groups."[11] It would be difficult to imagine a delegation representing a minority religion storming out of a presidential palace in any Muslim nation. It's difficult to imagine them being invited in, in the first place.

"We expect the White House to clarify why Abdullah al-Arian was excluded from the meeting and to apologize to him and to the Muslim community," said CAIR communications director Ibrahim Hooper.[12] The following month, al-Arian returned to the White House with the same group of Muslim leaders. They expressed their concern that no Muslim had been appointed to the White House team for the faith-based initiative. More noteworthy than this incident is the fact that his father, Sami al-Arian—now deported on charges of being a leader of Palestinian Islamic Jihad— had the previous week been "among a group of Muslim leaders admitted to the White House for a political briefing."[13] It was a sign that Islam was finally coming into its own in the United States— and that devout Muslims were at the vanguard.

In reference to a March 2002 attack against American churchgoers in Pakistan, journalist Stephen A. McDonald wrote: "As 'moderate' Muslims rolled six grenades down an aisle in a church packed with worshippers in the diplomatic enclave of Karachi, the message is clear."[14] McDonald noted that after 9/11, "most took counsel from the politically correct crowd as they repeatedly pronounced Islam as a 'religion of tolerance.'" Nothing could be farther from the truth. In every major speech President Bush has made since September 11, he has assimilated Islam into the global mainstream. Islam had no international voice before the attacks. Now scholars define the Western heritage as not the Judeo-Christian tradition, but as the Judeo-Christian-Islamic tradition. What? Where'd that come from?

In his book *Where is the Islamic Tolerance?*, McDonald wrote:

> Islam was given a soapbox on which to stand only days after the attacks at the World Trade Center. It looks to us like they have taken a good swing at the ball and used their new-found prominence to justify their "mainline" views to the world. The

position of prominence given to Islam around the airwaves, in print, and in cyberspace has done nothing to tone down the devout views possessed by their members; rather, it has done just the opposite, empowering a whole new voice of devout Muslims under the guise of educating the world in the virtues of Islam and the intolerance of Christianity and Judaism."[15]

According to Mordechai Nisan,

"Islamic civilization in itself provided a permanent outlet for aggressiveness by legitimating and obligating war against the infidels. This is a mechanism for mental health, avoiding the debilitations of guilt feelings and shamefulness. Thereby, Muslim armed aggression, or any other form of combat, is therapeutic and can be very effective and successful in particular against the restrained, psychologically entangled, morally inhibited West. The Western love of peace, a virtual badge of submission, is paraded proudly as a supreme value for inter-civilizational harmony. Jamal al-Din al-Afghani, the notable Muslim thinker and reformer in the nineteenth-century, was explicit in his comparison of Islam and Christianity on the power equation. He stated: "The Christian religion is based on making peace, and kindness prevails in everything . . . whereas Islam is based on an aspiration to victory, might, conquest and boldness."[16]

As Westerners/infidels, we must face these bitter truths, and face them together. Jihad is in every country in the Western world. Jihad may appear peaceful to you now, but its intentions are not. After reading this book, you should be able to identify some of the most common tactics of the jihadists and their allies, and to know that you are not required to passively approve of the destruction of your nation and culture.

11

RISING IN DEFENSE OF DEMOCRACY

On November 8, 2001, President Bush declared that we are waging "a war to save civilization itself." He added, "Our nation faces a threat to our freedoms, and the stakes could not be higher. We are the target of enemies who openly boast [in the Middle East] that they want to kill, kill all Americans, kill all Jews, and kill all Christians. We have seen that type of hate before, the only possible response is to confront it and to defeat it."[1]

Our enemies' hatred suggests that we have something that they do not. Call it freedom, call it liberty—it is what enables us to live productive lives within a reasonable, though admittedly imperfect, framework of rights and obligations. Our enemies would like to subjugate us and remake us in their own image. All our sophisticated weaponry cannot win the ideological struggle we face; if we are to have any hope of prevailing, we must renew our appreciation for the differences that set us apart from those who would conquer us. We must measure our freedoms against the degradation of totalitarian regimes and terrorist organizations, as well as against the principles of Islamic Sharia, from which our enemies derive the spiritual and ideological motivation to destroy us.

We have much to lose. The freedoms we enjoy rest on principles common only to Western democracies: the rule of law, equality under the law, individual rights as opposed to group rights, private property, an independent judiciary that recognizes the sanctity of human life and has regard for the rights of others, and the separation of church and state. We must also remember freedom of thought, of conscience, of expression, of association, and of religion. These freedoms allow us to change our religion, ridicule religion, or reject it entirely—rights denied to all Muslims living under Islamic regimes.

Our freedoms are tempered by responsibility. If we act responsibly within a framework of rights and obligations, we can follow our dreams and pursue happiness without having to do it in lockstep with the government. Western society is far from perfect, there is plenty of room for improvement. But because it guarantees the rule of law while upholding personal freedom as an ideal, the system works.

In contrast, among the world's fifty-seven Islamic states, it would be hard to find even one of the above principles being put into practice consistently. With few exceptions, Muslim countries are ruled by dictators who expect to hold on to their jobs for life.[2] Almost without exception, these dictators live in perpetual fear of a coup d'état or some other violent form of regime change. The rule of law in these countries is virtually nonexistent. Instead, their citizens live in perpetual *fear* of the law. The regime enforces or disregards laws at will, and does not protect the individual from the whims of the state. Every day the citizens live on shaky ground. Mix terrorism in with this totalitarianism and you get chaos and lawlessness.

Radical Islam is poised to destroy us, and current events are moving in its favor. Our task, therefore, is nothing less than to alter the course of history. All peoples targeted to be conquered, subjugated, and slain by Muslims determined to bring the world under the Islamic umbrella, must awaken. We do not carry weapons. We do not seek physical battle. We are ordinary people of goodwill who believe that if Americans and Europeans are made aware of the designs devout Muslims have on the world, they will not be content to sit idle.

Every individual must recognize that civilization itself is at stake. While the government conducts its war on terrorism on many fronts, U.S. residents must resist the ideological assault in progress within our own borders.

Devout Muslims are employing American democratic institutions in their campaign to destroy us. Syndicated journalist Cal Thomas writes:[3]

> Suppose our enemies have invaded the United States through immigration for the express purpose of organizing themselves politically? Suppose they present themselves as benign and seek to register voters, becoming politically active in order to elect their people to office and change U.S. policy in the Middle East?
>
> What if their intentions are the eventual destruction of this nation through its democratic processes and the imposition of a theocratic state? . . .
>
> In at least sixteen states, Muslim groups, by their own admission, are organizing voter-registration drives and political consciousness-raising events for this express purpose.[4]

Voter registration and the election of candidates as strategies for the acquisition of political power are perfectly legal. We must educate ourselves about the threat. We must learn to recognize the message that devout Muslims are spreading and understand how to reject its propaganda. This is our responsibility, and we must not expect the government to do it for us.

Remember that the other side has limitless energy, a limitless contingent of suicide cadres, seemingly limitless financial resources, and unwavering confidence in its identity and beliefs. Our confidence in Western civilization and its values must match our opponents'. Rest assured, our enemies are and will remain motivated. Their top priority is our destruction and they will not be distracted. The good life and the freedoms attainable only in Western democracies do not impress or entice them. They are committed to one purpose, a single goal to which they hold with utmost patience and determination. They count on our craving for immediate gratification, our famously short attention span and lack of determination, on our tolerance of any and all points of view, our hospitality, our guilt complexes, our weaknesses, and our lack of resolve to provide them with the club with which to clobber us.

"Our enemies have used our best character qualities against us—tolerance, inclusion, forgiveness and pluralism," Cal Thomas observed in May 2002. "They believe in none of these concepts and think anyone who does is an enemy of their god."[5]

"We are at war to the death," says former CIA chief James Woolsey. "There should be no mistake about this. September 11 galvanized us into serious action in exactly the same way that December 7, 1941, did."[6]

On September 11, the nightmare began. Although some years have passed without another successful attack on American soil, the conflict is far from over. If Western civilization emerges victorious, it will be because a critical number of individuals decided to assume personal responsibility for ensuring the survival of our way of life.

Will you be one of them?

• • •

Holy war has been declared on America and the West, and it's a very different kind of conflict from past wars. Because our enemy does not owe allegiance to a particular country, does not wear a military uniform, and uses women and children as part of its arsenal, we may be prone to forget that we are at war. We cannot forget. We must not.

And while this is a very different war from those of years past, one feature remains pertinent. Just as civilians assisted their nation's previous war efforts, so must we become active participants in this conflict. No matter which country in the West we reside, we share the same values of equality and respect toward humanity. Indeed, I submit that our active involvement as civilians in this war is even more essential than ever.

We are facing more than a relentless, tenacious, and determined enemy bent on either destroying or subjugating us. Because of the rise of political correctness we have the additional burden of facing people within our own borders—government officials, academics, journalists, and others—who dismiss the threat we're up against, blame America or Israel as the cause of the conflict, treat anyone who speaks out against Islamofascism as an "intolerant bigot," or treat Islamofascists as oppressed victims. These purveyors of political correctness are foolishly and dangerously aiding and abetting the rising tide of Islamofascism.

For this and other reasons, we cannot sit back, relax, and let the government fight this war for us. The sad and terrifying reality is that far too many elected officials, intelligence officials, military officers, and bureaucrats do not or will not see the true nature of the threat we face. Our societies and our governments are being infiltrated by Islamists who will resort to any means to bring about the imposition of Sharia law and restoration of the Islamic caliphate. The absence of successful terrorist attacks on our soil does not mean we are not under assault.

Civilians must defend our families, our communities, and our nations. By "defend" I am not speaking of armed violence. I am referring to exercising our rights and powers as citizens in free societies. For if we fail to act, if we allow the government to fight this war without us, I am convinced we will ultimately lose. To win we must make hard choices and often unpopular decisions.

In order to devise and implement the right civilian strategies and tactics to win this war it is necessary to identify each element of the opposition and define its role in this war. They are (1) the devout Muslims; (2) Muslim front organizations that work to silence any critique or criticism of Islam; (3) enablers of Islamic education—those who write, supply, and finance educational materials that have seeped into higher education and public schools and that whitewash the violent and conquering nature of Islam; (4) hate-mongers, those who, in Western mosques and madrassas, advocate violence, terror, and the overthrow of constitutional law and democracy; and (5) the PC propaganda machine, the purveyors of political correctness in the West.

THE DEVOUT MUSLIMS

The devout Muslims are the most obvious threat. This group includes clerics who pronounce calls to jihad, individuals, and organizations who fund and provide logistical support, and the leaders and foot soldiers who carry out the actual attacks.

MUSLIM FRONT ORGANIZATIONS

Muslim organizations have learned well how to use the tolerance, freedom, and legal systems in Western societies to stifle and even silence debate about and criticism of Islam. In the United States, such organizations labor tirelessly to shut down critiques of Islam and intimidate even the most objective and knowledgeable critics.

Such organizations facilitate the growth of the power and reach of Islamofascism. They may make statements renouncing acts of terror, but in their relentless assault on freedom of speech they are attempting to confiscate one of the more powerful weapons we have against the rising tide of Islamofascism—the freedom to speak the truth.

With every lawsuit intended to silence a journalist; with every condemnation of criticism of Islamic militancy as intolerant, extremist, racist, or Islamophobic, these organizations move us one step closer to the day when no public criticism of or debate about Islam will be tolerated. With every claim that criticism of Islamofascism and its political ideology of conquest is religious bigotry, they attempt to use the best of Western civilization against us. This is a classic strategy of shooting the messenger, demonizing anyone who is not cowed into silence. To a great extent they have succeeded in Western Europe and England, and there is abundant evidence that they continue to make significant strides in the United States.

These modern-day propagandists function as the advance guard of Islamofascism. They are softening us up for the frontal assaults yet to come. The very foundation of Western thought is based on the desire to evaluate, reason, and critique all claims to truth. The claims by apologists for Islam that it is a religion of peace are easily refuted by even the most cursory examination of its doctrines and its history. Thus, propagandists for Islam have no choice but to make every effort to shut down debate and silence criticism. In doing so they are preparing Western society for the ultimate conquest of Islam through jihad by cultural or violent means. This makes them every bit as dangerous, and perhaps even more so, than suicide bombers.

ENABLERS OF ISLAMIC EDUCATION

This third element works in tandem with those who attempt to silence criticism and shut down debate. It includes those who have written and are supplying higher education institutions and the public school systems of Western societies with educational materials that are heavy on pro-Islamist bias and anti-Western criticism and light on truth. Broadly speaking, such materials put a happy face on the history and doctrines of Islam that are simply at odds with reality. By placing such distortions into textbooks, for children of elementary-school age and older, they hope to bend the perceptions of the next generation of adults toward a tolerance for and affirmation of Islam.

At the college level, the pro-Islamic, anti-Western bias prevalent in Middle East Studies programs prepares students to be apologists for Islam in the military, government, academia, and media. Students in these programs are a major source of the politically correct behavior that has, for instance, infected the FBI and its flawed Arabic translators program. We are now seeing the result of Saudi-influenced education on America's children over the past sixteen years since the Saudis started giving millions of dollars to American universities to support Middle East Studies and Political Science departments. These Arab millionaires have taken advantage of the Title IV program instituted after World War II to teach students about foreign countries and languages. The result has been a new generation of Americans who have been heavily influenced by Arab propaganda. Pro-Arab, anti-Israel, and anti-American professors who teach in these departments have brainwashed our children into believing that Israel is the source of the problem in the Middle East and that America is a bad country because of its foreign policy.

HATE-MONGERS

Those in Western mosques and madrassas who advocate and/or distribute materials that advocate violence and the overthrow of constitutional law and democracy are causing the increased radicalization of moderate Muslims in America and other countries of the West. The impact is especially strong on younger Muslims.

The right to freedom of speech is being abused by these Islamist ideologues. It is unlawful to yell "fire" in a crowded theater, because the freedom of speech does not protect outcries that pose an imminent threat or danger. How can it then be lawful to preach violence and the overthrow of lawfully elected governments under the guise of "free speech"?

THE PC PROPAGANDA MACHINE

The fifth element consists of those primarily on the political left who have become useful pawns of the Islamofascist movement. Such people stand in league with Muslims and Muslim organizations who demonize anyone who dares to criticize Islam. Indeed, in America they are more concerned about what is deemed "hate speech" from the political right than about unequivocal exhortations of violence and sedition happening right under their noses.

Much of the political left in Europe and America, through its politically correct intolerance of ideas and philosophies with which it disagrees, aids and abets the rising tide of Islamofascism. The ultimate irony is that, should the Islamofascists win, they will purge societies of the political left and its values they find so abhorrent.

. . .

To plot a war on terror by focusing our efforts almost exclusively on the foot soldiers and their leaders misses the point for two reasons. First, it is not a "war on terror"—it is a war against an ideology that employs terror as one of many tools to advance itself. Second, the leaders and their foot soldiers who actually plan and perpetrate the terror are only one element of the enemy.

Our enemy has two more powerful allies: apathy and disbelief.

History reveals very clearly that the apathetic give way to the passionate and the complacent are subdued by the committed. This happens under conditions of actual physical battle and also in the world of politics. Apathy and complacency in Europe already has demonstrated once again that those who passionately believe in something will overcome those who are unwilling to fight for anything. As apathy grows in America, we leave the doors open to those who are ready to fight to the death for what they believe.

The second ally is disbelief. I find it to be common for Westerners to disbelieve that the generals and soldiers of Islamofascism actually mean what they say. Too many Westerners simply can't come to grips with the fact that an ideology as oppressive, brutal, and fanatical as Islamofascism can actually exist in the twenty-first century. Radical Islam seems to them to be a relic of some bygone age—and, ironically, they're right: Islamofascism proudly proclaims that its goal is to restore the principles of the true Islam of Mohammed and the fourteen centuries of conquest and subjugation that followed him.

THE WEAPONS OF OUR WARFARE

Understanding the truth about militant Islam and jihad and being able to accurately identify the enemy combatants are the first weapons of our warfare. You cannot successfully fight what you do not see or understand.

The second weapon is to recognize and comprehend both the strengths and the weaknesses inherent in democratic societies. An understanding of our strengths reveals to us strategies we can use to fight back, and an understanding of our weaknesses reveals what our enemies can and will exploit, if we allow them.

One of the greatest strengths of a free society is the marketplace of ideas. It is this exchange of ideas that is anathema to devout Islamists and their co-belligerents, the purveyors of political correctness. The political left has had no compunction whatsoever in debating the merits of or criticizing Judaism and Christianity. But there is a striking hypocrisy in how the left regards debate about Islam, debate that the left is intent on silencing.

The purveyors of political correctness, who, as I noted earlier, position themselves mostly on the political left in America and Western Europe, have resorted to every tactic of apology and rationalization to either ignore or dismiss the truth about Islam's militant, forceful nature and the terrorism that emanates from it. They claim that Islamic terrorists are victims of poverty and a lack of education, that Islamic terrorists are victims merely striking back at "Western oppressors," that American foreign policy has provoked terrorist actions, and that criticisms of Islamofascism are nothing more than religious bigotry and intolerance.

Therefore, it is imperative that Americans and citizens of other free countries object to such allegations. However, as individuals acting alone we are virtually powerless. People I talk to routinely tell me they wonder what one person can do, that they feel frustrated and angry.

As I travel around the world and correspond with people from different countries, I find that most people are concerned, upset, and disgusted at the erosion of our freedoms by a less tolerant, less enlightened, less civilized group of people who are causing death and destruction. That the barbarous strives to replace the civilized is so infuriating that most Westerners long to fight these ideological thugs and protect our values and way of life. This is not an issue of right and left, of conservative or liberal. Nor is this an American, French, British, Danish, Canadian, or Australian issue. It is one that encompasses all of us, including the moderate Muslims living among us and enjoying Western freedoms. With these freedoms and liberties under assault, the time to act is now.

In his excellent book *Future Jihad*, Walid Phares, a world-renowned expert on the Middle East and terrorism, has this to say about the necessity of citizen action to combat the spread of militant Islam:

> The concept of national resistance to jihadism is fundamental. . . . Just as local communities and authorities cooperate in fighting criminal and racist activities, everyone should be involved in fighting terrorism. . . . Today, more than ever, all adults should be alert and intellectually equipped to understand the threat at their level. A network of tens of millions of aware citizens around the country would shield society from penetration by an ideology that promotes violence. . . . When the population lacks information and is not mobilized, terrorists are able to fill the void.[7]

You are one of those "tens of millions" for whom I founded the grass-roots action organization called ACT! for America. One of the primary goals of ACT! for America is to empower and give a voice to the many individuals who now feel powerless. ACT! for America is empowering thousands of people by connecting each person to an organization much larger than themselves. As we build a formidable network of local chapters and millions of members, we will demonstrate to those in government, academia, and the media that we are not going to sit back and blithely allow our cherished freedoms to be eviscerated by the assault of political correctness, intimidation, and deception. As we speak with a powerful, unified voice, we will demonstrate that those who are trying to steal our freedom to speak are not a majority voice in America, but a small minority. We will demonstrate to those intent on spreading the vile ideology of Islamofascism that we have the will and the means to resist.

ELECTED REPRESENTATIVES AND GRASSROOTS POWER

History demonstrates the power grassroots organizations in America can exert. Indeed, any country that has freely elected government representatives has the potential to exert this kind of "bottom-up" power to dictate the course of public policy.

Why? Because elected officials care about being reelected. Indeed, in any body of elected representatives there is a substantial number who care more about getting reelected than adhering to principle. They constitute the "insincerely undecided" when it comes to controversial issues. They hold their fingers to the wind to see which way the wind is blowing, and only then decide what to do.

This is a weakness of democratic societies, one which Islamic apologists work to exploit. They know that many elected officials care more about their reelection prospects than adhering to principle, so they in effect threaten these representatives with negative publicity if they do not toe the politically correct line.

The old saying "Sticks and stones can break my bones, but words will never hurt me" is out the window. In today's PC world people turn the words of character assassination into bullets that kill. For instance, by planting publicity in the media that accuses an elected representative of being an Islamophobe, a religious bigot, or intolerant, Islamic apologists send a message—not only to the target of their attacks but to other elected representatives— that to take a stand against Islamofascism will exact a price in negative publicity. In America, members of Congress know all too well that the establishment media is a major mouthpiece for political correctness and is more than willing to advance the agenda of Islamism and use any politically incorrect quote to embarrass and attack. Consequently, far too many members of Congress are unwilling to speak out against the growing tide of Islamofascism, or are unwilling to be educated on the matter, because they do not want to be castigated as Islamophobes.

However, organized power at the grassroots level will trump the voices of political correctness. A grassroots uprising can be more powerful than the establishment media. A good example of this is the demise of the immigration reform legislation in the U.S. Congress in 2007. In spite of support from the media, the political left, and even some on the political right, the proposed legislation was shelved due to the outcry of citizens across America. In short, the voice of grass-roots America triumphed over the voice of the elite. Too many members of Congress began to fear they would lose reelection if they supported the legislation, and in responding to the spontaneous phenomenon of grassroots pressure they became part of an avalanche in Congress that doomed the bill.

We are not waiting for this phenomenon to occur in the war against Islamofascism. We are not simply hoping for a spontaneous grass-roots eruption that may or may not come. We are *making it occur* by organizing ACT! for America chapters and supporters across America. We are providing a vehicle through which Americans can become part of a movement to fight against the rising tide of Islamofascism and the political correctness that supports it. We will force elected representatives to choose—align themselves with the voice of grassroots America or the voice of political correctness.

As I told a group of congressmen on Capital hill, "I can be your worst enemy or your best friend." I believe that, as the failed immigration reform legislation demonstrates, the numbers favor us. When those in Congress who agree with us are joined by the "insincerely undecided" who are concerned that our grass-roots power threatens their political careers, we will create a working majority in Congress that will take the steps necessary to protect us.

HOW GRASSROOTS POWER WORKS

Another weakness of modern democratic societies is that their governments have grown so big that it's difficult for the average citizen to understand and keep track of what goes on in the national legislature. Many elected officials count on this. It's not uncommon for American senators and congresspersons to vote one way in Washington and talk differently when they are in their states and districts.

Thus, the key to success is knowing the truth and having an organization through which to disseminate it. This is why ACT! for America has created a "congressional scorecard" program and a voter-education project. We research bills we consider important to our national security and the threat of Islamofascism. We keep tabs on how each elected official votes on these bills. Then we create congressional scorecards that document the votes of every senator and representative and rate them according to those votes. The more they vote to protect our security and fight Islamofascism, the higher their scores.

We then distribute these scorecards via the ACT! for America chapter network and on our website. People can download the scorecards from our website or obtain hard copies from ACT! for America chapter activists. We make it easy for every voter in America to know exactly how their congresspeople voted. Indeed, the very existence of such scorecards has an impact on how elected representatives vote on legislation, because they know their votes will be recorded and disseminated to millions of voters. They know they are being watched. We don't endorse candidates or tell people how to vote. We arm individuals with objective, documented truth—and it is powerful. We provide them with the facts and the voters choose who they believe are the best decision-makers for the security of the free world.

We must hold our elected officials responsible for their actions and ACT! scorecards help make this possible. Elected officials know their votes and their positions will be observed and reported. They know that the citizenry is organized, and has representatives in every community and a national spokesperson. This forces elected officials to listen and work with the citizens who now have more power than any lobbyist to keep an elected official in office. A lobbyist who speaks for a handful of well-funded Islamic organizations will no longer have enough clout to pressure an elected representative in the face of this organized grass-roots power.

But organized grassroots power is not limited to having an impact on the national government. How long would a local public school push an Islamist agenda if hundreds of parents in the community descended on school board meetings and demanded that changes be made? How long would a university continue to promote an anti-American, anti-Israel, pro-Islamist bias, if a grass-roots boycott of the school led to decreased enrollment and alumni discontinuing their financial gifts? How long would a local newspaper continue to print a slanted view of the news if its major advertisers started pulling their advertising as a result of organized boycotts of their businesses?

Small wonder Islamic organizations and their politically correct allies are doing all they can to silence leaders who speak out. By intimidating leaders they hope to preempt organized grassroots activism that could resist what is happening. Ignorance, unorganized effort, and apathy are their allies. They know they cannot advance their agenda in the face of an informed, organized and mobilized force. Now that I have brought ACT! for America on line, I am determined to speak out boldly in the West, although no one spoke out for me and other Christians in Lebanon before. I've been there, experienced terror, and vow to never let it happen again. The only course for us from here on out is knowing the truth and "ACTing" on it to keep us free.

The strategies and tactics discussed in the following chapter will show you how you can make a difference no matter what country you live in.

12

WINNING THE WAR ON ISLAMOFASCISM: STRATEGIES AND TACTICS

I'm going to approach the question "What can we do?" from this perspective: if we are going to have any chance of being effective and successful in combating the spread of Islamofascism, we must do it as groups of people rather than individuals. Therefore, the first and most important tactic of successful grassroots action is . . .

THE POWER OF ORGANIZATION

Let me assure you that when it comes to being concerned about the rising tide of Islamofascism you are not alone. Within your sphere of influence are family members, friends, business associates, or members of your church or synagogue who agree with you and your concerns about our security. As we have seen with the Muslim Brotherhood Project, they have a plan to Islamize America and are connected and organized through their mosques and madrassas. But as citizens most of us have no plan, are not organized nor connected, which makes it nearly impossible to rise up against Islamofascism and infinitely easier for the Islamofascists to advance their goals.

This is why I recommend that the first tactic for successful grass-roots action is to *get organized*. There is strength in numbers and in unity of purpose. There is encouragement, the feeling of not being alone, and a sense of empowerment when one works with others toward common goals. When it comes to pushing against the tide of Islamofascism, it doesn't take massive numbers to effect changes at the local level.

Of course, I encourage every reader of this book who lives in the United States to join ACT! for America and become part of this grass-roots citizen action network. Our Web site (www.act foramerica.org) provides news and commentary on matters related to national security, terrorism, and the spread of Islamofascism. We focus only on the threat of Islam to world peace and national security. We offer citizens like you the opportunity to sign up for our e-mails and action alerts, to join an ACT! for America chapter, or start one near you. And you don't have to live in the United States to become part of our organization. We have chapters as well as members in France, England, Australia, Sweden, Canada, Spain, and many other countries.

We can connect you with people like yourself in your community. Wherever you are, I encourage you to begin reaching out to those around you and connect with others who are concerned. You can provide them with educational materials (such as this book) and invite them to join with you to create a local group of concerned citizens. Even if you begin with only a handful of people, you are already better positioned than if you try to go it alone. The most important point is for you to build a network of people who understand what is happening and who will join with you to educate your elected officials and others about the tide of Islamofascism rising around you. Remember, silence is golden for those who want to infiltrate and take us by surprise. Whether you become involved in a chapter of ACT! for America or a local citizens' group, there are some basic things you can do to get started and make a difference.

READY-SET-GO:
SIMPLE TIPS TO GET YOU STARTED

Contact Your Elected Officials

Program the telephone numbers of the White House or your congressperson into your cell phone. When you are stuck in traffic and listening to talk radio and fuming about a certain issue, call your elected officials and voice your opinion. Every call is counted and considered. This is how the White House and government keep tabs on the pulse of the nation. (The White House number is 202-456-1111.)

Read Books and Periodicals

Each month, choose a book about current affairs for your chapter to read and hold a monthly discussion about it. Stay informed by reading magazines and newspapers.

Show Videos

Make it a point to have your chapter sponsor a showing of one video dealing with Islamic terrorism. You can book your local theater or library as a venue for the event. Advertise the screening in all churches, temples, universities, and other public outlets in your community. There are plenty of videos on the market that deal with this subject, and we have an updated list of them on our Web site.

Meet Monthly with Your Elected Officials

Choose two representatives from your chapter to serve as your liaison with your elected officials. They should meet monthly with the elected officials in your area and develop a relationship with them. Remember, they are real people just like you. Present your concerns to them about one or two issues at a time and follow up monthly to monitor their progress in dealing with them.

Monitor Your Local Newspaper

Elect two or three representatives from your chapter to monitor your local newspaper. If it publishes any derogatory articles about the United States or Israel, immediately write a letter to the editor and bring it to the attention of the group via e-mail so they can do the same. If the editor won't respond, contact the paper's advertisers.

Monitor Your Local Universities

Assign volunteers from your chapter to sign up at your local college or university to monitor what the professors are teaching in their Middle East Studies and Political Science departments. You are there to point out when the professor is teaching something other than the truth. The students need to hear another point of view. They cannot stand up to the professor; if they do, they will get bad grades and they know it. With the knowledge and information you will be receiving from ACT! and your own research, you will be able to set the record straight and put any professor on notice that intellectual dishonesty and misleading teaching techniques will not be tolerated and will be reported to the administration if they continue.

THE POWER OF MOTIVATION

People are prompted to action by threats they perceive to be the most imminent to them and their families. Thus, an effective local citizens' organization is one that identifies such threats. A local mosque suspected of distributing literature that advocates violence against infidels and the overthrow of democratic government represents such a threat. A public school whose curricula and textbooks glorify Islam, blame America and Israel for the rise of militant Islam, and promote a message that anyone who criticizes Islam is a religious bigot is also an imminent threat. Bringing the truth out in the open about activities detrimental to our lives and way of life is one method of counterattacking.

Investigate carefully and thoroughly the types and nature of threats that exist in your area, and then decide which one or two demand the most immediate action. Others around you will be more motivated to act when it is made clear to them how the threats can and will affect them and their families.

THE POWER OF THE RIGHT STRATEGY

Determining which battles to fight and how to fight them constitutes good strategy. Guy Rodgers, ACT! for America's executive director, who has been a leader in dozens of political campaigns and grass-roots organizations, puts it this way:

> Not all problems are created equal. Not all solutions to those problems are created equal. Choose the problem you perceive to have the greatest imminent threat *and* the greatest prospect for solving with the wisest tactics. By evaluating every

prospective challenge through this lens, you maximize your prospects for an early victory and early success. And nothing builds momentum like success.

Here's an example. Suppose your local newspaper regularly prints editorials that downplay the threat of Islamic terror and blames America and Israel for Islamic violence. One strategic approach would be to go to the editor and describe the fallacy of their position. If they persist and their position seems rooted in PC or ideological thinking, identify one of the newspaper's advertisers that several people in your organization know and send a delegation to that business. Respectfully but firmly inform the advertiser of your concern and your discussion with the editor. After describing the negative impact you feel the newspaper is having in your community tell the business owner that your entire group will boycott their business and encourage others to do so unless they pull their ads from the paper.

The advertiser now has a powerful motivation to agree to pull his ads—the fear of a loss of revenue due to a boycott. Win over enough advertisers and the newspaper's publisher will be forced to take action. It is not uncommon for money to trump ideology.

The right strategy is the one that works. You shouldn't be afraid to think creatively or escalate your approach until you get the desired results.

THE POWER OF TECHNOLOGY

Thanks to remarkable advances in technology during the last twenty years, never has it been easier to organize people than it is today. We have unprecedented ability to communicate rapidly and efficiently. Learn how to use and apply modern technology and you will maximize your effectiveness as an individual and an organization.

With the click of a button, you can send an e-mail to ten, a hundred, or a thousand people in your address book. That e-mail could be a news story, an action alert, a notice regarding a bill being voted on the next day where immediate action is vital, and so on. If only a few of those recipients forward it to their own ten, hundred, or thousand contacts, hundreds of thousands can be informed. A couple of years ago, I gave a speech at Duke University, the text of which went out in an action alert. The speech circulated around the world for a year via the Internet, reaching millions. A year later I heard from someone who wanted to tell me how happy they were to read what I had said! Get information out there and let it move from one person to another.

THE POWER OF THE WIN-WIN SCENARIO

The premise behind the "win-win scenario" is the notion that selecting the right battles to fight or problems to solve will result in residual benefits to the organization even if the organization does not win the fights it directly engages in. The most important and direct residual benefit that can accrue to an organization is an increase in its size.

By choosing a battle to fight or problem to solve that stirs people to action, and using wise tactics to fight that battle, the organization can win respect and support even if it loses the battle. Thus, if a local organization adds thirty new active supporters as a result of its efforts, it has still gained. The organization is a little bigger and a little stronger. It is now better equipped for the next fight.

THE POWER OF PROPER PERSPECTIVE

Our perspective on the potential success of any endeavor is directly related to our expectations of success. Expectations have a tremendous impact as long as we are willing to work at that new endeavor. Unrealistic expectations can lead to disappointment, which typically leads to giving up. For instance, someone who goes on a diet with the goal of losing fifty pounds in two weeks, has unrealistic (as well as dangerous) expectations that are doomed to failure and can lead to abandoning the weight-loss effort altogether. The difference between expectation and reality is the degree of disappointment. Keep the degree of disappointment low.

Here is what we must expect regarding our efforts to roll back the tide of Islamofascism. This is not a conflict that will be won in one or two years. This is a marathon, not a sprint. The Islamofascists view this war in terms of decades, much like the Communists viewed the cold war. They think and strategize in the long term. This was not and is not an easy perspective for us in the fast-food West to get our minds around. We will ultimately beat the Islamofascists through our resolve to protect our freedoms, as the West presents a united front supported by information and a common purpose.

We too must have a long-term perspective—another reason that building and being part of an organization is so essential. Individuals will come and go, being more active or less active over time. A local chapter will in the long run be able to survive and grow in spite of the normal ebb and flow organizations experience. When everyone involved understands this, people won't pack up and declare victory because they were able to get one inaccurate and dishonest textbook pulled from a local school, nor will they pack up and surrender if they fail to get that textbook pulled.

The power of proper perspective also helps us see things from the point of view of those we are trying to influence and persuade. The person who explains to a legislator that taking a certain position is in the best interests of both the legislator and the voters will have the highest degree of success—because the legislator understands that the consequence of this position is a higher probability of getting reelected.

TACKLING THE PROBLEMS

The Devout Jihadists

We at ACT! for America are calling for numerous legislative and government actions to improve our security and provide greater protection from terrorists. These actions include:

- Drastically tighten border security and the monitoring of visas. Terrorists are infiltrating America through our porous borders and abuse of our work- and student-visa programs.
- Wage the war on terror as a real war, not as a police action. Enemy combatants whose goal it is to kill civilians should not be entitled to rights of due process accorded to American citizens in criminal proceedings. The president must have the tools of foreign surveillance and intelligence-gathering that such a war demands.
- Define jihadist ideology as terrorism. Anyone who promotes the ideology of violent jihad is inciting terrorism and should be defined as a terrorist, arrested, and charged. This kind of speech does not deserve to be protected.
- End FBI discrimination against Christians and Jews who are qualified Arabic translators. Despite its shortage of Arabic

translators the FBI insists on excluding virtually all non-Muslims.

- Improve training in counterterrorism agencies and improve coordination and cooperation between intelligence agencies and among the federal, state, and local governments.
- Perform thorough background checks and deny government positions and security clearances to Muslim activists.
- Increase scrutiny, such as financial auditing, of Muslim organizations that purport to be charitable or nonprofit organizations. Numerous Muslim organizations in North America have become masters at the nonprofit "shell game," where complex organizational structures exist to hide who is actually involved, where monies come from and where they go, and the sort of activities the organization engages in. Even if direct ties to terrorists cannot be proved, where sufficient evidence exists of the advance of the political ideology of Islam, such groups should be stripped of their nonprofit status and redesignated as political organizations.
- Enforce the oath of allegiance for immigrants who desire to become citizens, and include asking specific questions regarding whether they agree with the supremacy of the U.S. Constitution over Sharia law.
- Improve airport security by searching passengers who fit terrorists' profiles.
- Demand that taxpayer funds or tax-exempt status be cut off from any school that teaches hatred and violence against non-Muslims. Just as schools in the past have lost their tax-exempt status for teaching race hatred, so should Islamic schools lose tax benefits for preaching religious hatred and violence.

The Rising Flood of Islamic Educational Materials

Islam is celebrated as a religion of peace that has been somehow misunderstood for centuries. Muslims are characterized as victims.

A lie unanswered, and repeated often enough, comes to be believed. (This understanding of "the big lie" was the heart and soul of Goebbels' Nazi propaganda machine.) We cannot sit idly by and watch our children be spoon-fed historical revisionism, distortions, and outright falsehoods about Islam.

Typically, local government officials and educational authorities do everything they can to avoid controversy, which is one reason that sanitized lessons about Islam are taught in public schools. This is also why organized protests directed at such authorities can be successful. A group of concerned parents who meet with a school principal or the local school board to point out pro-Islamist bias can have a significant impact. I know of one case in California where a high school cancelled an "Islamic Awareness Week" celebration after complaints by parents.

Concerned parents should get involved in the PTA or run for school board. However you participate, the first line of defense is *alertness*—become aware of what is happening in your area's schools, what is being taught, and what is in the textbooks. This is another important reason for having a committee of concerned citizens, so that initiatives can be shared by several people instead of falling on the back of one.

Another consequence of the glorifying of Islam in educational materials is that it conditions people to more readily accept Islamist infiltration of society and Islamic refusal to assimilate within free societies. Western Europe's experience is most telling in this regard. To cite just one example, when the Muslim population of Britain reached approximately one million, key Muslim leaders set up a "Muslim parliament" and began passing laws applicable to

Muslims, which had their foundation in Islamic law. What's more, they demanded that Britain recognize the laws passed by this parliament as they applied to Muslims.[1]

This infiltration is cultural jihad. It is often overlooked and underestimated as a vehicle for the ultimate subjugation of a society by Islam because most people are concerned about terrorism. But this form of jihad will at best result in two parallel cultures and laws within the same society, and at worst will lead to the gradual imposition of Sharia law on all.

It is not religious bigotry to resist cultural jihad. It is resistance to a political ideology that will transform and ultimately dominate a culture. We must resist its advance in our universities and schools, in the media, and in government. In the United States, most government officials and elected representatives take an oath to uphold and defend the Constitution. They must be educated about the dangers cultural jihad presents to the Constitution, and pressured to uphold their oath to protect it. If they fail to do so, we need to vote them out of office. The same tactics must be utilized by concerned citizens in other free countries.

Speak Out Against Western Mosques and Madrassas that Advocate Violence

Push for laws that define jihadist ideology as terrorism, thus making the proclamation of this ideology unlawful. We should not have to wait until a terrorist acts before we define his act as terrorism. Those who advocate an ideology that calls for jihad and the forced imposition of Sharia law are calling for terrorism. They are just as responsible for acts of terror as those who commit them— perhaps more so. They should not be allowed invoke claims of "freedom of speech" or "freedom of religion."

In America, property deeds are public records, and researchers have learned that most mosques are owned by interests in Saudi Arabia. If there is a mosque or Islamic institution in your community, you can ascertain its ownership for yourself. Why is this important? Saudi-owned mosques are very likely to be using materials funded by the Wahhabis, who profess a very pure strain of Islam. Some online research will lead you to examples of Wahhabi literature. Provide this information to local authorities so they are alerted to the likelihood that a Saudi-owned mosque is using such materials.

FIGHT USING THE POWER OF THE DOLLAR

I encourage university alumni to withhold their contributions to their alma maters as long as political correctness with regard to Islam is permitted to run amok. I know of one American who, after Iranian president Mahmoud Ahmadinejad was invited to speak at Columbia University, called Columbia's president to inform him that as a result he had changed his mind about making a million dollar contribution. If enough donors took this kind of action, the financial pressure placed on colleges and universities would likely lead to efforts to provide a more balanced and honest presentation of Islam.

FINAL THOUGHTS

In this war that has been declared on us, there is no substitute for victory. Failure is not an option. Several months ago, a close friend of mine made a remarkable comment. She said, "If we choose to look the other way, or choose the path of acquiescence, our grand-children will demand to know why we didn't take action."

And they will have every right to.

Therefore I urge you to rise in defense of our freedoms, our democracy, and our way of life. I urge you to do so for the sake of humanity throughout the world. We must work together to create lines of defense in our communities and our country for the sake of national security.

I visited England recently and addressed members of the business community as well as members of the British Parliament. I got to speak with many people from all walks of life. I was shocked to see what has happened to Britain. I felt as if I was talking to people back in the days of the Soviet Union—people afraid that they are going to be arrested and thrown in jail if they opened their mouth and said something. The moment I mentioned Islamic terrorism people clammed up and looked around nervously, as if to continue the conversation would be dangerous. I sensed the steady drum-beat of Islamic intimidation at work.

On my way back home, I realized that it is up to us to save the world. Because the threat of Islamofascism is far more dangerous than any other enemy we have faced before.

The United States is not a geographical area only. It is a spirit, the spirit of the founding fathers who settled this great land and were willing to do whatever it took to accomplish what they thought was right and good for humanity. Americans embody that spirit, and it is what makes us different than the rest of the world. We are the leading champions for the freedom of mankind. We are born to be leaders, born knowing that we come from a great line of leaders who stood against all odds to live in freedom. We are united in a patriotic bond.

What we must do to save our world is not going to be easy. It will be challenging, it will be demanding, it will be frustrating, but it will also be fulfilling. For when we lay our head on the pillow at night we are all going to be able to say: I tried everything I can to make a difference in this world, to leave it better for our future generations. I stood up against evil, I fought for goodness, and I served my country with honor and pride when I was called upon, so that my children will be able to live in the greatest, freest country in the world.

One day, when we win our fight against Islamofascism, just as we won against Communism and Nazism and fascism, we will be able to say with pride: We were part of the greatest movement in America's history. We fought for our liberty and the liberty of our civilization. We triumphed over evil, and we were leaders who mobilized and lead our fellow citizens in defense of America and Western civilization.

A Note of Thanks

This book would not be complete without a special thank-you to our military.

Words tremble on my lips and emotions swell in my heart in my attempt to humbly thank you for all the things you do to protect America and the world. Words cannot express my depth of gratitude to your service, to your sacrifice, to all that you leave behind to go forth into the world and protect America's interests around the globe.

Let my grateful tears thank you for the nights you slept freezing in a tent or sweating in the desert, for the lonely days you spent missing your loved ones, for the hours you spent sick in pain and without someone holding your hand, for the moments of sheer fright in the heart of battle, for the wounds you have suffered fighting evil, for the endless days in hospitals undergoing painful surgeries, for the precious occasions you have missed back at home. For all of these sacrifices I thank you on behalf of millions of Americans who are so grateful for you. We truly appreciate these sacrifices.

A special thank-you is in order to your families, to the parents who raised you and made you be the man or woman you are today. I thank your wives, husbands, and your loved ones who stand by you and support you with their love and dedication.

And for those who returned in eternal sleep, may your legacy be honored for generations to come, may the tears shed over your coffins fertilize the fields of patriotism in our nation to raise a new generation built on strength and honor, able and willing to follow in your footsteps when duty calls to defend America. May your blood not have been shed in vain. May we prove worthy of your sacrifice. May we always honor your parents so they will always know that they are the parents of an American hero.

You are our brave ones, our heroes, and our national treasures. You are the pride of our nation, our strength and our foundation. Thanks to you, millions have been freed around the world. Thanks to you, those who criticize our country, burn our precious flag, and speak ill of you, are able to do so because their freedom is built upon your blood and your sacrifice.

I salute you one and all. I bow before you in respect and humility. May God bless you and bless America, land of the free and home of the brave, and the dream that became my address.

Acknowledgments

Writing a book is a daunting task that involves hundreds of hours and much energy and research. I would like to give special thanks to those who worked on research and development: my dear friends Joanna Chandler, Karen Freeman, Jerry Gordon, and Guy Rodgers. My assistant, Stephanie Reis. My researchers: Donnie Staggs, Kara Amestoy, and Susan Martin. My agent, Lynne Rabinoff, my editor, Nichole Argyres, and her assistant, Kylah McNeill, and the whole incredible staff of St. Martin's Press. I couldn't be more proud and fortunate to work with such an outstanding staff and a great publisher that supports my efforts. And last, a special thanks to my husband, who worked by my side night and day, and my children who give me the love, support, and freedom to be all I can be. I am forever grateful for their love and sacrifice.

Notes

Introduction

1. http://www.alarabiya.net/articles/2009/01/27/65087.html.

2. http://bighollywood.breitbart.com/mtapson/2009/04/09/the-post-american-president/.

3. http://www.centerforsecuritypolicy.org/p18084.xml.

4. http://article.nationalreview.com/?q=YjJmNjlmNjYxNWYyZDIyMWZjMTgyOTE0ZDIyZTg4MjA=.

5. http://article.nationalreview.com/?q=ZTMyNTY5YTk1ZDJhOGY2MWI0NGE1ZmU3ZTgwYWZkODE=.

6. http://www.washingtonpost.com/wp-dyn/content/article/2009/03/13/AR2009031302371.html.

7. http://www.washingtontimes.com/news/2009/aug/06/white-house-war-terrorism-over/?feat=home_headlines.

8. http://www.newsmax.com/kessler/napolitano_terrorism/2009/03/23/194888.html.

9. http://pajamasmedia.com/blog/get-ready-for-an-more-radical-iranian-regime/.

10. http://www.huffingtonpost.com/2009/06/02/obama-iran-nuclear-energy_n_210332.html, Huffington Post, Obama: Iran nuclear energy concerns legitimate, by Nancy Zuckerbrod, June 2, 2009. Read more at: http://www.huffingtonpost.com/2009/06/02/obama-iran-nuclear-energy_n_210332.html.

11. David Gollust, "Clinton Says U.S. Considers 'Defense Umbrella' to Deter

a Nuclear Iran," *Voice of America*, Phuket, Thailand, July 22, 2009, http://www.voanews.com/english/2009-07-22-voa8.cfm.

12. "The Americans Are Begging Iran for Dialogue," Middle East Media Research Institute (MEMRI), Special Dispatch No. 2467, July 31, 2009, http://www.memri.org/bin/latestnews.cgi?ID=SD246709., citing and quoting from *Kayhan*, Iran, July 27, 2009.

13. Ibid.

14. http://www.nydailynews.com/news/ny_crime/2009/09/16/2009-09-16_fbi_unit_set_for_more_antiterror_raids_in_queens_sources_fears_of_madridstyle_su.html.

15. http://www.investigativeproject.org/1062/shooting-of-two-soldiers-in-little-rock-puts.

16. http://www.investigativeproject.org/1107/terror-arrests-on-the-rise.

17. http://www.voanews.com/english/archive/2009-08/2009-08-08-voa7.cfm.

18. http://minnesota.publicradio.org/display/web/2009/09/11/somali-death/.

19. http://www.france24.com/en/20090913-more-britons-travel-somalia-jihad-report.

20. http://www.telegraph.co.uk/news/newstopics/religion/6083338/Sebastian-Faulks-The-book-I<->really-cant-put-down.html.

21. http://news.sky.com/skynews/Home/UK-News/Mohammed-Book-Firebomb-Attack-Charges-Trio-Accused-Over-Blaze-At-London-Publisher/Article/200810115112445.

22. http://www.nytimes.com/2009/08/13/books/13book.htm.

23. http://yalepress.yale.edu/yupbooks/KlausenStatement.asp, Statement by Yale University Press, August 14, 2009.

24. http://www.jihadwatch.org/2009/09/shame-on-the-netherlands-wilders-to-go-on-trial-january-2010.html.

25. http://www.dianawest.net/Home/tabid/36/EntryId/1012/Convicted-for-Islamic-Blasphemy-in-Finland.aspx.

26. http://www.investigativeproject.org/1095/hizb-ut-tahrir-in-america-preaching-hate-building.

27. http://news.bbc.co.uk/2/hi/asia-pacific/8254631.stm.

28. http://www.dailymail.co.uk/news/article-1197478/Sharia-law-UK–How-Islam-dispensing-justice-side-British-courts.html.

29. http://www.ajc.com/metro/content/metro/stories/2009/06/10/terrorism_trial_tech.html.

30. http://www.investigativeproject.org/1420/al-qaradawi-center-for-moderation.

31. http://www.investigativeproject.org/1088/pro-terror-group-to-meet-in-chicago-suburb.

32. http://www.dailymail.co.uk/debate/article-1141087/Britains-world-leader-sharia-banking–havent-grasped-sinister-dangerous-implications.html#ixzz0RWNyLGxB.

33. http://www.humanevents.com/article.php?id=31537.

34. http://www.dailymail.co.uk/debate/article-1141087/Britains-world-leader-sharia-banking–havent-grasped-sinister-dangerous-implications.html.

35. http://www.thenational.ae/article/20090711/FOREIGN/707109763/1002.

36. http://www.jpost.com/servlet/Satellite?cid=1248277924485&pagename=JPost%2FJPArticle%2FShowFull.

37. http://teaandpolitics.wordpress.com/2009/07/29/spain-moroccan-tries-an-honor-killing-stabs-20-times-his-daughter/.

38. http://www.adnkronos.com/AKI/English/Security/?id=3.0.3777791349.

39. http://www.humanevents.com/article.php?id=32869.

40. http://www.dailymail.co.uk/news/article-1201625/Cheating-wife-face-honour-killing-acid-poured-lovers-throat.html?ITO=1490.

41. http://www.foxnews.com/story/0,2933,494785,00.html.

42. http://www.centerforsecuritypolicy.org/p18157.xml.

1. Islam 101: The East Through Western Eyes

1. Yahiya Emerick, *Complete Idiot's Guide to Understanding Islam* (New York: Alpha Books, 2006), p. 17.

2. Philip K. Hitti, *History of the Arabs* (London: Macmillan, 1937), pp. 96–101.

3. Saifur Rahman, *Ar-Raheeq Al-Makhtum: The Lineage and Family of Muhammad* (Saudi Arabia/UK/USA/Pakistan: Dar-us-Salam Publishers and Distributors).

4. Ibid.

5. Emerson, *American Jihad.*

6. Ibid.

7. The Counterterrorism Blog, "Radical Indoctrination in the U.S. Prisons," August 25, 2005.

8. "Five Pillars of Islam," www.allaboutreligion.com.

9. "Islam: The Koran," http://library.thinkquest.org/28505/islam/koran.htm.

10. Yahiko Sagamori, "Peacemongers and Jihadeers," http://www.think-israel.org/sagamori.peacemongers.html, accessed November 3, 2007.

11. http://prophetofdoom.net/Islamic_Quotes.Islam.

12. *Jihad Encyclopedia,* MSN Encarta, http://encarta.msn.com/encyclopedia_761582255/Jihad.html.

13. Bernard Lewis, "The Revolt of Islam," *New Yorker,* November 19, 2001.

2. Islamic Terrorism: Then and Now

1. As someone who speaks Arabic as my mother's tongue, I read the Koran in Arabic, the language in which it was written. However, in this book I give an English reference to the Koran. The reference is http://prophetofdoom.net because it is the most accurate and closest translation to the Arabic version I have ever read.

2. "Battle of Uhud," *Encyclopedia of the Orient,* http://lexicorient.com/e.o/ uhud_b.htm.

3. S. Moninul Haq, *Ibn Sa'd's Kitab al-Tabaqat al-Kabir,* vol. 2 (Islamic Book Service/Idara Islamiyat-e-Diniyat/Kitab Bhavan) pp. 134, 136, 137.

4. Harry W. Hazard, *Atlas of Islamic History,* vol. 12 of *Princeton Oriental Studies,* edited by Philip K. Hitti (Princeton: Princeton University Press, 1954), pp. 6–9.

5. *Kitab al-Wagiz fi Fiqh Madhab al-Imam al-Safi'i,* English translation cited in Andrew Bostom, *The Legacy of Islamic Jihad,* (2005), p. 199.

6. The provisions of the Pact of Umar are cited as translated in Norman Stillman's *The Jews of Arab Lands: A History and Source Book* (Philadelphia: Jewish Publication Society of America, 1979), pp. 157–158.

7. Bat Yeor, *Islam and Dhimitude: Where Civilizations Collide* (Madison, NJ: Fairleigh Dickinson University Press, 2001), pp. 185–6, 191, 194.

8. *A History of the Crusades* (editor in chief, Kenneth Meyer Setton), vol. 3; *The Fourteenth and Fifteenth Centuries,* edited by Harry W. Hazard (Madison: University of Wisconsin Press, 1975).

9. "Urban II," *The Catholic Encyclopedia,* vol. XV (New York: Robert Appleton Company, 1912), http://www.newadvent.org/cathen/15210a.htm.

10. "Historic Figures, Napoleon Bonaparte (1769–1821)," BBC History, http://www.bbc.co.uk/history/historic_figures/bonaparte_napoleon.shtml.

11. Jamie Glazov, "The Infidel Revolution," *frontpagemag.com,* February 21, 2007.

12. Joseph Farah, "The Lessons of Al-Hudaybiyah," *worldnetdaily.com,* May 23, 2002.

13. Abbas Milani, "A Revolution Betrayed," Hoover Institution, *Hoover Digest,* www.hoover.org/publications/digest/3050786.html-31k.

14. Ibid.

15. Milton Viorst, The Time 100, Monday, April 13, 1998, http://www.time.com/time100/leaders/profile/khomeini.html.

16. Michael D. Evans, "Father of the Revolution," *Jerusalem Post* online edition, June 20, 2007, http://www.jpost.com/servlet/Satellite?cid=1181813077590 &pagename=JPost%2FJPArticle%2FShowFull.

17. "Carter Planted Seeds of Al-Qaida," *Investor's Business Daily,* Wednesday, May 23, 2007, http://www.ibdeditorials.com/special3.aspx.

18. Kenneth Morris, "Jimmy Carter, American Moralist: The Life Story and

Moral Legacy of Our Thirty-Ninth President," *Britannica Online Encyclopedia*, www.britannica.com/eb/article-9020545/Carter-Jimmy.

19. Farhad Mafie, "Yasser Arafat and the Islamic Republic of Iran: Birds of a Feather Flock Together," April 29, 2002, http:/www.spectacle.org/0602/mafia. html.

20. "EU's Ministers of Economic and Financial Affairs' Council Violate the Verdict by the European Court," NCRI Web site, February 1, 2007.

21. "Iran: Carter's Habitat for Humanity," *Investor's Business Daily*, May 24, 2007, Editorials and Opinions, http://www.investors.com/editorial/editorial content.asp?secid=1501&status=article&id=264899644231746&secure=1178.

22. Milani, "A Revolution Betrayed."

23. Plateau of Iran, "Father of the Iranian Revolution" (updated), June 21, 2007,   plateauofiran.wordpress.com/2007/06/21/father-of-the-iranian-revolution.

24. "Iran and the West: Sailing into Troubled Waters," Economist.com, April 4, 2007, www.economist.com/PrinterFriendly.cfm?story_id=8960313.

25. "Iran Hostage Anniversary," *CBS News*, January 18, 2001, www.cbsnews.com/stories/2001/01/18/iran/main265244.shtml.

26. "Who Murdered the Athletes of the Israeli 1972 Olympic Team in Munich?," Palestine Facts, Israel 1967–1991, Olympic Team Murdered, www.palestinefacts.org/pf_1967to1991_munich.php.

27. Richard Baehr and Ed Lasky, "Stephen Walt's War with Israel," *American Thinker*, March 20, 2006, www.americanthinker.com/articles.php?article_id=5342.

28. "Killer Jailed Over Poison Plot," *BBC News*, UK version, Wednesday, April 13, 2005, http://news.bbc.co.uk/1/hi/uk/4433709.stm.

29. "Transcripts, The Situation Room," Wolf Blitzer, CNN.com, aired August 10, 2006, http://transcripts.cnn.com/TRANSCRIPTS/0608/10/sitroom.03.html.

30. "Chechen 'Claims Belan Attack,'" Jill Dougherty, CNN Moscow bureau chief, CNN.com, September 17, 2004, http://edition.cnn.com/2004/WORLD/europe/09/17/russia.beslan.

31. American Jewish Committee, *Islamist Ideology and Terror: Part II: Actions*, October 2006, p. 6, available at www.ajc.org.

32. "Indepth: Toronto Bomb Plot," online interview, *CBS News*, October 22, 2007, www. cbc.ca/news/background/toronto-bomb-plot/index.html.

33. "Jail for Demark 'Honour' Killing," *BBC News*, UK version, June 29, 2006, http://news.bbc.co.uk/1/hi/world/europe/5128206.stm.

34. Maggie Farley, "US Will Still Pursue Iran Sanctions," Latimes.com, December 5, 2007, http://www.latimes.com/news/nationworld/world/la-fg-un5dec05,0,5853640.story?coll=la-home-center.

35. John R. Bolton, "The Flaws in the Iran Report," *Washington Post*, December 6, 2007.

36. Robert D. Blackwell, "Opinion: Forgive Russia, Confront Iran," *Wall Street Journal,* Thursday, December 6, 2007.

37. Elaine Sciolino and William J. Broad, "Report Raises New Doubts on Iran Nuclear Program," Newyorktimes.com, November 16, 2007, http://topics. nytimes.com/ . . . /organizations/i/international_atomic_energy_agency/index. html?offset=40&s=oldest.

38. Quoted in Amir Taheri's *Holy Terror* (Maryland: Adler & Adler, 1987), p. 24.

39. Islamic Republic News Agency, "President Ahmadinejad's Address at UNGA," found at "Weapons of Mass Destruction (WMD)," GlobalSecurity.org, full speech available at this link: http://www.globalsecurity.org/wmd/library/news/iran/2006/iran-060920-irna02.htm.

3. Purists Drink Their Islam Straight

1. Interview of the President by Al Arabiya, Oval Office, Colonnade, Map Room, *White House News,* October 4, 2007.

2. Interview with Tony Blair, *Newsweek* magazine, March 12, 2001.

3. Prime Minister Blair's speech to the Los Angeles World Affairs Council, August 1, 2006.

4. Prophet of Doom, Islamic quotes, Fighting, http://prophetofdoom.net/ Islamic_Quotes_Fighting.Islam.

5. Prophet of Doom, Islamic quotes, Paradise, http://ww.prophetofdoom. net/Islamic_Quotes_Paradise.Islam.

6. Jamie Glazov, "Schmoozing with Terrorists," frontpagemag.com, October 31, 2007.

7. "Bin Laden Lieutenant Admits to Sept. 11 and Explains Al-Qa'ida's Combat Doctrine," Middle East Media Research Institute (MEMRI), memri.org, February 10, 2002.

8. Ibid.

9. Ibid.

10. "Al-Qa'ida Activist, Abu' Ubeid Al Qurashi: Comparing Munich (Olympics) Attack 1972 to September 11," memri.org, March 12, 2002.

11. Ibid.

12. "Ibid.

13. Prophet of Doom, Islamic Quotes, Women, http://www.prophetofdoom. net/Islamic_Quotes_Women.Islam.

14. Prophet of Doom, Islamic quotes, Jihad, http://www.prophetofdoom. net/Islamic_Quotes_Jihad.Islam.

15. "Suicide Bombers Follow Quran, Concludes Pentagon Briefing," world netdaily.com, September 27, 2006.

16. Ibid.

17. Ibid.

18. Ibid.

19. Middle East Media Research Institute; memri.org.

20. Sarah Hall, Suzanne Goldenberg, and John Hooper, "Palestinian Joy, Global Condemnation," Guardian.co.uk, September 12, 2001; "Attacks Celebrated in West Bank," *Times* of London, September 11, 2001; "Palestinians in Lebanon Celebrate Anti-U.S. Attack," Agence France-Presse, September 11, 2001; Joseph Logan, "Palestinians Celebrate with Gunfire," Reuters, September 12, 2001; "AP Protests Threats to Freelance Cameraman Who Filmed Palestinian Rally," Associated Press, September 12, 2001; "Foreign Journalists 'Deeply Concerned' by PA Harassment," Associated Press, September 13, 2001; "Middle East Newsline," special to WorldTribune.com, September 12, 2001, and "Israel to AP: Release Film of Palestinian Celebrations," September 13, 2001; "Bin Laden Poster Seen at Gaza Rally," Associated Press, September 14, 2001.

21. Middle East Media Research Institute, memri.org.

22. The Mosque, The Lahore Ahmadiyya Movement for the Propagation of Islam, aaiil.org or ahmadiyya.ws or muslilm.sh or islam.It!

23. Middle East Media Research Institute, memri.org.

24. Howard Bloom, *The Lucifer Principle* (New York: Atlantic Monthly Press, 1995), p. 225.

25. Sergio Kieman, "Seeking the Truth: The AIMA Bombing Goes to Trial," American Jewish Committee; "U.S. on Highest Alert in Kuwait, Saudi Arabia," NewsMax.com, November 1, 2000; "Meanwhile in Iran," *Jerusalem Report*, April 7, 2003; Yehudit Barsky, "Hizbollah," American Jewish Committee, May 2003; Don Feder, "Dumb and Dumber in Chechnya," NewsMax.com, January 3, 2000; "U.S. Mountaineers Freed in Central Asia," United Press International, August 19, 2000; Matt Pyeatt, "Clinton Paid 'Lip Service' to Terror Attacks, Expert Charges," CNSNNews.com, December 6, 2001; "Dozens Killed as Taleban Overrun Town," United Press International, August 3, 2000; "Kashmir Massacres, 84 Dead," Agence France-Presse, August 2, 2000; Lev Navrozov, "Islam and CNN's Christiane Amanpour," January 7, 2002; "World Ignores Atrocities in Sudan," United Press International, April 5, 2001; John LeBoutillier, "Iran, Israel & 2004," NewsMax.com, May 27, 2003; "Egypt Air Secrecy and Spin—Piecing Together the Facts," NewsMax.com, November 10, 1999; "Suicide Attack in Chechnya Kills 40," NewsMax.com, May 12, 2003; Colonel Stanislav Lunev, "Moscow Siege Over, But War in Chechnya Goes On," NewsMax.com, October 22, 2002; "Yemen Links bin Laden to USS *Cole*," NewsMax.com, November 27, 2001; "Saudi Arabia Finally Added to Terror List," NewsMax.com, December 18, 2002; "Saudi Bombing Death Toll at 34," NewsMax.com, May 14, 2003; "Saudi Attack Feared Salient by Revived Al-Qaeda," NewsMax.com, May 15, 2003.

26. "U.S. Links Bin Laden to New Year Bomb Plot," United Press International, February 21, 2000.

27. "Islamic Terrorists Have Targeted Pope," NewsMax.com, October 15, 2001.

28. Abu Ubeid Al-Qurashi, "Fourth Generation Wars," *Al-Ansar*, February 2002, memri.org.

29. Ibid.

30. Richard T. Cooper, "General Casts War in Religious Terms," *Los Angeles Times*, October 16, 2003.

31. Norman Lieberman, "Civilization at Twilight," NewsMax.com, April 14, 2002; Cooper, "General Casts War in Religious Terms."

32. Al-Qurashi, "Fourth Generation Wars."

33. Christopher Ruddy, "Don't Demonize the Islamics," NewsMax.com, September 17, 2001.

34. Yael Shahar, "Al-Qaeda in Saudi Arabia: Coming Out of the Shadows," Institute for Counter-Terrorism, May 13, 2003.

4. The Muslim Brotherhood "Project" for North America

1. Patrick Poole, "The Muslim Brotherhood 'Project,'" frontpagemag.com, May 11, 2006.

NOTE: The English translation of The Project has been prepared by Scott Burgess and was first published in serial form by *The Daily Ablution* in December 2005 (Parts, I, II, III, IV, V, Conclusion). It is based on the French text of The Project published in Sylvain Besson, *La conquête de l'Occident: Le projet secret des Islamistes* (Paris: Le Seuil, 2005), pp. 193–205.

2. Ibid.

3. Ibid.

4. Ibid.

5. Frank Salvo, "Al-Taqiyya: The Islamist Terrorist Weapon of Deception," *The American Daily*, November 11, 2007.

6. www.Dawa.Net.com.

7. "Sharia Law in UK Is 'Unavoidable,'" *BBC News*, February 7, 2008.

8. "Homeland Security: 'Airport Admits Installing Foot-Washing Benches,'" worldnetdaily.com exlusive, May 1, 2007.

9. Ibid.

10. Rod Dreher, "What the Muslim Brotherhood Means for the US," Dallasnews.com, September 9, 2007.

11. Mark Pratt, "Shariah Comes to Old Crimson: Harvard Tries Women-Only Gym Hours," Associated Press, March 4, 2008.

12. Janet Levy, "State House Muslim Proselytism," frontpagemag.com, February 1, 2008.

13. Roger Yu, "Airport Check-Ins: Fare Refusals in Minnesota," *USA Today*, September 8, 2006.

14. "New York Public School Accused of Radical Islamist Agenda," CNN. com, September 4, 2007.

15. Paul L. Williams, Ph.D., "Radical Muslim Paramilitary Compound Flourishes in Upper New York State," *Canada Free Press*, May 11, 2007.

16. Patrick Poole, "Islamofacism Fraud at Wright State," frontpagemag.com, March 25, 2008.

17. The Search for International Terrorist Entities (SITE), siteinstitute.org, archives: fact sheet on Elashi Brothers and Info.com, December 18, 2002.

18. Nicholas Van Zandt, "An Insider's View of the Holy Land Foundation Trial," frontpagemag.com, July 19, 2007.

19. Ibid.

20. The Investigative Project on Terrorism (IPT), "Second HLF Trial Could Bring Change," *IPT News*, October 23, 2007.

21. Dreher, "What the Muslim Brotherhood Means for the US."

22. David J. Jonsson, "Islamic Economics and Shariah Law: A Plan for World Domination," *Global Politician*, December 21, 2006.

23. Joseph Myers, "Homeland Security Implications of the Holy Land Foundation," Americanthinker.com, September 18, 2007.

24. Eric Lichtblau, "Report Warns of Infiltration by Al Qaeda in U.S. Prisons," *New York Times*, May 5, 2004.

25. "Homeland Insecurity: Blacks Recruited for Terror by Al-Qaida: Pitch to African-Americans Invokes 'Martyr' Malcolm X," worldnetdaily.com, May 21, 2007.

26. Ibid.

27. Abdullah Al Araby, "Neither Black nor African," *Islam Review*, islamreview.com.

28. Francis Bok, *Escape from Slavery* (New York: St. Martin's Press, 2003).

29. Ibid.

30. The Nizor Project, Shofar FTP Archive File, Anti-Defamation League, "Hamas, Islamic Jihad and The Muslim Brotherhood: Islamic Extremists and the Terrorist Threat to America," 1993, New York, http:// www.nizkor.org/ftp. cgi/orgs/american/adl/hamas/hamas-islamic-jihad.

31. Judicial Watch Inc., "Hamas: Via Hand Delivery September 20, 2001," http://www.judicialwatch.org/cases/78/hamascomplaint.pdf.

32. Judicial Watch Inc., Special Report 2007, "Muslim Charities: Moderate Non-Profits or Elaborate Deceptions," http:// www.judicialwatch.org/archive/ 2007/SR_muslimorg.pdf.

33. Palestine Center.org, Hamas Charter, 1988, http://www. palestinecenter. org/cpap/documents/charter.html.

34. Ibid.

5. Madrassas in America and Abroad

1. Stanley Kurtz, "A Fundamental Front in the War," *National Review* online, Saudi in the Classroom [on Title VI and Middle East Studies], July 25, 2007.

2. Kenneth Adelman, "U.S. Islamic Schools Teaching Homegrown Hate," *Fox News,* February 27, 2002.

3. Joe Kaufman, "The School That Terrorism Built," frontpagemag.com, December 5, 2005.

4. John Mintz and Douglas Farah, "In Search of Friends Among the Foes: U.S. Hopes to Work with Diverse Group," September 11, 2004, http://www.washingtonpost.com/wp-dyn/articles/A12823-2004Sep10.html.

5. Kaufman, "The School That Terrorism Built."

6. Beila Rabinowitz, "US Dept of Education Awards Blue Ribbon for Excellence to Islamist School Where Pledge of Allegiance Is to 'Allah and His Prophet,'" *Militant Islam Monitor,* PipeLineNews.org, October 2, 2005.

7. Bureau of Islamic and Arabic Education. Pledge to Allah, June 22, 2006.

8. Beila Rabinowitz, "Islamist School Wins Dept of Education Award," *Militant Islam Monitor,* PipeLineNews.org, October 20, 2005.

9. www.DawaNet.com.

10. "The Shock of Islamic Indoctrination in American Classrooms," *Western Resistance,* March 14, 2007, http://www.westernresistance.com/blog/archives/003640.html.

11. "Judge Rules Islamic Education OK in California Classrooms," worldnetdaily.com, December 13, 2003.

12. Ibid.

13. First Amendment Center, http://www.firstamendmentcenter.org: Religious Liberty in Public Schools—topic.

14. First Amendment Center, "Religious Liberty in Public Life," http://www.firstamendmentcenter.org.

15. Paul Sperry, "Look Who's Teaching Johnny About Islam," worldnetdaily.com, May 3, 2004.

16. http:// www.theislamproject.org/education/Lessonplans.htm.

17. Sperry, "Look Who's Teaching Johnny About Islam."

18. George Archibald, "Muslim Explorers Preceded Columbus?" *Washington Times,* April 2004.

19. "Outlandish Claims in 'Arab World Studies,'" LittleGreenFootballs.com, April 16, 2004.

20. Dreher, "Islam: What Seventh-Graders in California Are Learning About Mohammad & Co."

21. Daniel Pipes, "Think Like a Muslim (Urges 'Across the Centuries')," *New York Post,* February 11, 2002.

22. William Bennetta, "Same Junk, Different Peddlers," review of *World Cultures: A Global Mosaic*, from The Textbook Letter, September/October 1999, The Textbook League, http://www.textbookleague.org/104glob.htm.

23. Gilbert T. Sewall, "Islam and the Textbooks: A Reply to the Critics," The American Textbook Council, December 2003.

24. Ibid.

25. Beila Rabinowitz and William A. Mayer, "Khalil Gibran School—A Jihad Grows in Brooklyn," *Militant Islam Monitor*, PipeLineNews.org, April 13, 2007.

26. Daniel Pipes, "The Travails of Brooklyn's Arabic Academy," *New York Sun*, May 22, 2007.

27. "Dhabah Almontaser & Lena al-Husseini Arab American Family Support Center Joins with Khalil Gibran School to Promote Islamism," *Militant Islam Monitor*, May 10, 2007.

28. AAFSC—Arab American Family Support Center, http://www.aafscny.org.

29. "Giuliani Rejects $10 Million from Saudi Prince," CNN.com, October 12, 2001.

30. "CAIR-NY Urges Support for Arabic Language School," IslamOnline.com, February 8, 2007.

31. Beila Rabinowitz and William A. Mayer, "Brooklyn's Khalil Gibran Madrassah Will Function as Jihad Recruitment Center," *Militant Islam Monitor*, August 7, 2007.

32. Cair Watch, "Omar Mohammedi (a.k.a. 9/11's Lawyer) President and Former General Counsel of CAIR-New York," http:// www.americansagainsthate.org/cw/profiles_cw.php.

33. "About Lebanon," Kahlil.org, http:// www.kahlil.org/aboutlebanon.html.

34. Linda Keay, "Muslim Scouts Political Program Raises Eyebrows," The Investigative Project on Terrorism, IPT news service, September 23, 2007.

35. Joe Kaufman, "Khalil Gibran's Muslim Brotherhood Advisor," frontpagemag.com, August 23, 2007.

36. http://www.AmericansAgainstHate.org.

37. Ibid.

38. Joe Kaufman, "A New Year's Jihad Retreat," frontpagemag.com, December 29, 2005.

39. Ibid.

40. Ibid.

41. Ibid.

42. Beila Rabinowitz and William A. Mayer, "Florida Islamic Conference Outed as Jihad-Fest," PipeLineNews.org, December 19, 2003.

43. Joe Kaufman, "Young Muslim's Secret Camp," frontpagemag.com, August 1, 2006.

44. Ibid.

45. Ibid.

46. Alex Alexiev (senior fellow, Center for Security Policy), "Wahhabism: State-Sponsored Extremism Worldwide," testimony before the U.S. Senate Subcommittee on Terrorism, Technology and Homeland Security, June 26, 2003, http://kyl.senate.gov/legis_center/subdocs/sc062603_alexiev.pdf. For details on Saudi funding of the madrassas see Alex Alexiev, "The Pakistani Time Bomb," *Commentary,* March 2003.

47. Nic Robertson, "Special Investigation Unit: Pakistan Terror Central," CNN, December 28, 2007.

48. "Inside Pakistan's Jihad Factories," *Jihad Watch,* September 9, 2006, http://www.jihadwatch.org/archives/013040.php.

49. Abdulla Muhammad Al-Zaid, *Education in Saudi Arabia: A Model with a Difference,* translated by Omar Ali Afifi (1982), p. 39. The author, Al-Zaid, is a former member of the teaching staff at King Abd Al-Aziz University, former chairman of the department of education, and former director general of education for the western province of Saudi Arabia.

50. "Saudi Arabia's Curriculum of Intolerance," report by Center for Religious Freedom and Institute for Gulf Affairs, Washington D.C., http:// www. freedomhouse.org/religion, http://www.www.gulfinstitute.org/IGA051605/IGA-FH-SaudiReport.pdf.

51. Ibid.

52. Ibid.

53. Ibid.

54. "Friday Sermons in Saudi Mosques: Review and Analysis," MEMRI special report, memri.org.

55. As reported in *Ain-Al-Yaqeen,* September 20, 2002, http://www.ain-al -yaqeen.com/issues/20020920/feat7en.htm.

56. United States Commission on International Religious Freedom, http:// www.uscirf.gov/index.php.

57. "Saudi Arabia's Curriculum of Intolerance," report by Center for Religious Freedom, Washington, D.C.

58. "Saudi Arabia's Curriculum of Intolerance," Freedom House, 2006, http://www.hudson.org/files/publications/CRF_SaudiReport_2006.pdf, http:// www.uscirf.gov/countries/publications/currentreport/2007annualRpt.pdf.

59. Nina Shea, "This Is a Saudi Textbook (After the Intolerance Was Removed)," Washingtonpost.com, May 21, 2006, http://www.washingtonpost. com/wp-dyn/content/article/2006/05/19/AR2006051901769.html.

60. Ibid.

61. Steven Stalinsky, "Teach Kids Peace—Saudi Education: Hatred of Christians & Jews," memri.org, Special Report—Saudi Arabia, http://www. teachkidspeace.org/doc3516.php.

62. *Ain-Al-Yaqueen* (a weekly news magazine published online by the Saudi royal family), March 1, 2002.

63. "From Nationalist Battle to Religious Conflict: New 12th Grade Palestinian Schoolbooks Present a World Without Israel," *Palestinian Media Watch*, http://www.pmw.org.il/BookReport_Eng.pdf. (For copy of report: info@pmw.org.il).

64. Itamar Marcus, "Presentation of Report on Palestinian Schoolbooks by PMW Director Itamar Marcus in US Senate Building," *Palestinian Media Watch*, PMW Political Impact, March 1, 2007.

65. Ibid.

66. "From Nationalist Battle to Religious Conflict" (see ch. 5, n. 63).

67. Itamar Marcus and Barbara Crook, "The Arab Media Is Now Monitoring PMW," *Palestinian Media Watch* bulletin, December 19, 2007, http://www.jerusalemsummit.org/eng/pmw.php?pmw=79.

68. "Behind the Headlines: Hamas' Mickey Mouse Teaches Children to Hate and Kill," Israel Ministry of Foreign Affairs, May 10, 2007, http://www.mfagov.il/ . . . /Behind+the+Headlines/Hamas+Mickey+Mouse+teaches+children+to+hate+and+kill+10-May-2007.htm.

69. Bob Unruh, "Scholastic Joins Education Industry's Campaign for Islam: Publication for Elementary Students Promotes Americans in Madrassas," worldnetdaily.com, January 3, 2007, http:// www.worldnetdaily.com/news/article.asp?ARTICLE_ID=53603.

70. Valerie Strauss, "Islamic Saudi Academy School Officials Say U.S. Panel's Call for Closure Hurt Image," Washingtonpost.com, November 16, 2007, p. B06, http://www.washingtonpost.com/wp-dyn/content/article/2007/11/15/AR2007111502324.html.

71. Andrea Stone, "Federal Panel Wants to Shut Islamic School in VA," *USA Today*, October 2007.

72. Valerie Strauss, "U.S. 'Studying' Islamic School Report," Washingtonpost.com, November 5, 2007, p. B04, http://www.washingtonpost.com/wp-dyn/content/article/2007/11/04/AR2007110401596.html.

73. "Teaching Hate," Washingtonpost.com, March 4, 2005, p. A20, http://www.washingtonpost.com/wp-dyn/articles/A5648-2005Mar3.html.

74. "Military: Wahhabi," GlobalSecurity.org, http://www.globalsecurity.org/military/world/gulf/wahhabi.htm.

75. Emmanuel A. Winston, "Seeing Islam Clear. Seeing Islam Muddy," *Think-Israel*, http://www.think-israel.org/winston.viewingislam.html.

76. Jacqueline L. Salmon and Joe Holley, "Federal Agency Recommends Closing Saudi School in VA," *Washington Post*, October 18, 2007, http://www.washingtonpost.com/wp-dyn/content/article/2007/10/18/AR2007101800024.html.

77. Ibid.

78. "Teaching Hate," Washingtonpost.com (see ch. 5, n. 73).

79. "Parameters," *U.S. Army War College Quarterly,* Winter 2005–2006, http://www. carlisle.army.mil/usawc/parameters/05winter/bowman.htm.

6. Reviving the Caliphate: One World Nation Under Allah; Supersizing the Muslim World

1. Ralph Braibanti, "The Structure of the Islamic World," International Strategy and Policy Institute, http://www.ispi-usa.org/braibanti/braibanti10.html.

2. James Brandon, "The Caliphate, One Nation Under Allah," *Christian Science Monitor,* May 10, 2006.

3. "Ayman al-Zawahiri Letter to Abu Musab Al-Zarqaqi," reprinted in *The Weekly Standard,* October 10, 2005.

4. Brandon, "The Caliphate, One Nation Under Allah." (see ch. 6, n. 2)

5. Al Qaeda Training Manual, http://www.fas.org/irp/world/para/ladin.htm.

6. Ibid.

7. Ibid.

8. Ibid.

9. Haroon Rashid, "Pakistan Taleban Vow More Violence," *BBC News,* http://news.bbc.co.uk/2/hi/south_asia/6292061.stm.

10. Yunis Al-Astal (Hamas MP and cleric), "We Will Conquer Rome, and from There Continue to Conquer the Two Americas and Eastern Europe," excerpts from address that aired on Al-Aqsa TV on April 11, 2008, available at www.memritv.org/clip_transcript/en/1739.htm.

11. Brandon, "The Caliphate, One Nation Under Allah." (see ch. 6, n. 2)

12. Aaron Klein, *Schmoozing with Terrorists: From Hollywood to the Holy Land, Jihadists Reveal Their Global Plans to a Jew!* (Medford, OR: World Net Daily Books, 2007).

13. Ibid.

14. Brandon, "The Caliphate, One Nation Under Allah" (see ch. 6, n. 2).

15. Ibid.

16. Ibid.

17. Ibid.

18. "Letter from al-Zawahiri to al-Zarqawi (dated July 8, 2005)" GlobalSecurity.org, Homeland Security, http://www.globalsecurity.org/security/library/report/2005/zawahiri-zarqawi-letter_9jul2005.htm.

19. Osama bin Laden, "State of Jihad," speech, Al-Jazera, reprinted in article by Walid Phares.

20. Jed Babbin, *In the Words of Our Enemies* (Washington, D.C.: Regnery Publishing Inc., 2007), (Sheikh Ibrahim Madhi), p. 26; (original source) Danielle

Pletka, "Why the American Reluctance?" The American Enterprise Institute, short publications, December 22, 2005.

21. Babbin, *In the Words of Our Enemies* (Sheikh Abdel Rahman), p. 60.

22. Simeon Kerr and Mariko Sanchanta, "Dubai Fund Takes Stake in Sony," *Financial Times*, November 26, 2007.

23. "Iran Leader's Messianic End-Times Mission," worldnetdaily.com, January 6, 2006.

24. Hizb ut-Tahrir, "The Khilafah Was Destroyed in Turkey 79 Years Ago; So Let the Righteous Khilafah Be Declared Again in Turkey," www.islamic-state.org, February 22, 2003.

25. Neil MacFarquhar, "Rising Tide of Islamic Militants See Iraq as Ultimate Battlefield," *New York Times*, August 13, 2003.

26. Brynjar Lia, *The Society of the Muslim Brothers in Egypt* (Ithaca, NY: Ithaca Press, 1998), p. 28.

27. Daniel Simpson, "British Moslem Radicals Urge Islamic Fightback," Reuters, March 6, 1999.

28. Robert Spencer, *The Politically Incorrect Guide to Islam (and the Crusades)* (Washington, D.C.: Regnery Publishing Inc., 2005), p. 190; partially reprinted in *Dallas News* blog, December 17, 2004.

29. Babbin, *In the Words of Our Enemies*, p. 82.

30. Daniel Pipes, "What Do the Terrorists Want? [A Caliphate]," *New York Sun*, July 26, 2005.

31. Ibid.

32. "Fanatics Around the World Dream of the Caliph's Return," *The Daily Telegraph* (update), August 1, 2005.

33. Michael Ireland, "Global Insecurity: 40% of Young UK Muslims Want Sharia Law," worldnetdaily.com, January 31, 2007.

34. Glen Beck, *An Inconvenient Book* (New York: Simon and Schuster, 2007), p. 44.

7. The Islamization of Europe

1. "Europe Celebrates 60 Years Since End of WWII," *International Herald Tribune*, May 8, 2005, http://www.iht.com/articles/2005/05/08/europe/web.0508EU.php.

2. "European Chart of Values," Europa-Union Deutschland, http://www.europa-web.de/europa/02wwswww/203chart/chart_gb.htm.

3. Ibid.

4. Paul Belien, "Eurabia Scholars Gather in the Hague," *The Brussels' Journal*, February 10, 2006, http://www.brusselsjournal.com/node/840.

5. CounterJihad Brussels 2007 Presentations, keynote speech, Bat Yeor,

CounterJihad Brussels 2007 Conference, October 18–19, 2007, http:// counterjihadeuropa.files.wordpress.com/2007/11/yeor-brussels-october-2007. pdf.

6. Ryszard Cholewinski, *Migrant Workers in International Human Rights Law: Their Protection in Countries of Employment,* (Oxford: Clarendon Press, 1997), p. 16.

7. Simon Kuper, "Head Count Belies Vision of 'Eurabia,' " *Financial Times,* August 19, 2007.

8. Robert S. Leiken, "Europe's Angry Muslims," *Foreign Affairs,* July/August 2005, http://www.foreignaffairs.org/20050701faessay84409-p40/robert-s-leiken/europe-s-angry-muslims.html.

9. Belien, "Eurabia Scholars Gather in the Hague" (see ch. 7, n. 4).

10. Max Steenberghe, "Muslim Forces Anesthetist from Operating Room," Religion News Blog, October 27, 2007, http://www.religionnewsblog.com/ 19778/islamic-extremism-13, also posted at Dhimmi Watch, November 13, 2007, http://www.jihadwatch.org/dhimmiwatch/archives/018782.php.

11. Robert S. Leiken, "Europe's Angry Muslims," *Foreign Affairs,* July/August 2005, http://www.foreignaffairs.org/20050701faessay84409-p40/robert-s-leiken/europe-s-angry-muslims.html.

12. Lorenzo Vidino, "The Muslim Brotherhoods' Conquest of Europe," *The Middle East Quarterly,* Winter 2005, vol. XXII, n. 1, http://www.meforum.org/ article/687.

13. Henryk M. Broder, "Hurray! We're Capitulating!" *Spiegel* Online International, January 25, 2007, http://www.spiegel.de/international/spiegel/0,1518, 462149-3,00.html.

14. Ibid.

15. Ibid.

16. Paul Jeeves, "Now Muslims Get Their Own Laws in Britain," *Daily Express,* May 1, 2007, http://www.express.co.uk/posts/view/5795.

17. Esther Pan, "Europe: Integrating Islam," Council on Foreign Relations, July 13, 2005, http://www.cfr.org/publication/8252/europe.html#5.

18. Leiken, "Europe's Angry Muslims" (see ch. 7, n. 11).

19. Michael Slackman, "Saudi Ties to Taliban Draw Retrospective U.S. Criticism," *Los Angeles Times,* January 20, 2002.

20. Paul Belien, "The Piggy Bank Ban and Selling Out to Muslims," *The Brussels Journal,* October 25, 2005, http://www.brusselsjournal.com/node/396.

21. Ibid.

22. Ibid.

23. "Multiculturalism 'Drives Young Muslims to Shun British Values,' " *Daily Mail,* January 29, 2007.

24. Leiken, "Europe's Angry Muslims" (see ch. 7, n. 11).

25. Shabee Nabil, "Muslims in Greater Europe," IslamOnline.net, December

29, 2005, http://www.islamonline.net/English/EuropeanMuslims/Politics/2005/12/07.SHTML.

26. Ibid.

27. Gary Cleland, "Hairdresser Sued over Muslim Headscarf Ban," *Daily Telegraph*, August 11, 2007, http://www.telegraph.co.uk/news/main.jhtml?xml=/news/2007/11/08/nhair108.xml.

28. Shireen T. Hunter, *Europe's Second Religion: The New Social, Cultural, and Political Landscape* (Westport, CT: Praeger Publishers, 2002), p. 77.

29. MEMRI, no. 447, December 6, 2002, memri.org.

30. Michel Gurfinkiel, "Islam in France: The French Way of Life Is in Danger," *Middle East Quarterly,* vol. IV, no. 1, March 1997, http://www.meforum.org/article/337.

31. "Islam in Europe," March 29, 2007, http://islamineurope.blogspot.com/2007/03/tilburg-imam-denies-allegations.html.

32. Ibid.

33. Ibid.

34. "Minister Welcomes Sharia in the Netherlands If the Majority Wants It," *NIS News Bulletin,* September 13, 2006, http://www.nisnews.nl/public/130906_2.htm.

35. Michael Manville, "Russia Has a Muslim Dilemma: Ethnic Russians Hostile to Muslims," *San Francisco Chronicle*, November 19, 2006, http://www.sfgate.com/cgiin/article.cgi?f=/c/a/2006/11/19/MNGJGMFUVG1.DTL.

8. The Subtle Islamization Agenda: Boiling the West Alive

1. Jerry Seper, "Terror Cells on Rise in South America, *Washington Times*, December 18, 2002.

2. Hector Tobar and Paula Gobbi, "Triple Border Region May be Ideal Hide-Out for Terrorists," *Los Angeles Times*, December 26, 2001.

3. Ibid.

4. "Patterns of Global Terrorism: 2001," U.S. Department of State, May 2002, pp. 44–45, http://news.findlaw.com/hdocs/docs/dos/trrpt2001/dostrrpt2001p5.pdf.

5. "Patterns of Global Terrorism: 2001," p. 50.

6. Ibid.

7. "Hamas, Hezbollah Find Haven in S. America," *Middle East Newsline*, May 5, 2002, http://menewsline.com.

8. Ibid.

9. "Patterns of Global Terrorism: 2001," p. 50.

10. "Terrorist Base South of Border," Joseph Farah's G2 Bulletin, December 1, 2003.

11. Jeffrey Goldberg, "The Party of God" (parts I and II), *New Yorker*, October 14 and October 28, 2002; Ed Blanche, "The Lebanese Link in Suspected Latin American Militant Fundraisers: U.S. Presses Governments to Crack Down on Alleged Terror Support Network," Lebanon Wire, July 1, 2003; Blanca Madani, "Hezbollah Global Finance Network: The Triple Frontier," *Middle East Intelligence Bulletin*, vol. 4, no. 1, January 2002; Brian Byrnes, "Argentina Placed on High Alert for Terrorist Attack," VOANews.com, November 26, 2003; Tim Johnson, "Hezbollah May Be Trafficking Drugs in South America," Knight Ridder Newspapers, May 23, 2003.

12. "Paraguay Arrests Suspected Link with Mullahs' Regime," Reuters, October 28, 1998; "Terrorist Network Being Broken in South America," informationwar.org, October 1998; Blanche, "The Lebanese Link in Suspected Latin American Militant Fundraisers" (see ch. 8, n. 11); "Lebanese Hizballah Member Arrested in Paraguay," www.ict.org.il, November 1, 1998.

13. Madani, "Hezbollah Global Finance Network."

14. *A Report Prepared by the Federal Research Division, Library of Congress under an Interagency Agreement with the Department of Defense*, The Library of Congress. A Global Overview of Narcotics-Funded Terrorist and Other Extremist Groups. May 2002.

15. Marc Perelman, "Brazil Connection Links Terrorist Groups," *Forward*, March 31, 2003.

16. "Hezbollah Agent Arrested on Way to Bomb Israeli Targets," WorldTribune.com, December 4, 2000.

17. Madani, "Hezbollah Global Finance Network."

18. Ibid.; Carmen Gentile, "Brazil Extradites Terror Suspect," *Washington Times*, November 19, 2003; "Alleged Hezbollah Financier Extradited by Brazil to Paraguay," Nahamet.com, November 20, 2003.

19. "Alleged Hezbollah Financier Extradited by Brazil to Paraguay."

20. Tobar and Gobbi, "Triple Border Region May Be Ideal Hide-Out for Terrorists."

21. "Patterns of Global Terrorism: 2002," U.S. Department of State, April 2003, http://usinfo.state.gov/topical/pol/terror/2002patterns/wha.htm.

22. Madani, "Hezbollah Global Finance Network."

23. "Brazil's Lula in Syria on First Leg of Historic Mideast Tour," *Jordan Times*, December 4, 2003.

24. "Former U.S. Official Says Bush Expected to Sign Sanctions Against Syria," Agence France-Presse, December 1, 2003.

25. "Brazil's Lula in Syria on First Leg of Historic Mideast Tour" (see ch. 8, n. 23).

26. "Bolivia Detains 16 Muslims on Terror Tipoff," Reuters, December 4, 2003.

27. "Invasion USA, Venezuelan IDs Help Terrorists Enter U.S.," worldnetdaily.com, October 26, 2006.

28. Ibid.

29. Ibid.

30. Brigitte Gabriel, *Because They Hate* (New York: St. Martin's Press, 2006).

31. Victor Mordechai, "Islamic Infiltration into the U.S. Along the Mexican and Canadian Borders," FreeRepublic.com, February 21, 2002; Joseph Farah, "Mexico: The New Lebanon?" worldnetdaily.com, June 22, 2001.

32. Farah, "Mexico: The New Lebanon?"

33. Ibid.

34. "Report: Chechens Entered U.S. via Mexico," United Press International, October 13, 2004.

35. "Mexico al-Qa'ida 'Back Door' to US," *The Australian*, October 16, 2004.

36. Richard Whittle, "Strikes Only First Steps, Rusted Says," *Dallas Morning News*, October 9, 2001; "Report Says Iran Gave Terrorists U.S. Arms," *New York Times*, January 12, 2002; Ken Silverstein, "Stingers, Stingers, Who's Got Stingers," Slate.com, October 3, 2001; "Iran Delivered Stinger Missiles to Terrorists," AFP, January 12, 2002.

37. Christopher J. Chipello, "Canada Investigates Link to Terrorist and Deadly Blast," *Wall Street Journal Europe*, May 3, 2002.

38. "Al Qaeda Claims Attack on Tunisia Synagogue," Agence France-Presse, April 15, 2002.

39. "Asian Organized Crime and Terrorist Activity in Canada, 1999–2002: A Report Prepared Under an Interagency Agreement," Federal Research Division, U.S. Library of Congress, July 2003, pp. 2–5, http://www.loc.gov/rr/frd/pdf -files/AsianOrgCrime_Canada.pdf.

40. Lee Berthiaume, "The Untold Story of Hasanville's Shadowy Past (Part 1)," *The Ottawa Citizen*, May 4, 2002.

41. "Muslims of the Americas: In Their Own Words," Anti-Defamation League (ADL), 2001.

42. Colin Nickerson, "In Canada, Terrorists Found a Haven," *Boston Globe*, April 9, 2001.

43. Gary Dimmock and Aaron Sands, "Toronto Shop Clerk Tied to World Terror," *Ottawa Citizen*, October 29, 2001.

44. Mike Robinson, "Former Boston Cabbie Arrested in Chicago by FBI," Associated Press, September 20, 2001; Tom Godfrey, "Marabh, Pilots Linked: In Regular Contact with Atta, al-Shehhi, U.S. Police Say," *Toronto Sun*, November 16, 2001.

45. Godfrey, "Marabh, Pilots Linked"; John Berlau, "Terrorist Haven," *Insight*, May 31, 2002.

46. Berlau, "Terrorist Haven."

47. "Canada Admits: We're Terror Haven," worldnetdaily.com, March 2, 2004.

48. Berlau, "Terrorist Haven."

49. "Asian Organized Crime and Terrorist Activity in Canada, 1999–2002," pp. 2–5 (see ch. 8, n. 39).

50. "Patterns of Global Terrorism: 2002" (see ch. 8, n. 21); "Asian Organized Crime and Terrorist Activity in Canada, 1999–2002," pp. 2–5 (see ch. 8, n. 39).

51. "Asian Organized Crime and Terrorist Activity in Canada, 1999–2002," p. 1 (see ch. 8, n. 39).

52. "Toronto Terror Plot Foiled," CNN.com, June 3, 2006.

53. Susan Bourette, "Can Tolerant Canada Tolerate *Sharia*?," *Christian Science Monitor*, August 10, 2004.

54. Ibid.

55. "Columbia University Plans to Host Iranian President Mahmoud Ahmadinejad," AP, *Fox News*, September 22, 2007, www.foxnews.com.

56. Samuel Estreicher and Michael J. Gray, "Religion and the US Workplace," *Human Rights* magazine, Summer 2006, http://www.abanet.org.

57. Daniel Pipes, "Ban the Burqa—and the Niqab Too," *Jerusalem Post*, August 1, 2007, http://www.danielpipes.org.

58. Bruce Bawer, "Europe in Denial" chapter 1 in *While Europe Slept* (New York: Doubleday, 2006), synopsis of violence in Europe, pp. 37–39.

59. *TD Monthly* and reprinted at http://www.toydirectory.com/monthy/.

60. Katherine Zoepf, "Bestseller in Mideast: Barbie with a Prayer Mat," *Damascus Journal*, September 22, 2004 (reprinted in *New York Times* and available at http://www.nytimes.com).

61. N. Ahmed-Ullah, "Fast-Food Giants Cater to Muslims," *Chicago Tribune*, January 5, 2007.

62. Debbie Hamilton, "Fast Food, Halal Food," Right Truth blog, http://www.righttruth.typepad.com, January 12, 2007.

63. Ibid., also available at Webloggin—Your Daily Source of Politics, Media and Culture, http://www.webloggin.com.

64. Ibid. (ch. 8, n. 62).

65. Starbucks Coffee Company, Date Frappuccino, www.albawaba.com; www.starbucks.com.

66. Marc Adams, "Showing Good Faith Towards Muslims," *HR* magazine, November 2000.

67. "Homeland Insecurity: Airport Adds Foot Basins for Muslim Cabbies," worldnetdaily.com, April 28, 2007, http://www.wordnetdaily.com; "University of Michigan Installing Foot-Washing Basins," FoxNews.com, The Big Story with John Gibson, July 30, 2007.

68. "Homeland Insecurity: Muslim Sensitivity Training for 45,000 Airport Workers," worldnetdaily.com, December 28, 2007, http://www.worldnetdaily.com; Daniel Pipes and Sharon Chadha, "George Soros Teaches the FBI Tolerance," frontpagemag.com, July 22, 2004, www.danielpipes.org.

69. Paul Sperry, "Homeland Insecurity: Airport-Security Firm at Mercy of

Muslims," worldnetdaily.com, November 9, 2001, http://www.worldnetdaily. com.

70. "The Arab and His Camel," The Baldwin Project, http://www.mainlesson. com/display.php?author=scudder&book=fables&story=arab.

71. "Columbia University Plans to Host Iranian President Mahmoud Ahmadinejad," Associated Press, September 22, 2007, also reported by Fox News, http://www.foxnews.com.

72. Joe Loconte, "Columbia University's 15 Minutes of Fame," BritainAndAmerica.com, http://britainandamerica.typepad.com/britain_and _america/.

73. "Free Speech in Iran: Crime and Punishment," CBS News, October 15, 2007, www.cbsnews.com.

74. "Homeland Insecurity," worldnetdaily.com, December 28, 2006, http:// www.worldnetdaily.com.

75. "Profile: CAIR," Investor's Business Daily, August 8, 2005.

76. Emerson, American Jihad, p. 2.

77. Jamaat ul-Fuqra (terrorism organization), South Asia Terrorism Portal, http://www.satp.org.

78. Mira L. Boland, "Sheikh Gilani's American Disciples," The Weekly Standard, vol. 7, issue 26, March 18, 2002.

79. MilitantIslamMonitor.org, http://www.militantislammonitor.org/article/ id/1794.

80. Jerry Gordon, "The Best Positioned Group to Help al-Qaeda Launch an Attack in the US," New English Review, April 2008.

81. Patrik Jonsson, "Flood of Knockoff Merchandise Triggers a Wider Crackdown Across the US," Christian Science Monitor, February 14, 2007, also on CBS News.

82. Jerry Gordon, "The War on Terror Comes to Cherry Hill," American Thinker, May 10, 2007.

83. Donna Leinwand, "FBI: Clerk 'Unsung Hero' in Fort Dix Plot," USA Today, May 9, 2007.

84. FBI, Los Angeles Field Division, Thom Mrozek, Public Affairs Officer, December 14, 2007.

85. Warner MacKenzie, "It's the Ideology, Stupid!," Islam Watch, July 12, 2007.

86. Sayeed Abdul A'la Maududi, "Jihad in Islam," reprinted by Islam Watch; MacKenzie, "It's the Ideology, Stupid!"

9. Islam's Contempt for Women and Minorities

1. Craig Winn, Prophet of Doom: Islam's Terrorist Dogmas in Muhammad's Own Words, (CricketSong Books, 2004).

2. Ibid.

3. Ibid.

4. Ibid.

5. "Beginning of Creation," translation of *Sahih Bukhari,* book 54,USC-MSA Compendium of Islamic Texts, University of Southern California, http://www.usc.edu/dept/MSA/fundamentals/hadithsunnah/bukhari/054.sbt.html.

6. James Arlandson, "Domestic Violence in Islam: The Quran on Beating Wives," *American Thinker,* February 14, 2005.

7. "Violence Against Women in Pakistan," Amnesty International, media briefing, April 17, 2002, http://www.amnesty.org.

8. "Chad Struggles to Pass New Family Law," *VOA News,* Bavier report, April 15, 2005.

9. Abdullah Yusef Ali, *The Quran* (Elmhurst, NY: Tahrike Tarsile Quran, Inc., 1997).

10. Mohammed Marmaduke Pickthall, *The Meaning of the Glorious Koran* (New York: Mentor, 1953).

11. Nessim Joseph Dawood, *The Koran* (London: Penguin, 1995).

12. Mohammed Habib Shakir, *The Quran* (Elmhurst, NY: Tahrike Tarsile Quran, Inc., 1993).

13. Arthur John Arberry, *The Koran* (Oxford: Oxford University Press, 1983).

14. Vivienne Walt, "Marked Women," *Time,* July 19, 2004.

15. Jessica Morgan and Muhammad Elrashidi, "Editorial/Opinions," *The Minnesota Daily,* January 29, 1999.

16. "Jordan Quashes 'Honour Crimes' Law," Al-Jazeera, September 7, 2003.

17. Morgan and Elrashidi, "Editorial/Opinions."

18. Ibid.

19. "U.N. Women's Rights Group Criticized Pakistan for Honor Killings, Trafficking," Associated Press, June 8, 2007.

20. "Europe Tackles Honor Killings," *BBC News,* June 22, 2004.

21. Stephen Brown, "Horror Under the Hijab," frontpagemag.com, December 14, 2007.

22. Andrew Walden, "Honor Killing in Dallas," frontpagemag.com, January 7, 2008.

23. Silas, "Muhammad, Aisha, Islam and Child Brides," http://www.answering-islam.org/Silas/childbrides.htm.

24. "Iran: Council of Guardians Rules 9 Years Is Girls' Marriage Age," from UN wire, Winter 2001, http://www.unfoundation.org.

25. Robert Spencer, "Banned in Pakistan," frontpagemag.com, January 9, 2007.

26. Ayaan Hirsi Ali, *Infidel* (New York: Free Press, 2007) pp. 31–3.

27. Sara Corbett, "A Cutting Tradition," *New York Times,* January 20, 2008.

28. Abul Kasem, "Sex and Sexuality in Islam" (part 1 of 6), *Islam Review,*

presented by The Pen Vs. the Sword, http://www.islamreview.com/articles/sexinislam.shtml.

29. Robert Spencer and Phyllis Chesler, "The Violent Oppression of Women in Islam," David Horowitz Freedom Center, 2007.

30. "King Pardons Saudi Rape Victim," *CNN World*, December 19, 2007.

31. "Saudi: Why We Punished Rape Victim," *CNN World*, November 20, 2007.

32. "Saudi Arabia," Country Reports on Human Rights Practices, Bureau of Democracy, Human Rights, and Labor, 2001.

33. "Women and Religious Oppression," The Committee to Defend Women's Rights in the Middle East, http://www.geocities.com/middleeastwomen.

34. Ibid.

35. Christopher Dickey and Rod Nordland, "The Fire That Won't Die Out," *Newsweek*, July 22, 2002, pp. 34–37.

36. Donna M. Hughes, "Islamic Fundamentalism and the Sex Slave Trade in Iran," Women's Studies Program University of Rhode Island, http://www.uri.edu/artsci/wms/hughes/iran_sex_slave_trade.

37. Ibid.

38. Ibid.

39. Ibid.

40. Ibid.

41. Andrew Lawrence, "My Sportsman Choice: The Child Camel Jockey," *Sports Illustrated*, November 12, 2004, http://sportsillustrated.cnn.com/2004/magazine/specials/sportsman/2004/11/12/camel.jockey/index.html.

42. www.digitalhistory.uh.edu/database/subtitles.cmf?titleID=25-78k-January 9, 2006.

43. www.wsu.edu/~dee/MESO/CODE.HTM

44. "Arab Racism and Imperialism in Sudan (Africa)," http://www.raceandhistory.com/historicalviews/09122001.htm.

45. Serge Trifkovie, "Islam's Wretched Record on Slavery," frontpagemag.com, November 20, 2002.

46. Ibid.

47. Ibid.

48. "Slavery in Islam," http://www. answering-islam.org.uk/Silas/Slavery.htm.

49. Robert Spencer, "The Persistence of Islamic Slavery," frontpagemag.com, July 20, 2007, www.frontpagemag.com/Articles/ReadArticle.asp?ID=29227.

50. Bok, *Escape from Slavery*.

51. Trifkovie, "Islam's Wretched Record on Slavery."

52. Ibid.

53. "Slavery in Islam," http://www. answering-islam.org.uk/Silas/Slavery.htm.

54. Moses Ebe Ochonu, "Arab Racism Against Black Americans," *The Nigerian Village Square*, July 19, 2005.

55. Bok, *Escape from Slavery*.

56. Trifkovie, "Islam's Wretched Record on Slavery."

57. Joseph R. Gregory, "African Slavery 1996," First Things, 63, May 1996, pp. 37–39, http://www.leaderu.com/ftissues/ft9605/articles/gregory.html.

58. D. Del Castillo, "A Sociology Professor in Mauritania Fights Its Slave System," www.geocities.com/collegepark/classroom/9912/modernholocaust.htm.

59. Trifkovie, "Islam's Wretched Record on Slavery."

60. D. Del Castillo, "A Sociology Professor in Mauritania Fights Its Slave System," www.geocities.com/collegepark/classroom/9912/modernholocaust.htm.

61. Bok, Escape from Slavery.

62. "U.S., International Community Failing to Pressure Sudanese Government, Panelists Say," Virginia Law, February 11, 2005, www.lawvirginia.edu/home2002/htm/news/2005_spr/sudan.htm.

63. Military: Darfur Liberation Front, Sudan Liberation Movement, October 24, 2007, www.globalsecurity.org/militaryworld/para/darfur.htm.

64. Kevin Davies, "Slave Trade Thrives in the Sudan," Associated Press, February 1998.

65. Bok, Escape from Slavery.

66. Ibid.

67. Michael Coren, "Slavery Lives on in the Sudan," Toronto Sun online, November 15, 2003.

68. www.crisisgroup.org/home/index.cmf?id=3582&1=1-3k, January 10, 2006.

69. Daniel Pipes, "The Problem with Saudi Slavery," New York Sun, June 16, 2005.

70. Elise Labott, "U.S. Cites 4 Gulf Allies in Trafficking," CNN.com, June 3, 2005.

71. Pipes, "The Problem with Saudi Slavery."

72. "Prohibited Identities: State Interference with Religious Freedom," Human Rights Watch Publications, chapter V, "Conversion and Freedom of Religion," vol. 19, no. 7 (E), November 2007.

73. Paul Marshall, "Islam: From Toleration to Terror," Whistlerblower magazine, November 2001.

74. Paul Marshall, Their Blood Cries Out: The Untold Story of Persecution Against Christians in the Modern World (Nashville, TN: Word Publishers, 1997).

75. MIPT Terrorism Knowledge Base: Gamat Islamiya.

76. Marshall, Their Blood Cries Out.

77. "Egypt: Coptic Church," About.com, http://atheism.about.com/library/FAQs/islam/countries/bl_EgyptCoptic.htm.

78. "Warning After Synagogue Attack," BBC News, http://news.bbc.co.uk/2/hi/uk_news/wales/2126569.stm.

79. R. Burton, "Muslim Genocide of Hindus in India," reader comment on article "Islamophobia?," danielpipes.org, December 2, 2005.

10. Tolerance: A One-Way Street

1. Paul Belien, "Europe Criticizes Copenhagen Over Cartoons," *The Brussels Journal*, December 21, 2005, http://www.brusselsjournal.com/node/589.

2. "The Clash of Values and the Ideology Behind Terrorism," FaithFreedom. org, http://www.faithfreedom.org/Articles/sinaawa1.htm.

3. Paul Farhi, "Talk Show Host Graham Fired by WMAL Over Islam Remarks," *Washington Post*, August 23, 2005.

4. "Prof. Thomas Klocek Free Speech Battle at DePaul Began One Year Ago Today," Freerepublic.com, http://www.freerepublic.com/focus/f-bloggers/1485392/posts.

5. Bill Gertz, "Inside the Ring," *Washington Times*, January 4, 2008.

6. "Letters to the Editor," *Washington Times*, January 17, 2008

7. Mordechai Nisan, *Identity and Civilization: Essays on Judaism, Christianity, and Islam.* (Lanham, MD: University Press of America, 1999) p. 151, 152.

8. "Terrorist Recruitment and Infiltration in the United States: Prisons and Military as an Operational Base," Senate Testimony of Dr. Michael Waller (Alamoudi, Islamists, & Muslim Chaplains), Senate Judiciary Committee: Subcommittee on Terrorism, Technology and Homeland Security, October 14, 2003.

9. "Wife of Sami al-Arian Was Founder/Director/Secretary of the World Islamic Studies Enterprise—Palestinian Islamic Jihad Terror Front," Militant Islam Monitor press release, June 9, 2005, http://www.militantislammonitor.org/article/id/674.

10. "Muslims Storm Out of White House Meeting," *Middle East Times*, June 29, 2001.

11. Ibid.

12. Ibid.

13. "Without Explanation," Smartertimes.com, June 29, 2001.

14. Stephen A. McDonald, "Where Is the Islamic Tolerance?," *Pravda*, forum in English, March 19, 2002.

15. Ibid.

16. Nisan, *Identity and Civilization*, p. 165.

11. Rising in Defense of Democracy

1. "Transcript of Bush Speech in Atlanta," CNN.com, November 8, 2001.

2. Bernard Lewis, *The Crisis of Islam: Holy War and Unholy Terror* (New York: Modern Library, 2003), pp. 113–118.

3. Cal Thomas, "The Threat Among Us," JewishWorldReview.com, May 20, 2003.

4. Ibid.

5. Thomas, "When Suicide Bombers Call," *Washington Times*, May 26, 2002.

6. Jeff Barak, "The Spymaster's Prescription," *Jerusalem Post*, December 21, 2001.

7. Walid Phares, *Future Jihad* (New York: Macmillan, 2005), pp. 249–250.

12. Winning the War on Islamofascism: Strategies and Tactics

1. Melanie Phillips, *Londonistan* (London: Encounter Books, 2006), pp. 97–98.

Index

"Brigitte Gabriel's words should be read, and studied carefully...by everyone who values freedom."

—ROBERT SPENCER, AUTHOR OF *THE POLITICALLY INCORRECT GUIDE TO ISLAM (AND THE CRUSADES)*

Because They Hate tells Gabriel's personal story of how she lost her childhood to militant Islam. Fiercely articulate and passionately committed, she warns that fundamentalist Islamic theology threatens the United States and that radical Islam will stop at nothing short of domination of all non-Muslim countries.

 ST. MARTIN'S GRIFFIN

Caliphate
One world nation
under allah